These are
really good!

love
Mary Ann
2003

FIVE ★ STAR
Recipes

FROM WELL-KNOWN
LATTER-DAY SAINTS

FIVE ★ STAR

Recipes

FROM WELL-KNOWN
LATTER-DAY SAINTS

COMPILED BY
ELAINE CANNON

EAGLE GATE
SALT LAKE CITY, UTAH

Library of Congress Cataloging-in-Publication Data

Cannon, Elaine.
    Five-star recipes from well-known Latter-day Saints / compiled by Elaine Cannon.
        p.   cm.
    Includes index.
    ISBN 1-57008-865-9
    1. Cookery.   I. Title.
    TX714 .C358   2002
    641.5—dc21   2002015206

Printed in the United States of America   72076-6981
Publishers Printing, Salt Lake City, Utah

10   9   8   7   6   5   4   3   2   1

Contents

Preface

As the time-tested recipes in this unique cookbook are nourishing your family and friends, a portion of the proceeds from the purchase price of this book will be used to aid poor and needy people throughout the world.

Five-Star Recipes from Well-Known Latter-day Saints is a collection of favorite recipes contributed by prominent LDS authors and artists, musicians and athletes, business executives and political leaders from all over the world. Nearly 150 well-known Latter-day Saints responded to our call for recipes and generously donated stories and instructions for their favorite foods, which include everything from exotic Middle Eastern dishes and classic chocolate chip cookies to comforting stews and warm peach cobblers.

Because these recipes are favorites, they have been tested over and over again. A classic apple pie recipe from Elaine Cannon, a crowd-sized shrimp noodle casserole from Stephen and Sandra Covey, a warm and hearty shepherd's pie from Jane Clayson, a tempting corn soufflé from Orrin Hatch, sweet glazed carrots from Steve Young, buttery pancakes from Michael McLean, and an authentic Italian lasagna from Michael Ballam are just a small sampling of the delicious recipes presented in these pages.

The publisher would like to thank Elaine Cannon for contacting hundreds of possible contributors and soliciting recipes, stories, biographies, and photographs; Carla Cannon for keying in the vast majority of recipes contributed; Jana Erickson for providing crucial support throughout the book's production; Janna DeVore for editing, organizing, and supervising production of the book; Cheryl Boyle, Debbie Wager, Amy Felix, and Lisa Mangum for providing expert help in the proofing stages of production; Shauna Gibby for designing the book; and Tonya Facemyer for typesetting the recipes.

Finally, the publisher thanks those who generously contributed to this great cause by allowing us to share your favorite recipes with Latter-day Saints everywhere and thus provide much-needed help and support to LDS Humanitarian Services.

A Little Something of Everything

SAVORY SAUCES,
APPETIZERS,
DIPS, AND
HORS D'OEUVRES

Al's Barbecue Sauce

AL ROUNDS

This recipe was stolen from my childhood friend's (Cy Walker) Southern mother. I would pray to spend the night there, hoping she would cook her famous barbecue chicken with this mouthwatering sauce. If I was lucky enough to stay over, Cy and I got the job of killing all the yellow jackets as the chicken was cooking on the barbecue. I became an expert at yellow jacket traps! Think of me when you are enjoying this wonderful sauce at your next summer barbecue—while battling your own yellow jackets.

1 envelope Lipton's® onion soup mix

½ c. water

½ c. apple cider vinegar

½ c. margarine or butter

¼ c. sugar

½ tsp. salt

1 tsp. pepper

½ tsp. dry mustard

1 c. Del Monte® ketchup (Dad's only choice, because he worked for Del Monte)

Combine onion soup mix, water, cider vinegar, and margarine in saucepan. In small bowl, mix sugar, salt, pepper, and mustard; stir into soup. Cook over medium heat 10 minutes, then add ketchup, mixing well. Sauce is best when served after overnight refrigeration—and without yellow jackets! Tip: Cy's mother's advice is to not use too much sauce at first. Cook it slowly so the ketchup won't burn.

Makes 2 cups.

Al Rounds can't remember a time when he didn't want to be an artist. And it's apparent that he has always been drawn to architectural landscape—his first grade teacher sent home a note to his mother asking if Al knew how to draw anything besides his house. Today, his favorite painting locations include upstate New York and Historic Nauvoo. Al's paintings of temples, pioneer landscapes, and Latter-day Saint historical sites are well known and well loved throughout the country. Al is the father of seven children and divides his time between Utah and Nauvoo.

Spaghetti Sauce

VIRGINIA H. PEARCE

This is a variation of a recipe given to my husband during his intern/residency years by a fellow intern who said he loved to make it because its all-day simmering was so comforting while he studied. We love it because not only does it provide comfort during the simmering time but it can also be plucked out of the freezer and quickly made into a meal to take to a sick neighbor. Freezer storage also makes it possible to feed hordes of children and grandchildren on a moment's notice. Add a salad and frozen peas and presto, you're there!

3 (24-oz.) cans tomato sauce

1 (10¾-oz.) can tomato purée

1 (6-oz.) can tomato paste

3 to 4 Tbs. Italian seasoning

2 cloves garlic, crushed

½ tsp. onion powder

Parmesan cheese, grated (optional)

Fresh basil, minced (optional)

Simmer first 6 ingredients in crockpot on low 4 to 5 hours or in a covered heavy pan several hours. If using pan, stir occasionally so sauce doesn't stick and burn. Freezes well. Serve on pasta (top with freshly grated Parmesan cheese and fresh basil), use as sauce for lasagna, or serve over mixed vegetables fresh from garden.

Makes 4 quarts.

Virginia Hinckley Pearce received a master's degree in social work from the University of Utah. She has worked as a therapist in both public agencies and private practice. She has taught classes in children's literature and is a free-lance writer, having authored several books. She edited the best-selling book about her mother, *Glimpses into the Life and Heart of Marjorie Pay Hinckley*. Sister Pearce has served as a member of the Young Women general presidency and the Primary general board. She and her husband, Dr. James R. Pearce, are the parents of six children and the grandparents of sixteen.

Mother's Chili Sauce

CAROL CORNWALL MADSEN

With a family of seven children, my mother usually cooked a large roast for Sunday dinner in order to have leftovers for sandwiches that night and for school lunch boxes the next day. The roast was always accompanied by homemade chili sauce. This small culinary tradition was so ingrained that the daughters of the family have continued it for their own families. They have also often made extra batches of chili sauce for their brothers, who are not always recipients of this long-held family tradition. One brother even cultivated a tomato garden in order to have the freshest home-grown ingredients for this delicious condiment. The recipe, which originated in my grandmother's generation, is now seasonally utilized by the fourth generation of family members, and bottles of chili sauce have been mailed to places as near as Provo, Utah, and as far away as Hamburg, Germany, to satisfy the cravings of family members. Mother's chili sauce has become one of those small but irreplaceable bonds that tie the family together. Mother's dog-eared, handwritten recipe is as much a treasure as the chili sauce itself.

1 peck (8 quarts) ripe tomatoes

6 large onions, ground

6 large green peppers, ground

4 c. cider vinegar

2 c. sugar

2 Tbs. salt

1 Tbs. cinnamon

1 Tbs. dry mustard

1 Tbs. cloves, ground

Blanch tomatoes to remove skins. Core and chop; place in large heavy kettle. Grind onions and green peppers; add to tomatoes along with remaining ingredients. Simmer until sauce reaches desired thickness (usually 4 to 5 hours). Stir often to avoid burning. Enjoy tantalizing aroma as chili sauce cooks. When done, pour into sterilized pint jars and seal immediately. Process bottles in steam or water bath until sealed (7 to 10 minutes). Store in a cool, dry place.

Makes 8 or 9 pints.

Carol Cornwall Madsen is a professor of history in the BYU Department of History and a research professor in the Joseph Fielding Smith Institute for Church History. She is a former president of the Mormon History Association and the author of several books, including *Journey to Zion: Voices from the Mormon Trail.* Carol and her husband, Gordon A. Madsen, are the parents of six children and live in Salt Lake City, Utah.

Cranberry Chutney

ELAINE JACK

1 (16-oz.) pkg. cranberries

2 c. sugar

1 c. orange juice

1 c. walnuts, chopped

1 c. celery, chopped

1 tsp. ground ginger

1 medium apple, chopped

1 Tbs. orange peel, grated

1 c. golden or dark seedless raisins

Put cranberries, sugar, and 1 cup water in kettle and heat to boiling. Reduce heat to low and simmer about 15 minutes. Remove from heat; stir in remaining ingredients. Cover and refrigerate until ready to serve.

Keeps forever and is good with or without meat.

Makes 7 cups.

Elaine L. Jack grew up in Cardston, Alberta, Canada, where she recently served as matron of the Cardston Alberta Temple. Sister Jack has also served as general president of the Relief Society, as a counselor in the Young Women general presidency, and has a great love for the women of the Church of all ages. She's involved in community service in the areas of education and children's literacy. She and her husband, Joseph E. Jack, are the parents of four sons and grandparents of fifteen children.

Smoot Family's Famous Flavor-All Dressing

MARY ELLEN SMOOT

This dressing is great for tossed salads, a topping for baked potatoes, a light sauce over vegetables, steak sauce, or a great chip dip. This is a longtime family favorite.

1 (35-oz.) bottle Best Foods®
   Real mayonnaise

1 (8-oz.) pkg. cream cheese

1 qt. buttermilk

½ tsp. onion salt

½ tsp. black pepper

½ tsp. garlic salt

Mix all ingredients thoroughly; pour into glass container and store in refrigerator.

Makes 1½ quarts.

Mary Ellen Wood Smoot served as general president of the Relief Society from April 1997 to April 2002. She loves family history and has written histories about her parents, grandparents, and their local community. She served with her husband, Stanley M. Smoot, when he was called as a mission president in Ohio, and they later served together as directors of Church Hosting. They are the parents of seven children and the grandparents of forty-seven.

Three-Quart Shrimp Cocktail

NORMAN AND COLLEEN BANGERTER

This recipe is a family holiday favorite—it's also easy and fast to make!

2 tall cans tomato juice

3 (6-oz.) cans shrimp pieces

1 (30-oz.) bottle ketchup

½ tsp. onion salt

5 tsp. mild horseradish

1 tsp. garlic salt

2 Tbs. sugar

2 Tbs. Worcestershire sauce

3 c. celery, diced

Mix all ingredients together and chill 24 hours. Heat before serving, or serve cold.

Makes 3 quarts.

Norman and Colleen Monson Bangerter served for eight years as governor and first lady of the state of Utah. Prior to entering politics in 1974, Governor Bangerter was a successful real estate developer and businessman. He then served in the Utah House of Representatives as assistant majority whip, majority leader, and twice as speaker of the house. In 1990, the Governor announced his retirement to private life. The Bangerters are the parents of six children and reside in Salt Lake City, Utah.

Tasty, Quick Appetizer

CHARLES AND DOROTHA SMART

This is my favorite for parties. It was given to me by a retiring caterer and takes only fifteen to twenty minutes to make. The cheese spread can be mixed the day before; then, just before serving on the day of the party, can be spread on the freshly sliced bread and broiled.

½ lb. Monterey Jack cheese, ,shredded

1 (4-oz.) can mild diced chilies, drained

4 to 5 Tbs. mayonnaise

1 baguette bread loaf, thinly sliced

Mix grated cheese, chilies, and mayonnaise thoroughly. Spread moderate amount on bread slices. Place on baking sheet under broiler 2 to 3 minutes, watching constantly until bubbles appear. Place on platter and serve while hot.

Serves 12 to 16.

Dr. Charles A. Smart is a pioneer in computerizing cancer research. He is the former chief of surgery at LDS Hospital and the founder of the Utah Cancer Registry. His wife, Dorotha Sharp Smart, has given many years of service to the Utah Symphony and has served as president of the Utah Symphony Guild. She chaired the search committee that appointed Keith Lockhart music director of the Utah Symphony. Together the Smarts have served on the Temple Square Concert Series Committee and have completed a service mission to Moscow, Russia. They are the parents of six children and the grandparents of twenty-six.

Wild Mushroom Appetizer

KELLY PARKINSON

When I was young and growing up in the foothills east of Provo, a member of our ward—Revel Philips—a forest ranger by profession, came to my mother to inform her that we had a highly-prized variety of edible mushroom growing on our property. My mother, a child of the Depression, was not about to let this gourmet food go to waste. So, the children—my brothers, sisters, and I—were taught to gently harvest the mushrooms after every spring and summer rainstorm, and even into the fall. It had to be carefully done, so as not to disturb the mother plant. There were often grocery bags full of mushrooms—many more than we could use. Sometimes we gave them to our neighbors, who undoubtedly wondered why we were trying to poison them. We enjoyed some delicious meals featuring these wonderful wild mushrooms; and for a delicious appetizer, we would sauté them in butter, mix in a little sour cream, and spoon them onto toast.

1 to 2 French baguette loaves

Olive oil

1 lb. mushrooms, cleaned

1 Tbs. butter

2 to 3 Tbs. sour cream

Salt and pepper

Slice baguette on diagonal into small rounds. Spread with olive oil and broil on baking sheet 1 to 2 minutes until barely brown. Slice mushrooms thinly and sauté in butter until soft and light brown. Stir in sour cream and salt and pepper to taste. Spoon onto toasted rounds and serve.

Serves 12 to 15.

Kelly Clark Parkinson, violin soloist for Ballet West, grew up in Provo, Utah, and began violin studies at age seven. She attended the Peabody Conservatory and holds degrees in violin performance from BYU and UCLA. As a soloist and chamber musician, Kelly has performed throughout the United States and Europe. She and her husband, Dr. Brett Parkinson, are the parents of four children.

Hot Crab Dip

MARGARET D. NADAULD

This was on the menu for our wedding reception July 19, 1968. It was a hit with our guests that night, and we have continued to serve it over the years to our guests, especially during all the entertaining years when my husband served as president of Weber State University.

1 (6-oz.) can crab meat (or 6-oz. pkg. frozen crab meat)

½ c. sour cream

1 (3-oz.) pkg. cream cheese, room temperature

1 Tbs. lemon juice

1 tsp. horseradish

2 Tbs. green bell pepper, minced

1 Tbs. pimiento, minced

French bread (or baguette), thinly sliced

Crackers or potato chips (optional)

Drain and flake crab meat into small bowl (frozen crab meat must first be thawed in refrigerator overnight); cover and set aside. In medium saucepan, combine sour cream, cream cheese, lemon juice, and horseradish, stirring to blend. Add green pepper, pimiento, and flaked crab meat. Cook over low heat, stirring gently, until bubbly. To serve, keep warm in small fondue pot or heat-proof dish on hot tray. Use as dip for small bread slices, crackers, or chips.

Makes 2 cups.

Margaret D. Nadauld is the former general president of the Young Women organization and a former member of the board of trustees of Brigham Young University. She has taught piano lessons as well as high school English and is the author of *Write Back Soon: Letters of Love and Encouragement for Young Women*. She and her husband, Stephen D. Nadauld, a former member of the Second Quorum of the Seventy, are the parents of seven sons and the grandparents of eight.

Fantastic Party Dip

JAMES B. WELCH

Tired of the same old party dips? Then try this one. It always gets rave reviews.

1 (8-oz.) pkg. Philadelphia® cream cheese, softened

1 tsp. curry

½ bottle peach chutney (Old Calcutta® or other)

5 green onions, sliced thin

½ lb. bacon, cooked crisp and crumbled

Mix cream cheese with 1 teaspoon curry (or less—the curry flavor should be light). Form into brick again and chill until 1 hour before serving. Then layer curried cream cheese brick as follows:

Pour chutney over top.

Sprinkle with onions.

Sprinkle with bacon bits.

Serve with unflavored crackers or vegetable sticks.

Serves 8.

James Welch, University Organist at Santa Clara University in the San Francisco Bay Area, is a frequent performer at guest recitals on Temple Square. His musical career has taken him around the world, where he has performed in concerts at Notre Dame Cathedral, Paris, and in the cathedrals of Würzburg, Germany; Lausanne, Switzerland; Salzburg, Austria; Wellington, New Zealand; Olomouc, Czechoslovakia; and Beijing, China. He is the composer of "Bless Our Fast, We Pray" (*Hymns*, no. 138). James and his wife, Deanne, are the parents of two sons and reside in Palo Alto, California.

Mexican Cheese Roll

ALBERT AND MARILYN JEPPSON CHOULES

We don't know the origin of this recipe, but Albert has been making it for a long time. He makes this one best himself.

- 1 lb. Velveeta® Mexican cheese (mild or hot), room temperature
- 1 (8-oz.) pkg. cream cheese, room temperature
- 1 small can diced green chilies, drained

Place softened Velveeta cheese between 2 pieces of waxed paper and roll to thickness of ¼ to ⅜ inch. Remove waxed paper and spread cream cheese gently to cover Velveeta cheese. Sprinkle green chilies on top of cream cheese. At one end, begin rolling the three layers in jelly-roll fashion. Chill until firm. Serve with favorite crackers.

Serves 6 to 8.

Albert Choules, Jr., has been a member of the Second Quorum of the Seventy, a Regional Representative, and president of the New York, New York City Mission. He is the senior vice president of Coltrin and Associates, a New York City-based public relations firm. He was married to the former Rosemary Phillips, who passed away in 1984. Albert married Marilyn Jeppson in 1987. Marilyn has a Ph.D. from BYU and is a counselor in private practice in Salt Lake City. Together, the Choules have twenty-two grandchildren.

Cheese Ball

HILARY WEEKS

I remember having this old family favorite at many family get-togethers in Colorado—especially when we celebrated Thanksgiving. This cheese ball recipe is from the kitchen of my aunt, Gayle Buckwalter, who is a wonderful cook. After our family moved to Alaska, my mother continued to make the cheese ball for special occasions. Now I make it for my family. We love it anytime, but we always have it on the buffet table at Thanksgiving and New Year's Eve. I hope my children will pass the recipe on to their children—so I can come over and enjoy it!

1 (8-oz.) pkg. cream cheese

1 (5-oz.) jar Kraft® Old English Cheese

1 (5-oz.) jar Kraft® Roka Bleu Cheese

2 to 3 green onions, diced

2 tsp. Worcestershire sauce

Pecans, chopped

Crackers of choice

In mixer, thoroughly combine cheeses, green onions, and Worcestershire sauce. Form into ball; wrap and chill. When ball is firm, roll in chopped pecans until covered. Serve with favorite snack crackers.

Serves 12.

Music was a family affair in the Alaskan home where singer/songwriter Hilary Weeks was raised. Hilary began piano lessons when she was eight years old. Her two older brothers took lessons and Hilary specifically remembers asking her mother if she could have lessons, too. Mom agreed, and the rest is history. Hilary has four solo CD releases, including *I Will Not Forget, Lead Me Home,* and *Christmastime.* She has been honored by the Faith Centered Music Association with multiple Pearl Awards, including Songwriter and Female Vocalist of the Year. She and her husband, Tim, have three daughters.

Fruit Salsa with Sugar Cinnamon Chips

CHAD HAWKINS

The years 1999 and 2000 were a time in my career that I will never forget. In that season of unprecedented temple construction, I produced over forty paintings of temples throughout the world. In addition to my drawings and paintings, I had the privilege of touring and researching the histories of twenty-one newly completed temples. Some of my choicest memories center on the friends I made at that time. During a visit to the Fresno California temple, the owners of a local LDS bookstore invited me into their home for dinner. Elbert and Cheryl Cox served this appetizer that has since become a tradition in my home.

FRUIT SALSA

2 Granny Smith apples

1 Bartlett pear

1 c. strawberries

1 mango

2 Tbs. fresh lemon juice

1 Tbs. brown sugar, packed

CINNAMON CHIPS

6 large flour tortillas

4 Tbs. sugar

1 Tbs. cinnamon

To make salsa, peel, core, and chop apples. Wash and chop pear, strawberries, and mango. Place fruit in medium bowl and stir in lemon juice and brown sugar to coat. Chill in refrigerator. You can mix and match any of your favorite fruits to make this salsa.

To make cinnamon chips, preheat oven to 375° F. Combine cinnamon and sugar in small bowl. Using water spray bottle, lightly spray tortillas and sprinkle with cinnamon-sugar mixture. Using pizza cutter, cut each tortilla into 8 wedges. Place tortilla wedges on baking sheet and bake 10 to 12 minutes or until crispy. Remove from oven and cool.

Serves 6.

Chad Spencer Hawkins began creating his unique series of temple prints in 1989, at age seventeen, to support his mission. Upon returning from the Germany Frankfurt Mission, Chad pursued an education in fine art at Weber State University. His paintings hang in galleries and private collections throughout the world, and his original work of the Vernal Utah Temple is on permanent display inside that edifice. His artwork has been selected for placement in twelve of the cornerstones of the Church's temples. Chad is the author of the bestselling book *The First 100 Temples* and *Youth and the Temple*. He and his wife, Stephanie, live in Layton, Utah, with their children.

Bread for Life

WARM

AND FLAKY

BREADS

AND ROLLS

Jessie Evans Smith's 90-Minute Bread

SUSAN EVANS MCCLOUD

I grew up with this recipe, which was handed down through the family, since Jessie was my great aunt, and I knew her well as a child and young woman. I use it always when I am in a hurry but want to make good, warm, homemade bread. I always use it for rolls on Thanksgiving Day, because it requires so little work.

4 c. warm water

4 yeast cakes (or equivalent in yeast granules)

4 tsp. salt

8 Tbs. sugar

4 Tbs. oil

7 to 8 c. flour

Dissolve yeast in 1 cup of the warm water. Mix in remaining ingredients, including the rest of the water, until dough is soft but not sticky. If needed, use more flour and knead to proper consistency.

Cut into 4 parts. Let stand 15 minutes. Using handle of butcher knife, pound each piece of dough 1 minute.

Form into 4 loaves and put each into a greased 4½x8½x2½-inch bread pan. Let stand, covered, at least 30 minutes. Bake 30 minutes at 400° F.

Makes 4 loaves.

Susan Evans McCloud has published more than forty books, including several biographies, children's books, and dozens of works of fiction. Her work also includes several screenplays, tape narratives, and the lyrics to two hymns: "Lord, I Would Follow Thee" and "As Zion's Youth in Latter Days." Susan and her husband, James, are the parents of six children and six grandchildren. They reside in Provo, Utah.

Gramine's Lovely Homemade Bread

ELLIOT AND MAXINE CAMERON

As a newlywed, I explained to Elliot that my talents were not in the kitchen. One evening when we sat down to eat one of our first meals together, I guiltily told him I could make only pancakes or meatloaf. He gazed at his plate and politely asked, "Which is this?" It was clear to me that I had to learn to cook. I started making homemade bread.

During the time Elliot served as president of Snow College and stake president, President Joseph Fielding Smith and his wife, Jessie Evans Smith, were guests in our home. I was honored to accompany Sister Smith's vocal solo in our stake conference. We all ate bread and milk after the conference.

President Harold B. Lee was also a guest in our home. His only request after conference meetings was for a bowl of bread and milk. Because of those experiences I continued to improve my bread-making skills, and I was thrilled in later years to hear my four teenagers say, as they walked through the door from school, "Umm-m-m, homemade bread!"

Our grandchildren are the best test I have for my food, so I included the foods they like most. They would rather have a slice of my homemade bread than a slice of pizza. During a visit to our family in the east, I was prevailed upon to make bread. At the conclusion of the evening meal, our daughter-in-law asked her small daughter if she would like something more to eat. The little girl said, "Yes, I'd like another slice of Gramine's lovely homemade bread!"

2 Tbs. dry yeast

½ c. lukewarm water

1 tsp. sugar

3½ c. skim milk, scalded

¾ c. canola oil

4 eggs, slightly beaten

¾ c. honey

2 (scant) Tbs. salt

9 to 10 c. whole wheat flour

1 c. white flour (optional)

Grind enough wheat to make about 10 cups whole wheat flour. You can also use whole wheat flour. Sift flour twice and set aside. Mix yeast in lukewarm water and stir in sugar. Mix milk, oil, eggs, honey, and salt in large bowl or bread mixer (not bread maker). Stir in yeast mixture. Gradually add flour one cup at a time; dough must not be too stiff. (Flour measurements are approximate. I usually add 1 cup white sifted flour.) Knead dough or mix on medium speed about 10 minutes. Cover dough with plastic wrap that has been sprayed with vegetable oil. Let rise until doubled in bulk.

Spray 5 small (4x7½-inch) loaf pans with vegetable spray. Divide dough into 5 equal parts and shape into loaves. Place in pans. Cover with plastic wrap that has been sprayed with vegetable oil. Let rise to about 1½ inches above pan edge. Preheat oven to 400° F. Place bread loaves on middle rack and reduce heat to 300° F. Bake 1 hour. Cool loaves on rack.

Makes 5 small loaves.

Elliot Cameron has served as president of BYU–Hawaii, commissioner of the Church Educational System, and president of the Provo Temple. His wife, Maxine Petty Cameron has served by his side as first lady of BYU–Hawaii and matron of the Provo Temple. She is an accomplished pianist and organizer of Forty Fingers, a piano quartet that plays for benefits, devotionals, and other programs throughout Utah. The Camerons have four children, one foster son, twenty-three grandchildren, and six great-grandchildren.

My Mother's Bread Recipe

JAKE GARN

I grew up with a wonderful mother who also happened to be a fantastic cook and baker. I knew I could live with many changes in my life as I left home to be married and serve as a Navy pilot; but I also knew I could not exist without my mother's whole wheat bread. I asked my wife if she planned to bake bread just like my mother's, and her answer was: "No!"

There was only one solution to this problem and that was to ask my mother to teach me how to bake bread and continue the family tradition. She told me it was not easy to bake good bread, that every batch would be somewhat different; so I would have to learn how to feel the dough to determine when it was just right. She also stated that her recipe was rather general because it did not make any difference what the specific ingredients were because bread-making was an art not a science.

So, decades ago, with much trial and error I became a baker. While I was mayor of Salt Lake City, and during all the years that I had the honor of representing Utah in the United States Senate, I baked at least four loaves of bread a week to keep my family supplied with their grandmother's bread. In fact, one son became so addicted to my bread that, once or twice a month, I would Federal Express two loaves for overnight delivery to Calgary, Canada, where he was serving his mission.

There was another benefit to my bread baking. Often, in the Senate, I could put in an eighteen-hour day and, at the conclusion of the session, ask myself what had been accomplished that day. The answer would be "nothing." At home, when my bread came out of the oven, however, there was a sense of accomplishment. I could smell the wonderful aroma and see the hot loaves and say, "I did that!" It gave me a tangible sense of accomplishment.

My mother wrote and framed her recipe for homemade bread. These are her directions, with my recommendations in brackets:

Take a yellow bowl that is chipped around the edges, add five cups of [warm] milk or water, a handful of salt [about 2 tablespoons], one and a half if your hand is small (mine isn't), three-fourths cup of sugar, one-half cup melted butter, [3 tablespoons liquid lecithin], two yeast cakes dissolved in a little warm water. Mix together and add enough [whole wheat] flour to make the dough stiff enough to mold, but not sticky. While kneading the dough, look out the window and be grateful for the beautiful world you live in and the good things in it. Then put the bowl in a warm place; let rise until double in bulk. Shape into three loaves; let rise again until the loaves are rounded above the pans. Bake in a 350-degree oven for 30 to 35 minutes, or until your good judgment tells you that it is done. As the fragrance sifts through the house, do not grumble if little folks want to cut a slice.

I love you! Grandma G. (5-12-1957)

Jake Garn retired from the United States Senate on 3 January 1993, after eighteen years in Congress. Prior to his election to the Senate, he served as mayor of Salt Lake City, Utah. Senator Garn had the singular distinction of flying as a payload specialist on flight 51-D of the space shuttle Discovery in 1985. Senator Garn and his late wife, Hazel Thompson, had four children. He is now married to Kathleen Brewerton, and they are the parents of three more children.

Monkey Bread

MARY ELLEN SMOOT

I also use this for rolls—a family favorite.

2 c. lukewarm water

½ c. sugar

1 Tbs. salt

1 Tbs. yeast

2 eggs, beaten

7 c. Wondra® flour (may substitute presifted flour)

4 Tbs. oil

½ c. butter

Preheat oven to 400° F. In large glass mixing bowl, mix water, sugar, salt, and yeast; let rest 10 minutes. Add eggs and 3 cups of the flour. Mix well with mixer. Add oil and remaining 4 cups flour, mixing until flour is absorbed.

Let rise in bowl 2 hours. Roll out dough ½-inch thick; cut out pieces of dough with an 11-ounce orange juice can. Melt butter in 2 Bundt pans. Stack pieces on their sides all around pans. Let rise 3 to 4 hours. Bake at 400° F. for 20 minutes.

Serves 8.

Butter Pastry Rolls

MARY ELLEN SMOOT

I received this recipe from a neighbor in Upper Arlington, Ohio, just before she passed away. It has become a family favorite.

1 pkg. yeast

1 c. lukewarm water

4½ c. flour

½ c. sugar

Pinch of salt

1 (scant) c. butter

2 eggs

Slivered almonds

Dissolve yeast in lukewarm water. Set aside. In a large bowl, combine flour, sugar, and salt. Cut in butter with pastry blender. In a separate bowl, beat eggs; add yeast mixture. Stir liquid into flour mixture with spoon. Let rise about 1 hour, then stir down. Let rise again.

Divide dough in two parts. Roll or pat out dough into a circle on a very lightly floured board. Spread with butter. Cut as a pie, then roll each piece from wide edge. Place rolls on buttered cookie sheet and let rise. Bake at 350° F. about 15 minutes. Do not brown or overbake. When slightly cooled, dust with confectioner's sugar and slivered almonds on top.

Makes 2 dozen rolls.

Mary Ellen Wood Smoot served as general president of the Relief Society from April 1997 to April 2002. She loves family history and has written histories about her parents, grandparents, and their local community. She served with her husband, Stanley M. Smoot, when he was called as a mission president in Ohio, and they later served together as directors of Church Hosting. They are the parents of seven children and the grandparents of fifty.

Sharon's Rolls

SHARON G. LARSEN

These rolls are always my food assignment at family gatherings. I try to make extra so that people can take some home, but there are rarely any left. Served with butter and jam, they are better than dessert!

1 c. butter or margarine

2 pkgs. dry yeast

2 Tbs. sugar

2 c. lukewarm water

1 c. sugar

6 eggs, beaten

8 c. flour

1½ tsp. salt

Melt butter in large mixing bowl and set aside. Mix yeast with 2 tablespoons sugar and water; add butter, sugar, and eggs. Mix well. Stir in flour and salt; let rise at least 2 hours. Stir down, cover with plastic wrap or tea towel, and refrigerate overnight.

Remove from refrigerator and place on floured board or pastry sheet. Separate dough into quarters. Roll each into a large circle; brush with butter and cut like a pie into 12 wedges (a pizza cutter works well). Roll up from wide end to tail end. Place rolls on buttered baking sheet, making sure tail side is down so it will not unroll as it rises. Let rise 4 to 5 hours. Bake at 375° F. for 10 minutes. Using a pastry brush, spread on melted butter after rolls come out of oven.

Makes 4 dozen rolls.

Sharon Greene Larsen attended the University of Alberta and graduated from Brigham Young University with a bachelor of science degree. She taught in elementary schools in Utah and Missouri. She wrote, produced, and starred in programs for the Utah Network for Instructional Television. She has twice served on the Young Women general board and in the Young Women general presidency and served as the national president of Lambda Delta Sigma. Sister Larsen taught institute at two colleges. She and her husband, Dr. Ralph T. Larsen, are the parents of two children and grandparents of three.

Butterhorn Rolls and Variations

WINNIFRED C. JARDINE

A variety of rolls—plain or fancy—can be made with this basic soft bread recipe.

1 package (1 Tbs.) active dry yeast

¼ c. warm water (115° F.)

1 c. butter, melted

¾ c. milk, scalded

½ c. sugar

¾ tsp. salt

3 eggs, well beaten

4 to 5 c. flour

In large mixing bowl, soften yeast in warm water. Combine ½ cup of the melted butter and scalded milk. Stir in sugar, salt, and eggs. Cool. Stir in softened yeast and enough flour to make soft dough. Cover; allow to rise 2 hours or until double in bulk. Turn out onto lightly floured board; knead just to coat dough with flour. Dough is very soft and should remain so. Divide dough. Roll each half into a 14-inch circle. Spread each circle with half of the remaining melted butter. Cut pie-fashion into 12 to 16 wedges. Roll each piece loosely from large end to small. Place on greased baking sheet. Allow to rise 2 hours or until double in bulk. Bake at 375° F. 12 to 15 minutes or until lightly browned.

These rolls and the variations that follow may be frozen ahead of time by shaping as desired, immediately placing rolls on baking sheet, and quick-freezing. Remove frozen rolls from baking sheet; place in heavy plastic freezer bag. Twist bag closed; keep up to 2 weeks. Six hours before baking time, remove from freezer and arrange on greased baking sheet or in greased muffin tins, according to recipe. Allow to thaw and rise 5 to 6 hours. Bake as directed.

Makes 24 to 32 rolls.

VARIATIONS

For variations on this recipe, follow preceeding instructions until it is time to roll out the dough. Then roll each half into an 8x14-inch rectangle. Follow filling instructions then roll loosely, starting from long side; pinch edges together. Slice into 12 pieces and place cut side down in buttered muffin pans. Allow to rise 2 hours or until double in bulk. Bake 12 to 15 minutes. While hot, brush with powdered sugar icing. (Butterscotch rolls do not need frosting.) Remove from pans.

STATLER HOUSE FILLING

½ c. butter, melted

4 Tbs. sugar

¼ c. raisins, chopped

Spread each rectangle with ¼ cup melted butter, 2 tablespoons of the sugar, and ⅛ cup of the raisins.

BUTTERSCOTCH FILLING

½ c. butter, melted

1 c. brown sugar

Spread each rectangle with ¼ cup melted butter and ½ cup brown sugar.

ORANGE FILLING

½ c. butter, softened

½ c. sugar

Zest from one orange

Cream together butter and sugar; stir in orange zest. Spread half of mixture on each rectangle.

CHRISTMAS TEA RING

Follow directions for Butterhorns until it is time to roll out dough. Roll out each half into an 8x14-inch rectangle; spread each half with ¼ cup melted butter; sprinkle 2 tablespoons sugar, and a variety of candied fruit and nuts atop the butter. Roll up each rectangle, starting from the long side. Shape each roll into a circle on a buttered baking sheet, pinching ends together. With scissors, make cuts two-thirds into the circle at 1-inch intervals; then twist each 1-inch piece one-half to left to make tea ring. Allow to rise 2 hours or until ring has doubled in bulk; bake as for rolls. Drizzle with powdered sugar frosting and decorate with candied cherries and nuts.

POWDERED SUGAR ICING

1 c. powdered sugar

1 Tbs. warm water

½ tsp. rum extract

For icing, combine powderd sugar, water, and rum extract to a smooth consistency.

Winnifred Jardine graduated from Iowa State University in technical journalism and foods and nutrition. For thirty-six years she served as food editor of the *Deseret News*. Prior to that time she served, among other things, as a home economist in the Martha Logan Test Kitchen, Swift and Company, Chicago; as director of home economics at the American Meat Institute in Chicago; and as instructor of foods and nutrition at the University of Utah. She is a past president of the Utah Association of Family and Consumer Sciences and the Utah State Nutrition Council. She is the author of many cookbooks. Winnifred and her husband, Stuart, live in Salt Lake City, Utah.

Buttermilk Banana Bread with Raisins

DAVID LINDSLEY

My wife's family has had this recipe for at least three generations—but without the raisins. I love juicy raisins in other baked goods and suggested that my wife use them instead of nuts. It was delicious! We often double it when the bananas on the counter have changed from perfect yellow to unappetizing brown-black. Buttermilk Banana Bread is my favorite snack recipe—and my personalized piece of family tradition. For a lighter version, try substituting half of the butter with ¼ cup applesauce. We love this moist version just as well.

1⅔ c. flour

½ tsp. salt

1 tsp. baking soda

½ c. butter

1 c. sugar

2 eggs

1 tsp. vanilla

¼ c. buttermilk

1 c. ripe bananas, mashed

½ to 1 c. raisins

Spray muffin pan and small loaf pan with cooking spray. Preheat oven to 350° F. Mix dry ingredients together in large mixing bowl and set aside. In separate bowl, cream together butter, sugar, and eggs. Stir in vanilla, buttermilk, bananas, and raisins to creamed mixture. Add this mixture by thirds into dry ingredients, stirring until well blended. Pour batter into muffin cups, filling each one-half to two-thirds full. Remaining batter will make one small bread loaf. (Otherwise, recipe will make one large bread loaf.)

Bake 20 to 25 minutes for muffins, 35 to 40 minutes for small loaf, or until browned and toothpick comes out clean. (For large loaf of bread, bake about 50 to 60 minutes.) Remove from pan and cool on rack. When cool, wrap in plastic wrap or foil. Freeze or serve fresh.

Makes 12 muffins and 1 small loaf or 1 large loaf.

Born and raised in California, David Lindsley exhibited artistic talent at an early age and has earned recognition and many awards. He has been painting portraits for over thirty years and is a member of the Portrait Society of America and the American Society of Portrait Artists. From 8x10-inch miniatures to 8x10-foot murals, he works exclusively in oils and has created commissioned works for private collections, colleges, publications, and corporations. Among his paintings are portraits of Joseph Smith and the Savior, Jesus Christ. David and his wife, Sherilyn, have four children.

Banana Bread

BARBARA B. SMITH

When we were all home together, I baked eight loaves of bread twice a week, had scones at noon for those who wanted to run home from school for the lunch hour, gave a loaf or two to neighbors, and had enough and to spare for our family, which included not only the seven children and the two of us but my father, Aunt Martha, and always a friend or two. This delicious bread recipe is my mother's.

2 c. flour
1 tsp. baking soda
1 c. sugar
¼ c. butter
½ tsp. salt
3 ripe bananas, crushed
2 eggs
½ c. chopped nuts

Preheat oven to 350° F. Sift together flour and soda, then mix all ingredients together and pour into a greased 8x2½x4½-inch loaf pan and bake 1 hour.

Makes 1 loaf.

Barbara Bradshaw Smith served as general president of the Relief Society from 1974 to 1984. She has also served as national president of the American Mothers, Inc., and on President Jimmy Carter's White House Advisory Committee for the Conference on Families. She is married to Douglas H. Smith, a former member of the First and Second Quorums of the Seventy and President of the Asia Area. Brother and Sister Smith have sent out thirty-five missionaries from their immediate and extended family. They have served on every continent of the world with the exception of Antarctica, and there is no mission there.

Conference Potato Doughnuts

DANTZEL W. NELSON

While giving a talk at the priesthood session of general conference, my husband—Elder Russell M. Nelson—mentioned that the women and children of our family were at home making doughnuts. This was a tradition of ours; when the men arrived home after the meeting we would all sit together and munch on the doughnuts and share one special thought that each priesthood holder had learned at the meeting. Since Elder Nelson's talk, many people have asked us: "How were the doughnuts?" Some have asked for the recipe. Here it is. I

clipped the recipe from the *Deseret News* years ago. Thanks to William S. Holmes. We still make the doughnuts twice a year and have many happy memories stored up as a family.

3 c. milk

1 c. shortening

4 tsp. salt

1 c. sugar

2 c. mashed potatoes (salt before cooking)

2 Tbs. (2 pkgs.) dry yeast

1 c. warm water

6 eggs, beaten

12 to 13 c. flour (more as needed)

2 tsp. lemon juice

2 tsp. lemon rind, grated

½ tsp. nutmeg

Glaze (see recipe)

GLAZE

1½ c. powdered sugar

¼ c. warm water (1 Tbs. at a time)

1 tsp. vanilla

¼ tsp. cream of tartar

1 Tbs. Karo® syrup

Combine milk, shortening, salt, sugar, and mashed potatoes in a large saucepan; heat to lukewarm. In large mixing bowl, dissolve yeast in warm water; then stir in beaten eggs. Stir in potato mixture. Add 6 cups flour and beat until well-blended and smooth. Add lemon juice, grated rind, and nutmeg. Then stir in remaining flour to make a soft, firm dough (firm enough to roll). Knead dough until smooth. Cover and let rise until doubled in bulk.

Punch down and divide dough in half. Roll out ½-inch thick and cut with a doughnut cutter. Cover and allow to rise until doubled, or about 30 to 40 minutes.

Fry in deep fat at 375° F. until golden on each side. Drain on absorbent paper; then dip in prepared glaze and set on waxed paper until ready to serve.

Recipe can be halved or doubled, depending on the size of the crowd. You can also dip the doughnuts in granulated sugar instead of glazing them.

Makes about 100 doughnuts.

For glaze, combine all ingredients together in medium bowl. Coat doughnuts.

Dantzel White Nelson, born in Perry, Utah, received her bachelor's degree from the University of Utah. She taught school in Salt Lake City, Utah, and Minneapolis, Minnesota, and has been a full-time mother and homemaker since 1948. She has served in Primary, Young Women, and Relief Society callings in Washington, D.C., Boston, Minneapolis, and Salt Lake City. She was a member of the Mormon Tabernacle Choir for twenty years. In 1999 she received the Exemplary Woman Award from Ricks College. She is married to Elder Russell M. Nelson of the Quorum of the Twelve Apostles. They have ten children (nine daughters and one son) and fifty-four grandchildren. Their great-grandchildren are just beginning to grace their family circle.

Cinnamon Rolls

JANENE WOLSEY BAADSGAARD

I like to make cinnamon rolls because I love the feel of the dough when I work with it. They also make my home smell heavenly. Our family especially enjoys the rolls on Christmas morning, along with hot chocolate and an orange from our Christmas stockings.

1 c. milk

1 stick butter

1 Tbs. yeast

½ c. warm water

1 tsp. sugar

¼ c. sugar

¾ tsp. salt

3 eggs, beaten

5½ c. flour

FILLING

2 Tbs. cinnamon

Sugar to taste

½ c. butter, melted

FROSTING

2 c. powdered sugar

½ c. milk

Melted butter, if desired

Heat milk in a small saucepan until hot; add stick of butter and set aside to cool. In a small bowl, combine yeast with warm water and 1 teaspoon sugar. (For quicker rising dough, double yeast measurement.) In large bowl, mix cooled milk and softened yeast mixture. Add ¼ cup sugar, salt, beaten eggs, and flour, mixing constantly to blend. Knead dough until smooth; cover and allow to rise. Meanwhile, spray baking sheet lightly with cooking oil.

Punch down dough and divide in half; roll out one half to oblong shape on floured surface. Mix cinnamon and sugar with melted butter; spread half of mixture over dough. Carefully roll up dough; pinch seam and place seam-down on floured cutting board. Slice to desired thickness and place rolls flat on prepared baking sheet. Let rise while following same procedure with other half of dough. Preheat oven to 325° F.; bake 20 minutes. Remove from tray and cool slightly before frosting.

Makes 2 dozen small or 1 dozen large rolls.

Janene Wolsey Baadsgaard is a homemaker and free-lance writer. She has been a columnist for the *Deseret News* and has taught English and literature classes at Utah Valley State College. Her work ranges from humorous and practical advice for mothers and fathers to clever and hilarious fiction. Her next project is a comprehensive book on mothering called *The LDS Mother's Almanac*, which will be published in April 2003. She and her husband, Ross, are the parents of ten children and the grandparents of three. They live in Spanish Fork, Utah.

Soup's On

SOUPS,
CHOWDERS,
STEWS,
AND CHILI

Joseph Robinson's Lentil Soup

KARL-HEINZ SCHNIBBE

My wife's father, Joseph William Robinson, was a longtime Alta Club chef—where tastes were sophisticated, the food plentiful, and its presentation elegant. But at home, her dad taught her the basics of food preparation and healthful eating. This recipe from her father's collection is for a nutritious soup our family has often enjoyed. I suggested adding a touch of vinegar—a German thing—and we now prefer it that way.

2 Tbs. olive oil or butter

1 onion, diced

2 carrots, diced

2 celery stalks, diced

2 qt. beef broth, heated

2 c. rinsed lentils

2 Tbs. Worcestershire sauce

1 large tomato, peeled, chopped

½ tsp. paprika

1 c. diced cooked meat: ham, bacon, or wieners

Salt and pepper to taste

1 tsp. MSG (optional)

2 Tbs. vinegar (optional)

Sauté onion, carrots, and celery with olive oil in soup kettle. Add hot broth and lentils. Then add Worcestershire sauce, tomato, paprika, MSG, and vinegar. Simmer 1½ hours. During last 15 minutes, add diced meat of choice, then season with salt and pepper to taste. If soup is too thick, add 1 to 2 cups water.

Serves 6 to 8.

Karl-Heinz Schnibbe emigrated from Germany to the United States after having survived seven years of imprisonment and hard labor in Germany and Russia during and immediately after World War II. He is a skilled craftsman and gold leafed Abravanel Hall in Salt Lake City and several Angel Moroni statues. His story is recorded in *The Price: The True Story of a Mormon Who Defied Hitler*. Karl-Heinz is married to Joan Robinson Schnibbe.

Sunday-Monday Soup

RICK AND MARIAN WARNER

Now that our children have their own homes, we're interested in simpler meals. This is a newly discovered, time-saving recipe for Sunday dinner and Monday soup. It eliminates the tedious task of removing the fat and meat off the ham hocks. The soup also freezes well. Even if there are no corned beef leftovers from Sunday, the flavoring in the broth, combined with the beans and vegetables, will satisfy.

1 (20-oz.) pkg. fifteen-bean soup

1 3- to 4-lb. corned beef brisket

2 to 4 potatoes, peeled, cut in chunks

3 to 4 carrots, chopped

1 onion, cut in chunks

¼ head cabbage, cut in chunks

Saturday Night: Cover opened beans with water in large bowl. Let stand overnight.

Sunday Morning: Pour off water and refill repeatedly until foamy residue disappears; cover with water and continue soaking. In roasting pan, prepare corned beef per directions for baking in oven, adding an extra inch of water. Place large chunks of potato, carrots, and onion around edges of pan, then bake as directed. When ready to serve, remove meat and vegetables from broth and place in covered serving dish. Add chunks of cabbage to cooking broth; let steam until tender. Serve meat, vegetables, and cabbage together. (For Monday's soup, reserve broth and some of the vegetables in covered container and refrigerate.)

For Monday's Dinner: Pour off final soaking water from beans. Add beans to saved broth in large kettle, increasing water to recommended amount; simmer until tender. Add fresh or frozen vegetables and seasonings as per package directions. To serve, add to soup any remaining chunks of corned beef.

Corned beef dinner serves 6 to 8.
Soup makes 1 to 2 quarts.

Richard L. (Rick) Warner retired in 1995 from a career in the automobile business operating fourteen franchises in the Salt Lake area. From 1995 to 1997 he and Marian served a mission in the temple presidency at Laie, Oahu. Earlier Rick served as a bishop and stake president, as a counselor in the Sunday School general presidency, and as a Regional Representative. He is currently a sealer in the Salt Lake Temple. He continues to play tennis daily and loves mentoring his forty-five grandchildren in the sport. Marian Nelson Warner graduated with a bachelor's degree in English literature from the University of Utah after spending her sophomore year at UCLA and junior year in New York City studying piano. Marian and her husband, Rick, were recently released as ward family history specialists. The couple has four sons and five daughters, all living in Salt Lake City.

Gazpacho

PAUL POLLEI

While we were in Florida in the 1970s, our friend Joyce Williams shared this recipe with us.

½ (20-oz.) can tomatoes

1 (10½-oz.) can beef broth

¼ c. lemon juice

⅓ c. olive oil

1 clove garlic, minced

½ onion, chopped

1 Tbs. paprika

1 Tbs. sugar

1 Tbs. salt

1 tsp. pepper

½ cucumber, diced

½ green pepper, diced

1 stalk celery, diced

Combine tomatoes, broth, juice, oil, garlic, onion, paprika, sugar, salt, and pepper in blender and blend well. Pour into bowl or pitcher. Add diced cucumber, green pepper, and celery; stir. Cover and refrigerate several hours (or overnight). When ready to serve, pour cold gazpacho into blender, mixing thoroughly.

Paul C. Pollei is the founder and artistic director of the Gina Bachauer International Piano Foundation, sponsoring annual international competitions and festivals in Salt Lake City and worldwide. He is a founding member of the American Piano Quartet, a group of four pianists dedicated to the performance of music for two pianos/eight hands. He is an emeritus professor of piano studies following a lifelong teaching career at Brigham Young University. In addition, Dr. Pollei lectures, adjudicates international competitions, and presents master classes, workshops, and concerts worldwide. His wife, the former Norene Barrus, was the costume director for the Theatre and Music Departments of Brigham Young University and became the director of costuming for the original Donny and Marie Osmond television productions and the *Touched by an Angel* series. They are the parents of two children and the grandparents of one.

Mexican Soup Bar

PETER VIDMAR

1 lb. bacon

1 large onion, diced

2 cloves garlic, minced

3 qt. chicken broth

2 (16-oz.) cans tomatoes

4 medium carrots, diced

4 medium potatoes, diced

2 tsp. sugar

1 Tbs. salt

1 tsp. pepper

4 avocados, peeled, sliced

Sour cream

Green onion, chopped

3 hard-boiled eggs, peeled, diced

Tortilla chips, crumbled

Green taco sauce (or tomatillo sauce)

1 lb. cheddar cheese

1 lb. Monterey Jack cheese

In large kettle, fry bacon; crumble and set aside. Sauté onions and garlic in some of the bacon grease for 10 minutes. Add to kettle broth, tomatoes, carrots, potatoes, sugar, salt, and pepper. Bring to boil; simmer until vegetables are tender. Put avocados, sour cream, onion, eggs, tortilla chips, and green sauce into serving bowls as condiments. To serve, sprinkle cheeses in bottom of bowl, ladle in soup, and top with condiments.

Peter Vidmar captained the U.S. Men's Gymnastics Team to its first-ever Olympic gold medal in 1984. He also captured the gold in the pommel horse, scoring a perfect 10, and he became the first American to take a medal (silver) in the individual all-around men's competition. His winning performances average 9.89, making him the highest-scoring U.S. male gymnast in Olympic history. He now lives in California with his wife, Donna, and their five children. He translates his skills as a leader and motivator into inspirational presentations for Fortune 500 companies looking to benefit from his gold-medal performances.

Taco Soup

JANE CLAYSON

This is a great recipe for a cold winter day. And it's easy, too. You can throw all your ingredients into a pot and forty minutes later . . . there's dinner. And leftovers are even tastier the next day.

1 lb. hamburger

2 medium onions, chopped

2 stalks celery

4 c. stewed tomatoes

2 (15-oz.) cans kidney beans, undrained

1 (15-oz.) can corn, drained

1 (8-oz.) can tomato sauce

1 pkg. taco seasoning

Sour cream

Corn chips

Brown hamburger and onions in a large pot. Cook celery in microwave until soft; add to hamburger mixture along with tomatoes, kidney beans, corn, tomato sauce, and taco seasoning. Simmer 30 to 40 minutes. Serve immediately with a dollop of sour cream and a handful of corn chips.

As an anchor and correspondent for CBS News, Jane Clayson provides in-depth, original reporting for *48 Hours* and the "Eye on America" segments of the *CBS Evening News*. Previously, Jane co-anchored, with Bryant Gumbel, *The Early Show* on CBS. She has also been a correspondent for *ABC Network News* in Los Angeles (1996–99), reporting for *World News Tonight* and *Good Morning America* network broadcasts. Between 1990 and 1996 she anchored and reported for KSL-TV in Salt Lake City. Her work has received numerous awards from the Society of Professional Journalists, as well as an Emmy and the prestigious Edward R. Murrow Award from the Radio and Television News Directors Association.

Chicken Tortilla Soup

RUTH TODD

This soup is a quick and easy crowd-pleaser at parties when served with a big selection of condiments. It can easily be doubled or trippled for large groups. As a family meal, if we need something hot and hearty in a matter of minutes, this is the ticket! Even when the only condiments we have on hand are cheese and crushed chips, it doesn't disappoint. If there's no fresh cilantro on hand, use dry flakes—or just skip it altogether. My kids love it as a left-over, too. Moms on the go, bookmark this one!

6 c. chicken broth

2 c. cooked chicken, cubed

2 small cans chopped green chilies

1 (15-oz.) can corn, drained

¼ c. fresh lime juice (or to taste)

½ tsp. cumin

Salt and pepper to taste

1 bunch fresh cilantro, chopped

Choice of condiments: grated cheeses (Monterey Jack, cheddar), crushed tortilla chips, chopped tomatoes, chopped olives, chopped green onions, chunky salsa, guacamole.

Prepare soup bowls with your favorite condiments. Heat broth. Add chicken pieces, chilies, corn, lime juice, seasonings, and cilantro. Cook to boiling; then pour soup over condiments in bowls.

Serves 6 to 8.

A graduate of Brigham Young University, Ruth Todd anchors the 10 o'clock news on Salt Lake City's ABC affiliate, KTVX-4. Ruth was born and reared in Arizona and loves Southwestern and Mexican cuisine. She is married to Bryan Todd, a Salt Lake City attorney, and they are the parents of four daughters and one son. The Todd family likes to snow ski and water ski.

Tinker Toy Potato Soup

GEORGE DURRANT

Potato soup will always be a memorable meal because of the Christmas when my new tinker toys fell in the pot as my mother prepared the soup for our family dinner. After fishing what she thought was the last piece of plastic out of the soup pot, Mom brought the kettle to the table and proceeded to serve the meal. Dad was eating his potato soup when a shocked look came onto his face. We all sensed that he had encountered something unusual. But only Mom and I knew right away what it was. "What in tarnation is this?" he asked, as he slammed down the toy on the table.

Mother seemed a bit timid as she explained how I'd put the box of toys away on the shelf above the stove and set the stage for a small disaster. Dad was mad for just a little while. Then I noticed that he nearly smiled as he casually said, "Please pass the Tinker Toy soup." I haven't been able to call it anything else since.

8 potatoes, peeled and sliced in ¼-inch rounds

½ c. butter

½ c. all-purpose flour

8 c. milk

8 oz. sour cream

½ c. cheddar cheese, shredded

¼ c. onion, diced

Salt to taste

Ground black pepper to taste

Bacon bits, for topping

Cheddar cheese, grated, for topping

Microwave potato slices in deep casserole dish in small amount of water 7 to 10 minutes, until easily pierced with fork. While microwaving potatoes, melt butter in large soup kettle over medium heat. Add flour and milk, stirring until smooth and slightly thick. Blend in sour cream, shredded cheese, onion, and seasoning as needed. Add cooked potatoes and continue to cook about 5 minutes or until heated through. Top with bacon bits and additional grated cheddar cheese if desired.

George D. Durrant is a popular homespun author and teacher. He has served as president of the Missionary Training Center in Provo, Utah, and as president of the Kentucky Louisville Mission. He has taught family history at BYU and is a co-author of *Family History for the Clueless*, a comprehensive guide to researching your family history and preparing names for submission to the temple. Brother Durrant and his wife, Marilyn, are the parents of eight children and the grandparents of thirty.

Chicken Soup with Homemade Noodles

C. TERRY WARNER

Nearly thirty-five years ago, when all ten of our children were at home, we also had a college student living with us. One night she made a large pot of soup for our dinner. There were thirteen of us around the table, and when we finished, every drop of the delicious soup was gone. This hearty dish has become a family favorite often requested by our children. Many guests have also requested the recipe. On a cold winter night when this soup is on the menu with hot rolls or French bread, there are never any leftovers. By our good luck those many years ago we happened upon this *real* chicken soup for the soul.

1 whole chicken (or chicken pieces)

2 to 3 bay leaves

Pinch of salt

6 chicken bouillon cubes

3 Tbs. dried parsley (fresh is even better)

8 carrots, chopped

7 to 8 celery stalks, sliced diagonally

1 to 2 onions, chopped

Salt and pepper to taste

Homemade noodles (recipe follows)

Place the chicken in a large pot of water. Add a few bay leaves and a pinch of salt. Slow boil until meat begins to fall off bones (usually about 2 to 3 hours). Separate chicken from broth. Remove meat from bones, tearing or cutting into bite-sized pieces. Place meat in bowl, discarding bones and skin. Set aside.

Add enough water to the broth to make about 10 cups of liquid. Add bouillon cubes and parsley, then carrots, celery, and onions; bring to a boil. When vegetables are almost cooked, season with salt and pepper to taste. (Bouillon cubes are heavy with salt, so be careful not to oversalt.) Drop noodle strips one by one into boiling soup, stirring so noodles do not stick together. It takes about 6 minutes for noodles to cook in boiling soup. Return chicken pieces to soup, just to heat through. Serve in large bowls.

HOMEMADE NOODLES

2 c. flour

1 tsp. salt

2 large eggs, beaten

4 Tbs. milk (approximately)

To prepare homemade noodles, measure flour into bowl. Add salt, beaten eggs, and milk. Mix, adding enough drops of milk to make dough that can be kneaded. Knead dough about 10 minutes or until pliable. Roll out on floured board into large rectangle about ⅛-inch thick. Use sharp knife to cut rolled dough into 1-inch-wide strips to make long noodles.

Dr. C. Terry Warner holds a Ph.D. from Yale University and is a professor of philosophy at Brigham Young University. He has been a visiting senior member of Linacre College, Oxford University, and in 1979 founded The Arbinger Institute, a widely respected group that devotes itself to helping organizations, families, and individuals. He is the author of *Bonds That Make Us Free: Healing Our Relationships, Coming to Ourselves.* Dr. Warner and his wife, Susan, are the parents of ten children.

Chicken or Beef Soup with Danish Dumplings

LAEL LITTKE

My grandmother came from Denmark with her family when she was nine years old. She didn't remember a lot about Danish ways, but she did pass along her mother's recipe for Danish soup with dumplings. My mother, Ada Petersen Jensen, made it frequently, and it is one of my favorite childhood memories. It was especially good on those icy Idaho days when we rode home from school in an unheated bus. My mother had it simmering on the old coal stove when we came shivering in. There were few joys to match slurping down that good soup in Mother's warm and fragrant kitchen where geraniums bloomed profusely on the windowsills year round. I have served it to my own family over the years. Now, when my Jewish son-in-law visits, he almost always asks for "that soup." This is the recipe that my mother gave me when I was a young bride.

Chicken or beef bone

1 tsp. salt

5 large carrots, chopped

1 large onion, diced

2 stalks celery, chopped

Fresh parsley (optional)

Dumplings (see recipe)

In large kettle or soup pot, cover chicken or beef bone with water and bring to a boil. Skim off scum that rises as water boils. Cook 1 hour or so, then add salt. Cook until meat is partly tender, then add carrots, onion, and celery. Cook until vegetables and meat are done; remove soup bone but put meat pieces back in pot. Make dumplings while soup is cooking.

DUMPLINGS FOR 4

1 c. milk

¾ to 1 c. flour

½ tsp. salt

1 to 2 eggs

To make dumplings, pour milk into frying pan and bring to a boil. Sift in enough flour for a soft dough and stir rapidly. When flour is moistened and lumping together, pull pan off heat; mix in salt and unbeaten egg. If dough is sort of stiff, mix in second egg. Stir or mix with electric mixer. With soup at a boil, sprinkle in a few sprigs of parsley for color if desired. Drop walnut-sized balls of dough by teaspoon into boiling soup. The dumplings swell as they cook. When all the dough is in, cover kettle and simmer 5 minutes. Dumplings will rise to surface of soup when they are done. Serve with hot bread.

Serves 4.

As a young girl, Lael Jensen Littke dreamed of becoming a writer. She planned to live in a penthouse in New York City, wear leopard-skin pants, and date Cary Grant for exquisite dinners at fancy restaurants. And while Lael did indeed become a writer—she even lived in New York City for a time—she still hasn't found a good pair of leopard-skin pants. Lael has authored thirty-six books for children and young people and lives in Pasadena, California. Her books include *Lake of Secrets, Haunted Sister, There's a Snake at Girls Camp,* and *Blue Skye.* Her latest venture, *Stories from the Life of Joseph Smith,* which she co-authored with Richard Turley, will be out in May 2003.

Homemade Chicken Noodle Soup over Mashed Potatoes

BRUCE AND CHRISTINE OLSEN

When we went to Bruce's parents' home for Thanksgiving, his mother had all the regular holiday food, as well as homemade noodles in soup that was used instead of gravy over the potatoes. I refused to follow her example in our own home. It was just too much work. But I soon came to love the rather old-fashioned tradition of soup over mashed potatoes, and developed my own concoction. Again, this has become a family favorite. When I ask the men in my family what they want for their birthday dinner, this is their request. I once even served it to President and Sister Hinckley.

1 large chicken

1 onion, quartered

2 carrots, chopped

2 stalks celery

2 cloves garlic, minced

1 Tbs. chicken bouillon granules

2 carrots, grated

¼ c. fresh parsley, minced

1 pkg. fresh linguine noodles, cut in 2-inch pieces

1½ c. petite peas, frozen

Place chicken in large pot and cover with water. Add onion, chopped carrots, and celery stalks. Bring to a boil; simmer gently about two hours or until tender. Remove chicken from stock, let cool; then remove meat from bones. Cut up chicken and store in the refrigerator until ready for use. Strain broth and chill. Remove fat from top of cooled broth.

About 30 minutes before serving, place broth in pot, adding garlic, bouillon, grated carrots, and minced parsley. Add more water as needed to make enough broth. Bring to a boil; then add chicken pieces, linguine noodle pieces, and peas. Cook until noodles are done. Serve in bowls over mashed potatoes.

Serves 8 to 10.

Bruce L. Olsen is the managing director of the Public Affairs Department for The Church of Jesus Christ of Latter-day Saints. His assignment includes direction of worldwide government affairs, community relations, and media relations programs of the Church. He has previously held positions as director of corporate communications for Geneva Steel and assistant to the president for university relations at Brigham Young University. His wife, Christine Payne Olsen, is a nurse at the University of Utah Women's Center and has served on the general board of the Young Women organization. From 1982 to 1985, Brother and Sister Olsen presided over the Massachusetts Boston Mission. They are the parents of five children and the grandparents of nine.

Marvelous Minestrone Soup

GEORGE I. AND ISABEL H. CANNON

This soup has been a favorite of ours ever since we first tasted it on a wintry trip to Baltimore. Upon accompanying our son's wife and children back to Baltimore after Christmas (our son had flown in earlier because of professional obligations) we arrived during one of the coldest spells they had ever had in Baltimore. Chesapeake Bay had even frozen over! It was wonderful to have the family reunited, but we arrived home to their spartan apartment in the intern housing very weary, with two bewildered and tired little children. The whole atmosphere changed when a neighbor, Joan Petty, arrived with a steaming pot of minestrone soup, a tossed salad, and hot bread. Suddenly the cold and weariness disappeared, and the wonderful comfort food did its work. Joan shared this recipe with us and we have served it often to family and friends. They always seem to enjoy it. We never eat the soup without remembering it as a gift of love that warmed and fed not only our bodies but our spirits as well.

1 lb. ground sausage

1 qt. water

2 garlic cloves, minced

2 large onions, chopped

2 to 3 carrots, cut up

2 stalks celery, cut up

2 (15-oz.) cans chopped tomatoes

2 (8-oz.) cans tomato sauce

2 (10-oz.) cans beef bouillon broth

½ tsp. dried basil

1 tsp. dried oregano

1 Tbs. dried parsley flakes

¼ tsp. sugar

Salt and pepper to taste

1 (15-oz.) can cut green beans, undrained

1 (15-oz.) can garbanzo beans, drained

1 handful macaroni (uncooked)

Parmesan cheese for topping

Bring water to a boil in large kettle. Add sausage by breaking it up and dropping it into boiling water. Stir and mash sausage as it cooks, boiling until it loses its pink color. (I sometimes boil the sausage the day or morning before cooking the soup. After boiling, strain off and chill broth, discarding the hardened fat that collects. Otherwise, skim fat off top of soup after it has cooked.) Add remaining ingredients, except the canned beans and macaroni. Simmer slowly 3 to 6 hours.

At least 20 minutes before serving, add cans of beans and macaroni. Stir occasionally so macaroni doesn't stick. Top with Parmesan cheese when serving. This soup is excellent, even after being reheated.

Serves 10 to 15.

George I. and Isabel Hales Cannon are both graduates from Brigham Young University, where George majored in business and Isabel in foods and nutrition. When their family was young, George presided over the Central British Mission for three years. Later he was a counselor in the YMMIA general presidency. In 1986, following George's retirement as an insurance executive, he was called to the Quorum of the Seventy. In this capacity, George and Isabel lived for a year in Hong Kong and three years in Manila, Philippines. Since that time they have served as president and matron of the Salt Lake Temple and as Church service volunteers assigned to visit temples. They are the parents of seven children, the grandparents of twenty-eight, and the great-grandparents of four.

Bacon and Corn Chowder

DIAN THOMAS

Our connection with the past and to our ancestors comes alive whenever soups, stews, and other old-fashioned one-pot meals are served. When it is comfort food you are looking for, corn chowder is a good one to meet the need. This has been published before in my own book, *Recipes for Roughing It Easy.* To really enjoy the meal, try this chowder on your camp stove out in the wilds.

4 slices bacon, diced

1 medium onion, minced

6 medium potatoes, peeled and cubed

2 c. chicken broth

2 (15-oz.) cans creamed corn

1 c. heavy cream or milk

½ tsp. salt

½ tsp. pepper

In a 2-quart saucepan over medium heat, sauté diced bacon and onion. Pour off drippings, then add potatoes and cook 10 minutes. Add broth and corn; cook, stirring occasionally, for 40 minutes or until potatoes are tender. Blend in cream, salt, and pepper; cook just until heated throughout.

Serves 6 to 8.

Dian Thomas is an outdoor enthusiast and cooking specialist. She is the author of eleven books, including the *New York Times* bestseller, *Roughing It Easy.* Dian spent eight years doing bi-weekly television spots for the Today show on NBC and six years on ABC's *Home Show.* Dian has also appeared on *The Tonight Show, Good Morning America,* over five thousand local and national shows, and a host of other feature programs. Her ingenuity and enthusiasm have earned her the title "America's First Lady of Creativity."

Bratten's Clam Chowder

MILTON WEILENMANN

2 (6½-oz.) cans minced clams

1 c. onion, finely diced

1 c. celery, finely diced

2 c. potatoes, diced

¾ c. butter

¾ c. flour

1 qt. half & half

1½ tsp. salt

Pepper to taste

Drain juice from cans of clams and pour liquid over vegetables, adding enough water just to cover. Simmer over medium heat until vegetables are barely tender. Melt butter in heavy saucepan. Add flour, making a roux; blend until smooth. Stir constantly while slowly adding half and half. Cook and stir with wire whisk until thick and smooth. Add vegetables, juice, and clams. Heat through. Add salt and pepper.

Serves 8.

Milton L. Weilenmann is best known for his popular Bratten's Grotto chain of restaurants. Milt's fresh fish bar, gourmet side dishes, best-ever chowder, and hot cocktail sauce made Bratten's a success for more than thirty years (1953 to 1988). He also developed Della Fontana, a popular Italian restaurant in Salt Lake City between 1967 and 1994. Milton has also served as chairman of the Utah State Democratic party and was the first director of the Utah Department of Economic Development. He and his wife, Diane, are the parents of seventeen and the grandparents of forty-eight.

Baked Beef Stew

WENDELL AND BARBARA SMOOT

Our greatest joys are the memories of Smoot Haus in Island Park, Idaho, and the many summers congregating with our children and grandchildren at our cabin home there, enjoying together the beauty of the trees, the river, the blue skies, the fluffy white clouds, and beautiful sunsets. The peace and tranquillity of lazy summer days and cool nights were a balm to our souls. Included in those memories are the meals we shared—a different menu from what we had in our city home. One of the joys was Barbara's Baked Beef Stew—easy to prepare and then leave in the oven to bake while we went out hiking, boating, fishing, swimming, or just swinging in a hammock. Nothing compares to a beautiful setting of nature and good food with your loved ones and friends. We have much to be thankful for.

1 lb. stew beef

2 tsp. salt

2½ Tbs. minute tapioca

1 Tbs. sugar

3 medium onions, peeled and sliced

1½ c. carrots, sliced

5 medium potatoes, cubed

1½ c. celery, chopped

¾ c. V-8® juice

Preheat oven to 250° F. Trim fat from meat, cut into hunks, and place in roasting pan. Mix salt and tapioca with sugar; sprinkle over meat. Add onions, carrots, potatoes, and celery. Pour V-8 juice over all. Cover tightly and bake 5 hours—no peeking!

Serves 6.

Wendell Smoot served as president of the Mormon Tabernacle Choir for seventeen years and was instrumental in recently organizing the Orchestra at Temple Square. He and his wife, Barbara, have traveled with the Choir to over twenty-five countries on six continents, showcasing the beauty of the Choir's musical talents to the people of the world. He has spent fifty-seven years in the investment counsel business. He and his wife have five children and fourteen grandchildren.

Oyster Stew a la Richard L. Evans

STANFORD P. DARGER

Elder Richard L. Evans made a singular and unique contribution in nearly every broadcast and concert given by the Mormon Tabernacle Choir. His messages on *Music and the Spoken Word* made indelible impressions on all who listened.

During his busy years with the Choir, Elder Evans rarely ate dinner prior to a concert. Consequently, following concerts he was always famished and would ask me, as the business manager, where I thought he could get a bowl of oyster stew. After the first unsuccessful search, I added to my list of things to do upon arriving in a concert city finding a restaurant or hotel dining room open after 10:30 P.M. that would serve oyster stew. It was perhaps not surprising that I was seldom able to find a restaurant that stayed open late and also had oyster stew on its menu. To solve the problem, we began providing the eating establishments with the recipe—and sometimes with the can of oysters, too! This much stew would adequately serve two people, but Elder Evans often ate the whole thing.

¼ c. roux thickening

1 pt. whole milk, heated

1 (15-oz.) can oysters, drained

1 Tbs. butter

Seasonings to taste

Add roux to milk, stirring until slightly thickened. Add drained oysters. Heat almost to boiling. Add butter and seasonings. Serve with a large bowl of soda crackers.

A conscientious cook might add 2 tablespoons minced onion, ½ cup diced celery, and 1 diced potato, the vegetables having been cooked separately to the al dente stage. Elder Evans was very content, even delighted, to eat it simply as a bowl of milk with oysters, with lots of soda crackers broken into it.

Serves 2.

Stan Darger was the business manager of the Mormon Tabernacle Choir for seventeen years, arranging the Choir's tours and concerts around the world and negotiating recording contracts. During this time the Choir presented concerts in fifty-eight cities in the United States, Canada, Mexico, and Europe, performed in five world's fairs, received a Grammy, and participated in the Inaugurations of Presidents Lyndon B. Johnson and Richard M. Nixon. Stan is married to the former Arlene Barlow, who served as first counselor in the Young Women general presidency. From 1989 to 1990, Stan and Arlene served a mission as executive secretary to the Europe Area Presidency in Frankfurt, Germany. They are the parents of five children and have twenty grandchildren.

Webb Chili

JULIE WEBB

This recipe has been in the Webb family for four generations and is always a party hit. For that reason I asked my husband, Allen (the really good cook in the family), if he would make a large pot of chili for the Olympic dress rehearsal party. I was on the choreography team for Opening and Closing Ceremonies for the 2002 Winter Olympics. The chili was a hit, but I had forgotten about the tight security that day. My chili had to go through five security checks.

2 lbs. (4 c.) red beans

2 lbs. ground beef

¼ tsp. chili powder (½ tsp. for more spice)

3 c. ketchup

6 onions, finely chopped

1 Tbs. salt

Wash red beans and put in a pressure cooker-type pan on stove. Cover with 3 times the water and boil down 3 to 4 hours until soft. Drain (keep beans covered with water and save reserve if needed for thinning) and set aside. Season ground beef with chili powder and brown in skillet. Drain off fat and pour into a large kettle. Mix together ketchup, onions, and salt. Mix with browned hamburger in kettle and add red beans. Cook over medium heat until well heated throughout.

Serves 12.

Julie Johansen Webb received a master's degree in education and teaches marketing courses at Roy High School and Weber State University. She is also a free-lance choreographer, directing and choreographing many special events, including: "The Bob Hope Special with Bill Clinton," the "Stadium of Fire" (for ten years), NFL and Fiesta Bowl half-time shows (for ten years), the World Congress on Families in Switzerland, and dance teams in Barcelona's Summer Olympics. Most recently Julie was senior production manager over cast and first assistant choreographer for the Opening and Closing Ceremonies of the Salt Lake 2002 Winter Games. She and her husband, Allen, are the parents of five children and the grandparents of two.

From the Garden

FRESH IDEAS FOR
VEGETABLES,
FRUITS, AND SALADS

Cannon Cabbage

EDWIN AND JANATH CANNON

This recipe comes from a cookbook published by an American group living in Ghana and was presented to us during our mission to West Africa in 1978 through 1979.

2 c. fresh cabbage, shredded

6 scallions, finely chopped

½ c. milk

½ tsp. salt

2 Tbs. butter

4 to 5 c. cooked white potatoes or
    yams (West African), mashed

Cook cabbage until tender. Simmer scallions in milk until tender. Add salt, butter, and potatoes to scallions and milk. Add cabbage. Mix well and place in buttered casserole dish. Reheat in oven until hot and ready to serve.

Serves 6 more or less hungry people.

Edwin Q. Cannon and Janath Russell Cannon have a lifelong legacy of Church and community service. With Janath, Brother Cannon has presided over the Switzerland Mission, the Hamburg Mission, the Frankfurt Germany Temple, and the Nauvoo Visitor's Center. Janath served as a counselor to Barbara B. Smith in the general Relief Society presidency and is a co-author of *Women of Covenant: The Story of Relief Society*. They count as one of their most dramatic experiences the opportunity to go as representatives of the International Mission to Ghana and Nigeria in 1978, the first in West Africa with authority to baptize and organize "without regard to race or color."

Mustard-Glazed Carrots

STEVE YOUNG

2 lbs. carrots, peeled and sliced

1 Tbs. salt

6 Tbs. butter

6 Tbs. prepared mustard

½ c. brown sugar

Place carrots in a pot of salted water; bring water to a boil. Cover and cook carrots until tender; drain. In small saucepan, combine butter, mustard, and brown sugar. Cook over medium heat until syrupy (about 3 minutes). Pour over carrots and simmer 5 minutes.

Steve Young is best known as the former quarterback for the San Francisco 49ers. His achievements include recognition as the highest-rated quarterback in NFL history, Super Bowl XXIX's Most Valuable Player (MVP), and the NFL's MVP in 1992 and 1994. Off the field, Young is founder and chair of the Forever Young Foundation, a charity devoted to the development, security, strength, and education of children. Steve and his wife, Barbara, are the parents of one son.

Kathryn Katseanes's Potato Salad

KORY KATSEANES

Since I grew up on a potato farm in Idaho, this recipe is part of my cultural as well as culinary heritage. Cancer took my mom much too early; but whenever we re-use one of her great recipes, it seems to bring her back a little, and helps keep her memory alive.

¼ c. sugar

¼ c. vinegar

¼ c. water

¼ tsp. salt

Dash pepper

Combine sugar, vinegar, water, salt, pepper, and mustard in a small saucepan and bring to a boil. Reduce heat; gradually add the beaten eggs. Cook, stirring constantly, until slightly thickened, about 5 minutes.

1 tsp. prepared mustard

2 eggs, beaten

1 c. salad dressing

4 c. (2 lbs.) potatoes, boiled and
    cubed

2 hard cooked eggs, chopped or
    sliced

½ c. cucumbers (or pickles), chopped

1 Tbs. minced onion

1 Tbs. radishes (or green peppers),
    chopped

Remove from heat, pour into a large mixing bowl, and add salad dressing. Stir in potatoes, eggs, and vegetables with the dressing.

Serves 8 to 10.

Kory Katseanes is the director of orchestras at the Brigham Young University School of Music, where he conducts the Philharmonic and Chamber orchestras in Utah and on their regular tours throughout the world. From 1987 to 2002 he was the assistant conductor of the Utah Symphony, collaborating with guest artists such as the King's Singers, the Chieftans, Nancy Griffiths, Riders in the Sky, Kathy Mattea, Michael Martin Murphy, Judy Collins, Art Garfunkel, Maureen McGovern, and Marvin Hamlisch. He played violin with the Utah Symphony for twenty-six years and teaches private violin lessons and coaches chamber music. He and his wife, Carolyn, are the parents of four children.

Karl's Red Cabbage

KARL-HEINZ SCHNIBBE

Karl-Heinz was born to faithful LDS parents in Hamburg, Germany, and grew up during the Nazi era. However, when he was about seventeen years old, a friend of his from Church, Helmut Huebner, asked him if he would like to listen to a BBC broadcast on a short-wave radio. Even though short-wave radios were forbidden by the Nazis, Helmut had access to one, and had been listening to the news from London. Karl and another friend, Rudy Wobbe, listened to the broadcasts with Helmut, and all three boys were convinced that the British were telling the truth and that the Nazis were lying. Helmut proposed that they spread the truth by passing out leaflets (surreptitiously) that contained summaries of the BBC news. They did so for a number of months. Eventually, though, they were caught and tried for their crime. Helmut was beheaded in Berlin in October 1942. He was seventeen years old. Karl and Rudy were imprisoned in various concentration camps until the end of World War II. Three weeks before the war ended, Karl was inducted into the German army—Germany was desperate for men by that time. Unfortunately, he was captured by Russian forces and sent to Siberia for another four years. He finally was able to return home in 1949. They were very poorly fed in Siberia, and one of the things that he really longed for was his mother's Red Cabbage. He still loves this dish and makes it frequently.

3 to 4 Tbs. canola oil

2 heads red cabbage, cored, washed, and chopped

1¼ c. white vinegar

2 small onions, chopped

2 small apples, peeled and chopped

7 (heaping) tsp. sugar

1 can beef broth

5 cloves, whole

3 bay leaves

5 to 6 peppercorns

Salt to taste

2 small cans V-8® juice

In large pot (6 quarts or larger) heat oil, then stir in chopped cabbage. Each piece of cabbage must be covered with oil or color will fade. Add vinegar and chopped onions and apples.

Sauté until cabbage is somewhat soft; add sugar, beef broth, and spices. Simmer, covered, until cabbage is soft; add V-8 juice. Remove cloves, bay leaves, and peppercorns before serving.

Serves 6 to 8.

Karl-Heinz Schnibbe emigrated from Germany to the United States after having survived seven years of imprisonment and hard labor in Germany and Russia during and immediately after World War II. He is a skilled craftsman, whose work includes gold leafing the balconies in Abravanel Hall in Salt Lake City and several Angel Moroni statues. His story is recorded in *The Price: The True Story of a Mormon Who Defied Hitler*. Karl-Heinz is married to Joan Robinson Schnibbe.

Nauvoo Green Beans

KATHLEEN H. BARNES

In 1978, I had the privilege of participating in the dedication of the Nauvoo Monuments to Women. At the time I was serving as a ward Relief Society president in the Wilmette, Illinois Stake. Our food assignment for that special dedication included this green bean dish.

1 (14-oz.) pkg. frozen French-style green beans

4 slices bacon

2 stalks celery, sliced

1 onion, diced

1 (8-oz.) can hearts of palm

¼ c. mayonnaise

Salt and pepper to taste

Steam beans until just tender. Fry bacon until crisp, reserving fat. Crumble bacon into small pieces and set aside. Sauté celery pieces and onion in bacon fat until transparent. Mix all ingredients together and pour into 1-quart casserole dish. Bake 20 minutes at 350° F.

Serves 6.

Kathleen Hinckley Barnes, a daughter of President Gordon B. and Marjorie Pay Hinckley, received a degree in education and has owned and operated her own business. She has been an active business and community leader, having served on several boards, including Bonneville International Corporation. With her sister Virginia, she has written a number of children's board books, including *Prayer Time, Sacrament Time*, and *I Love to See the Temple*. She and her husband, the late Alan Barnes, are the parents of five children and grandparents of fourteen.

Tomato Pie

JANE CLAYSON

This may be my very favorite dish. Years ago my mom ordered it at a restaurant in San Francisco and persuasively talked the chef into giving her the recipe. It is so easy and delicious. Don't waste a minute thinking about this one. Trust me. Get cookin'!

Frozen 9-inch deep-dish pastry shell

4 to 5 large roma tomatoes

¼ c. scallions, chopped

¼ tsp. dried basil

¼ tsp. salt and pepper

1 c. grated Swiss cheese

¼ c. mayonnaise

Preheat oven to 425° F. Cook pastry shell for 5 minutes. Let cool. Cut tomatoes into bite-sized cubes. Extract seeds and juicy parts and discard. Mix all ingredients together and cook at 400° F. for 35 minutes.

Serves 8.

As an anchor and correspondent for CBS News, Jane Clayson provides in-depth, original reporting for *48 Hours* and the "Eye on America" segments of the *CBS Evening News*. Previously, Jane co-anchored, with Bryant Gumbel, *The Early Show* on CBS. She has also been a correspondent for *ABC Network News* in Los Angeles (1996–99), reporting for *World News Tonight* and *Good Morning America* network broadcasts. Between 1990 and 1996 she anchored and reported for KSL-TV in Salt Lake City. Her work has received numerous awards from the Society of Professional Journalists, as well as an Emmy and the prestigious Edward R. Murrow Award from the Radio and Television News Directors Association.

Spinach Casserole

CLOY KENT

Mrs. Clayton Stapleton was the wife of the Iowa State University athletic director in Ames, Iowa. I did pastel portraits of their two children. When the paintings were completed, she invited my husband and me to lunch. She served this wonderful casserole and presented me my now famous *Gridiron Cookbook*, containing recipes of well-known coaches' wives.

2 (16-oz.) cartons cottage cheese

6 eggs, beaten

½ lb. American cheese, cut in large pieces

½ c. butter or margarine cut in large pieces

1 (10-oz.) pkg. frozen spinach, cut in large pieces

6 Tbs. flour

Grease casserole dish and preheat oven to 350° F. Place cottage cheese in large mixing bowl; add beaten eggs and stir mixture, adding American cheese and butter chunks. Add spinach, sprinkle flour on top, and mix well.

Pour into 2-quart glass casserole dish and bake for 1 hour.

Serves 8 to 10.

Cloy Kent began doing portrait work out of her home during World War II. As she perfected her skills as a pastel and oil artist, she also reared six children. Her work now hangs in galleries and homes throughout the country. She has been commissioned on numerous occasions by The Church of Jesus Christ of Latter-day Saints to paint such leaders as Barbara Smith, Ardeth Kapp, President Thomas S. Monson, and Elder Joseph B. Wirthlin. She is married to Jim Kent and lives in Bountiful, Utah.

Spinach Parmesan

SALLY BRINTON

This is a great way to get children to eat their spinach. Delicious!

3 lbs. fresh spinach

6 Tbs. Parmesan cheese

6 Tbs. minced onion

6 Tbs. heavy cream

5 Tbs. butter, melted

1 tsp. salt

⅛ tsp. pepper

½ c. buttered bread crumbs

Cook spinach in large saucepan with small amount of water until tender. Drain thoroughly. Add other ingredients, except bread crumbs. Arrange in shallow baking dish and top with buttered crumbs. Bake 10 to 15 minutes at 450° F.

Serves 6.

Sally Peterson Brinton first performed as a piano soloist with the Utah Symphony at age eleven. She has since been featured nine times with the symphony. Sally was named Miss Utah in 1972 and went on to compete in the Miss America pageant, where she won the Talent Award and was named Miss Congeniality. She has a master's of music degree from the Juilliard School of Music in New York City and is a member of the Mormon Tabernacle Choir. She and her husband, Dr. Gregory S. Brinton, are the parents of seven children and reside in Salt Lake City.

Bacon-Shrimp Potato Salad with Cayenne Pecans

LINDA MAMONE

As an artist, vibrant colors play a very important part in everything I do. Cooking is no exception. I have a lot of fun in creating visual feasts for all to enjoy. The unexpected colors and textures in my food are as important as the tastes. I always love to challenge people to be brave; try tasting everything at least once; put some excitement into your own visual feasts. This delicious salad is even more tempting when you use a mixture of potatoes. Using purple potatoes is a visual delight—when cooked, the potatoes turn a light violet. They are not hard to find and hold up very well. Also, don't use baby shrimp, they're too fishy. Serve the dish warm or at room temperature, not cold.

Cayenne pecans (recipe follows)

Hot Bacon Dressing (recipe follows)

2 lbs. potatoes, a mixture of purple, red, or Yukon gold

¼ c. green scallions, chopped

½ to 1 lb. cooked shrimp, medium or large, tails off

Prepare Cayenne Pecans and Hot Bacon Dressing; set aside.

In a large pot, cover whole potatoes with skins in salted water. Bring to boil and cook for 15 to 20 minutes, until tender (not mushy); drain. Pan dry them (leave potatoes in pot over low heat for a minute or two). When cool enough to touch, slice the potatoes. If using purple potatoes, pull off skins.

Dress potatoes while still warm to allow them to absorb more flavor. Pour two-thirds of the dressing over potatoes; sprinkle with half of the crumbled bacon from the dressing recipe and ¼ cup scallions. Let stand at room temperature for 1 hour. Toss shrimp in remaining third of dressing; keep in refrigerator until ready to use.

When ready to serve salad, toss dressed potatoes with shrimp, remaining bacon, and pecans, placing some attractively on top.

Serves 6 to 8.

CAYENNE PECANS

½ to 1 c. pecan halves

¼ tsp. salt

⅛ tsp. ground cayenne pepper

⅛ tsp. ground cumin

2 tsp. butter, melted (more, if using more nuts)

Preheat oven to 350° F. Prepare cayenne pecans by combining nuts, seasonings, and butter; spread on baking sheet; bake for 15 minutes. Set aside to cool. (Rather than baking the pecan mixture, it can also be sautéed in a non-stick pan until browned.)

HOT BACON DRESSING

7 strips bacon

½ c. green scallions, minced

½ c. sherry vinegar

1 tsp. mustard seeds, crushed

2 Tbs. honey

⅛ tsp. salt

½ tsp. pepper

2 Tbs. fresh parsley, chopped

1 Tbs. fresh dill, chopped (or 1 tsp. dried dill)

½ c. olive oil

To make dressing, sauté bacon in skillet until crispy. Drain on paper towels, crumble, and set aside for later use. Remove all but 1 to 2 tablespoons of drippings. Sauté scallions in drippings until soft. Remove pan from heat; whisk in sherry vinegar, crushed mustard seeds, salt, pepper, honey, parsley, and dill, until thoroughly mixed. Add oil in a slow stream, whisking until blended; set aside.

Linda Andelin Mamone is an artist, floral designer, and interior designer. Her vibrant and rich paintings are displayed in galleries throughout the United States, including the Mamone Galleries at Fisherman's Wharf in San Francisco. Her floral design and catering business is widely known throughout the Wasatch Front, and she teaches regular cooking classes at Thanksgiving Point in Lehi, Utah. Linda serves the Church as supervisor and head designer in charge of fresh floral designs, live plants, Christmas displays, and other staged events at Church headquarters in Salt Lake City. She has designed the costumes for the life-size Nativity on Temple Square. She is married to Frank C. Mamone. They are the parents of five children and grandparents of eight.

Rachel's Grilled Pineapple

CHAD HAWKINS

This recipe, named after my daughter Rachel, is the ideal dessert to make after barbecuing chicken (see recipe on pages 120 and 121 of this book), while the grill is still hot and everyone is ready for something sweet to eat.

1 whole pineapple, ripe

½ c. unsalted butter, melted

¾ c. sugar

1 tsp. grated lime zest

1 tsp. ground cinnamon

⅛ tsp. ground cloves

Preheat grill. Twist leafy top off pineapple, then cut off rind. Slice fruit horizontally into 8 or 10 even rounds. Using pineapple corer or paring knife, remove core from each round. When ready to cook, place melted butter in shallow bowl; combine sugar, lime zest, cinnamon, and cloves in separate bowl. Place both bowls at side of grill. Oil grill grate. Dip each slice of pineapple first in melted butter, then in sugar mixture, shaking off excess. Grill pineapple slices, turning with tongs, until browned and sizzling (5 to 8 minutes per side). Transfer to serving platter, arranging slices in overlapping fashion.

Serves 8 to 10.

Chad Spencer Hawkins began creating his unique series of temple prints in 1989, at age seventeen, to support his mission. Upon returning from the Germany Frankfurt Mission, Chad pursued an education in fine art at Weber State University. His paintings hang in galleries and private collections throughout the world, and his original work of the Vernal Utah Temple is on permanent display inside that edifice. His artwork has been selected for placement in twelve of the cornerstones of the Church's temples. Chad is the author of the bestselling book *The First 100 Temples* and *Youth and the Temple*. He and his wife, Stephanie, live in Layton, Utah, with their children.

Norene's Grapefruit-Avocado Winter Salad

PAUL POLLEI

4 pink grapefruit (about 1 per person)

Fresh lettuce leaves

3 to 4 avocados, peeled and sliced

2 (11-oz.) cans mandarin oranges

½ c. sliced almonds, toasted

1 (6-oz.) pkg. Mariani® Harvest Medley dried fruit, Craisins®, or dried cherries

2 kiwis, peeled and sliced

Bianni's® Poppy Seed Dressing

Peel skin off grapefruit. With grapefruit knife, remove sections from grapefruit at membrane, dropping into bowl. When ready to assemble for serving, place a lettuce leaf or two on serving plates; then make a bed of grapefruit slices on each plate. Layer with 4 or 5 slices of avocado, mandarin oranges, and a sprinkle of toasted almonds. Next, sprinkle with dried fruit of choice. Top with slices of kiwi to add color. Dress with poppy seed dressing.

Serves 4.

Paul C. Pollei is the founder and artistic director of the Gina Bachauer International Piano Foundation, sponsoring annual international competitions and festivals in Salt Lake City and worldwide. He is a founding member of the American Piano Quartet, a group of four pianists dedicated to the performance of music for two pianos/eight hands. He is an emeritus professor of piano studies following a lifelong teaching career at Brigham Young University. In addition, Dr. Pollei lectures, adjudicates international competitions, and presents master classes, workshops, and concerts worldwide. His wife, the former Norene Barrus, was the costume director for the Theatre and Music Departments of Brigham Young University and became the director of costuming for the original Donny and Marie Osmond television productions and the Touched by an Angel series. They are the parents of two children and one grandson.

Make-Ahead Green Party Salad

STEPHEN AND SANDRA COVEY

If you are having family, a party, or a large group over, this salad is delicious, nutritious, and can be prepared in advance.

- 1 head iceberg lettuce, cut in chunks
- 1 head romaine lettuce and/or spinach leaves, torn into serving pieces
- 1 pkg. frozen green peas, thawed and drained
- 1 can water chestnuts, sliced
- 1 to 2 avocados, sliced
- 1 (14.5-oz.) can cut green beans, drained
- 1 c. celery, diced
- 1 bunch green onions, sliced
- 1 (16-oz.) jar Best Foods® Real mayonnaise

In very large bowl or punch bowl, layer vegetables in any order, pressing down each layer to compact. Repeat layering until bowl is full. Spread top with mayonnaise until no greenery shows. Cover with plastic wrap and refrigerate several hours or overnight. Before serving, stir mayonnaise through salad.

Serves 20.

Stephen R. Covey is co-founder/co-chairman of FranklinCovey Company, the largest management and leadership development organization in the world. His book, *The 7 Habits of Highly Effective People*, is a *New York Times* number-one bestseller and has sold more than 14 million copies in thirty-three languages and seventy-five countries throughout the world. Dr. Covey and his wife, Sandra Merrill Covey, have a lifelong legacy of service to the Church and community. Together they presided over the Irish Mission for The Church of Jesus Christ of Latter-day Saints. Dr. Covey has also served as a regional representative of the Twelve and on several general Church leadership committees. The Coveys are the parents of nine children and the grandparents of thirty-eight. They reside in Provo, Utah.

Spinach Salad

2 eggs

2 to 3 strips bacon

2 qts. (2 bunches) spinach, washed
   and drained well

Toasted Sesame Seed Dressing
   (recipe follows)

TOASTED SESAME
SEED DRESSING

¼ c. red or white wine vinegar

½ c. white sugar

1 tsp. salt

¼ tsp. paprika

¼ c. olive oil or other salad oil

1 Tbs. onion, chopped

1 Tbs. sesame seeds, toasted

Hard-boil eggs; let stand in cold water, then peel and chop. Fry bacon; cut in small strips or crumble. Wash or soak spinach leaves to remove grit; drain well. Mix egg and bacon bits with spinach leaves in large salad bowl. Serve sesame seed dressing separately or pour over entire salad; tossing together lightly until blended.

To make dressing, boil vinegar, sugar, salt, and paprika in a small saucepan. Shake oil and onion in a jar, then add other ingredients. Shake vigorously.

Peter Vidmar captained the U.S. Men's Gymnastics Team to its first-ever Olympic gold medal in 1984. He also captured the gold in the pommel horse, scoring a perfect 10, and became the first American to take a medal (silver) in the individual all-around men's competition. His winning performances average 9.89, making him the highest-scoring U.S. male gymnast in Olympic history. He now lives in California with his wife, Donna, and their five children. He translates his skills as a leader and motivator into inspirational presentations for Fortune 500 companies looking to benefit from his gold-medal performances.

Grandmother's Green Salad

ALAN AND MONA SNELGROVE LAYTON

In 1957, Charles R. and Fidella Snelgrove were among the first missionaries of the Northwestern States Mission to serve in Nauvoo, Illinois. During their two-and-a-half years in Nauvoo, Sister Snelgrove collected many recipes as she attended the monthly luncheon meetings of the Nauvoo Ladies Society. Because one dish was a great favorite of the Elders, she always served this recipe at the missionary conferences in Nauvoo, under President Richard Stratford. Since that time, it has been a tradition for this salad to be served at all of our family gatherings. It is a great favorite of the grandchildren.

1 (3-oz.) pkg. lime Jell-O®

1 (3-oz.) pkg. lemon Jell-O®

2 c. boiling water

½ c. sugar

Juice of 1 lemon

1½ c. canned crushed pineapple

1 pt. whipping cream

1 c. sharp cheddar cheese, grated

Maraschino cherry on top (optional)

Dissolve lime and lemon Jell-O in boiling water. Let cool. In small saucepan, bring to a boil sugar, lemon juice, and crushed pineapple (with some juice). Let cool. Combine Jell-O and fruit mixtures in large bowl. Refrigerate until quivery. In mixing bowl, whip cream. Gently fold whipped cream and grated cheese into salad gelatin. Let gelatin set in a fancy glass bowl and top with maraschino cherry if desired.

Serves 12.

Alan W. and Mona Snelgrove Layton have a long tradition of church and community involvement. Alan is founder of Layton Construction Company, the builders responsible for several high-profile buildings, including: the LDS Conference Center, the Nauvoo Temple, the Utah Olympic speed skating oval in Kearns, the LaVell Edwards Stadium at BYU, and the Rice-Eccles Stadium at the University of Utah. Active in the Boy Scouts of America, Alan received the Silver Beaver Award. Mona has served in ward and stake auxiliaries, as well as on the Young Women general board. Together they have fulfilled four missions. Alan and Mona are the parents of ten children. They have fifty-eight grandchildren and forty-four great-grandchildren.

Rainbow Jell-O

JEFFREY MARSH

This multicolored Jell-O rainbow may take the better part of a day to finish, because each layer has to set before the next can be added. Begin with the darker-colored gelatins and move to the lighter. Though it takes time, the end result is worth the wait.

2 (3-oz.) pkgs. of each of these Jell-O® flavors: black raspberry, grape, cherry, orange, lime, lemon

12 c. boiling water (1 c. per Jell-O® package)

4 c. sour cream or yogurt (⅔ c. per Jell-O® flavor)

Starting with the black raspberry Jell-O, mix one small package with 1 cup boiling water and ⅔ cup sour cream or yogurt. Pour in a 9x13x2-inch dish or mold, then refrigerate until firm. Once the first layer is set, mix second black raspberry gelatin with 1 cup boiling water. Pour on top of previous set layer. Continue this process through remainder of flavored gelatins, proceeding from dark to light colors. Allow each layer to set before adding next.

Serves 12 to 15.

W. Jeffrey Marsh is an associate professor of ancient scripture at Brigham Young University and a popular speaker at BYU Education Week. He is the author of several books about the Savior and Joseph Smith, including *His Final Hours* and *The Light Within: What the Prophet Joseph Smith Taught Us about Personal Revelation*. He is married to Kathie Paul Marsh, and they are the parents of six children.

Margaret's Ginger Ale Salad

DOUGLAS PULLEY

This recipe is a family favorite from Katherine's mother, Margaret Jacobsen Bennion. Be sure to use *fresh*, not canned, pink grapefruit for spectacular results in this delicious salad!

2 Tbs. dry Knox® gelatin

4 Tbs. water

½ c. boiling pineapple juice

½ c. sugar

⅛ tsp. salt

1 pt. ginger ale

Juice of 1 lemon

1 (16-oz.) can pineapple chunks, well-drained

2 c. fresh grapefruit sections (without membranes)

1 (11-oz.) can mandarin oranges, well-drained

2 c. Thompson seedless or seedless red grapes, halved

Soak the gelatin in water; then dissolve it in the boiling pineapple juice. Add the sugar, salt, ginger ale, and lemon juice. Cool—then combine with the canned pineapple, fresh grapefruit, mandarin oranges, and grapes. Place salad in wet mold and chill to set.

Serves 10.

Douglas and Katherine Pulley live in Los Gatos, California, the perfect place to plant a garden and raise vibrant orchids. Doug is an ophthalmologist and graduate of the UCLA medical school. He is also the world's biggest breeder of Stanhopea Orchids. Stanhopeas are fragrant orchids that grow in trees in the jungle and bloom downward. Doug has made more hybrids of this type of orchid than anyone else in the world. While Doug's babies are his orchids, Katherine reared their other five children: three sons and two daughters.

Cool Cups
and Hot Mugs

PUNCHES, SLUSH,
AND OTHER
REFRESHING BEVERAGES

Mint Julep

SUSAN EVANS MCCLOUD

It is so difficult to find refreshing drinks that are also interesting, different, and pleasing to the eye. But it is easy to grow mint, and mint may even be purchased from grocery stores. So I always keep this syrup on hand. When people drop in unexpectedly—as they often seem to—they are always delighted and impressed when I serve this drink with ice in tall glasses, and usually with a metal stirring spoon that is also a straw!

1 c. water

1 c. sugar

2 Tbs. lemon rind

½ c. fresh lemon juice

1 c. fresh mint leaves, washed and chopped fine

Ginger Ale

Boil water, sugar, and lemon rind for 5 minutes. Remove from heat and stir in juice. Bruise mint leaves and add to mixture, stirring. Let stand for a few hours; then strain into a jar with lid. Refrigerate until serving. (May store 2 to 3 weeks.)

When making the julep, pour ginger ale into glasses and add syrup to taste (2 to 4 tablespoons per serving). Garnish with mint leaves or fresh raspberries.

Serves 10 to 15.

Note: This recipe can easily be doubled or quadrupled for use at parties or for serving large numbers of guests.

Susan Evans McCloud has published more than forty books, including several biographies, children's books, and dozens of works of fiction. Her work also includes several screenplays, tape narratives, and the lyrics to two hymns: "Lord, I Would Follow Thee" and "As Zion's Youth in Latter Days." Susan and her husband, James, are the parents of six children and the grandparents of six. They reside in Provo, Utah.

Piña Colada Cocktail

BARBARA B. SMITH

Quick, easy, and delicious!

1 (46-oz.) can pineapple juice

6 c. milk

1 c. sugar

1½ tsp. coconut extract

Blend ingredients and freeze in a 9x13-inch pan. Remove from freezer an hour before serving; chop and mash into slush. Serve in small glasses

Serves 12.

Barbara Bradshaw Smith served as general president of the Relief Society from 1974 to 1984. She has also served as national president of the American Mothers, Inc., and on President Jimmy Carter's White House Advisory Committee for the Conference on Families. She is married to Douglas H. Smith, a former member of the First and Second Quorums of the Seventy and President of the Asia Area. Brother and Sister Smith have sent out thirty-five missionaries from their immediate and extended family. They have served on every continent of the world with the exception of Antarctica, and there is no mission there.

Strawberry Punch

MARY ELLEN SMOOT

This is a very refreshing party punch.

3 c. sugar dissolved in 12 c. water

2 (6-oz.) cans frozen pink lemonade concentrate

2 pkgs. frozen strawberries, sliced

1 qt. vanilla ice cream, cut in chunks

2 to 4 L. 7-Up®

Mix sugar, lemonade, and strawberries in blender and freeze. Before serving, let mixture thaw slightly. Remove to large punch bowl, add ice cream chunks and 7-Up.

Serves 50.

Mary Ellen Wood Smoot served as general president of the Relief Society from April 1997 to April 2002. She loves family history and has written histories about her parents, grandparents, and their local community. She served with her husband, Stanley M. Smoot, when he was called as a mission president in Ohio, and they later served together as directors of Church Hosting. They are the parents of seven children and the grandparents of forty-seven.

Paul's Fruit Cooler

PAUL JAMES

The perfect accompaniment for the Cougarito Burgerito (see pages 156 to 157 of this book) is this iced concoction of your choice of fruit flavors. It never needs to be the same. It's so delicious, that Paul's sister Betty Thompson once included it in her cooking column for a Northern California newspaper.

1 qt. fruit or herb tea, or instant decaf iced tea (not too diluted)

Sugar or sweetener to taste

3 to 4 Tbs. lemon juice (fresh or bottled concentrate)

1 (6½-oz.) can frozen peach daiquiri mix, or cranberry (or your favorite flavor)

Lots of crushed ice

A drop or two of mint or almond extract (optional)

Mix all ingredients together; adjust the proportions to taste.

For thirty-seven years Paul James was the voice of the BYU Cougars, calling plays for KSL radio in Salt Lake City. Paul retired with Coach LaVell Edwards at the end of the 2000 season. With Bob Welti and Dick Nourse, Paul James formed a noteworthy trio of broadcasters that Utahns will remember for years to come. Paul now spends his time painting, caring for the orchids in his greenhouse, and learning to play the piano. He and his wife, Annette, are the parents of four children and reside in Salt Lake City.

Raspberry Slush

RICHARD M. SIDDOWAY

If you want something wonderful to serve with pizza, try this recipe for raspberry slush.

2 c. sugar

3½ c. water

1 c. orange juice

1 (1-lb.) can crushed pineapple with juice

2 (10-oz.) pkgs. frozen raspberries

7-Up®

In saucepan, heat sugar and water; stir until sugar dissolves. Cool, then add orange juice, pineapple, and raspberries. Stir until well mixed. Freeze, stirring once while slushy. To serve, scoop into a glass with 7-Up—add a slice of lime, if desired.

Serves 16 when added to 7-Up.

Richard M. Siddoway is the best-selling author of *The Christmas Wish*, which was produced as a made-for-TV movie starring Debbie Reynolds and Neil Patrick Harris. A professional educator for more than forty years, Richard is currently the director of Electronic High School for the State of Utah and a three-term member of the Utah State Legislature. He is the author of several memorable and touching books, including *Christmas Quest, Christmas of the Cherry Snow*, and *Twelve Tales of Christmas*. He and his wife, Janice, are the parents of eight children and the grandparents of sixteen plus. They reside in Bountiful, Utah.

Kieth Merrill's Elixir of Perpetual Youth

KIETH MERRILL

Making movies has provided some remarkable adventures and significantly impacted the way I eat and the foods that I enjoy. Traveling the world making films has exposed me to unexpected foods, both pleasurable and repulsive. None of them are written as recipes, as I was never inclined to swap the secret Mormon recipe for *Fruit Trapped in Green Jell-O* for the mixture of natural herbs stuffed in the jungle rat I ate in Brazil.

Because I don't have time to spend hours in the kitchen cooking up creative meals—and because Dagny and I agreed when the last of our eight kids left home that it was time for

her to retire as chief cook and bottle washer—I have no favorite recipes per se. The results: My favorite foods are simple and fast, but a very long ways from "fast food."

My Elixir of Perpetual Youth emerged from my first postular of epicurism: The blender does it all.

I carry a blender in my suitcase when I travel. If I forget to put one in I go to Wal-Mart and buy another one. I have a strange collection of really cheap blenders on the top shelf in the pantry. I've been using a blender to create liquid meals for so long I should get royalties from all these Johnny-Come-Lately Smoothie Shops and Juice Joints.

1 c. frozen berries (any kind of berries will do)

2 c. nonfat milk

½ ripe banana

1 to 2 eggs

1 packet of Vanilla Cream MyoPlex® Deluxe Nutrition Shake

10 ice cubes

Nonfat milk or water, as needed

Dump the frozen berries into the blender. Add nonfat milk—just slosh it in to about halfway. Throw in half a banana—or whole if you need potassium. Add an egg or two. Start blender—forget all those buttons—hit FULL POWER. Slowly add a packet of Vanilla Cream MyoPlex Deluxe Nutrition Shake while the blender is mixing to keep it from caking up on the sides. (I've tried them all—this shake mix from EAS is best.) Add ice cubes; then, if needed, slowly add additional nonfat milk or water. The goal is to create the consistency of a malted milk from 1958.

Serves 1.

Kieth Merrill is an Academy-Award-winning director, writer, and producer. He has written and produced twelve IMAX films, including *Grand Canyon, the Hidden Secrets*. His large format films include *Testaments of One Fold and One Shepherd* and *Legacy*, which have been seen by millions of people from all over the world. His work has garnered one Oscar, two Academy Award nominations, an Emmy nomination, a Clio, and the coveted NCHF Wrangler Award. He is married to Dagny Johnson Merrill, and they are the parents of eight children and the grandparents of twenty. The Merrills live in the Sierra foothills of California's gold country.

Cranberry Ice

BRENT AND BONNIE JEAN BEESLEY

This recipe from another generation makes a spectacular dinner appetizer.

2 c. fresh or frozen cranberries

2 c. water

¼ c. orange juice

½ c. lemon juice, or to taste

Sugar, to taste

Ginger ale

Steam cranberries in saucepan with water until soft, then mash. Heat mixture to boiling point. Remove from heat and let stand. When cranberry mixture is cool, add orange juice, lemon juice, and sugar to taste. Add a small amount of water, if needed for consistency. Pour into a large, shallow freezer tray and cover. Place in freezer. Open freezer occasionally to stir and soften the mixture. Set out to thaw an hour or two before serving. Serve alone in small custard cups or in goblets with ginger ale.

Brent Beesley is chairman and CEO of Heritage Bank, in St George, Utah. He holds a BA from BYU and an MBA and JD from Harvard University. During the savings and loan crisis in the early 1980s, Mr. Beesley was the director of the Office of the Federal Savings and Loan Insurance Corporation, Washington, D.C. He has been the president and CEO of the Farm Credit Corporation of America, in Denver, Colorado, which was the central entity of the nationwide Federal Farm Credit System. He served a mission in Argentina and now teaches the Gospel Doctrine class in his ward. He is married to the former Bonnie Jean Matheson. They have seven children.

Tomato Orange Cocktail

TRUMAN AND MARILYN CLAWSON

My mother had wonderful parties. Her graciousness made everyone feel at home. I especially liked to sample the food she created. It was always beautiful, and oh so yummy! This versatile drink can be served hot or cold; therefore, it works for all seasons. Best of all, it is fast and easy, and can be prepared almost as the guests are ringing the doorbell.

1 c. orange juice (not from concentrate)

1 (10¾-oz.) can tomato soup

½ c. water

¼ tsp. sweet basil

Salt & pepper to taste

Sour cream (opt.)

Blend together the orange juice, tomato soup, and water. Season with basil, salt, and pepper. Garnish with a dollop of sour cream, if desired.

Serves 5 to 8.

Truman Clawson graduated from the University of Utah law school. He is the owner of Clawson Travel Service and is chairman of the board of Hickory Travel Systems, an international travel service organization. He has served as chair of the Salt Lake Convention and Visitor's Bureau and the Utah State Travel Council, as well as vice-chair of Salt Lake Valley Hospitals for Intermountain Healthcare. His wife, Marilyn Jackson Clawson, is a home economist and served a mission with him as director of the Mormon Trail Center at Winter Quarters in Omaha, Nebraska, and the Kanesville Tabernacle in Council Bluffs, Iowa. They are the parents of eight children and the grandparents of fifteen.

Wonderful Wassail

HOMER R. WARNER

Our mission to Frankfurt, Germany, was a most unique experience as we traveled throughout Europe finding capable doctors for our missionaries and introduced new methods for keeping computerized records about the health problems of the missionaries. We celebrated our last Christmas in Frankfurt with twenty-five of our German neighbors in our apartment. We couldn't communicate in German, but the spirit we felt made us friends forever. One guest insisted on serving the hot wassail and cookies my wife had prepared; he became a waiter with a napkin over his arm. He had been a prisoner of war in Iowa during World War II and loved Americans. This was his way of saying thank you.

46 oz. apple juice

1 cinnamon stick

Zest of 1 lemon

⅔ tsp. nutmeg

1 (6-oz.) can frozen lemonade concentrate

1 (6-oz.) can frozen orange juice concentrate

½ c. honey (sugar may be substituted)

¼ c. fresh lemon juice

Heat apple juice, cinnamon stick, zest, and nutmeg almost to boiling. Reduce heat and simmer for 15 minutes. Stir in lemonade and orange juice concentrates, honey, lemon juice, and zest. If wassail simmers too long or becomes too concentrated in flavor, water may be added.

Makes 18 6-oz. servings.

Dr. Homer Richards Warner, a medical pioneer, established the world's first department of Medical Informatics at the University of Utah and served as department chair for thirty-one years. He also worked as chief information officer for the University of Utah's Health Sciences Center. Dr. Warner's work sent him all over the world as he helped the international community break into the field of computer diagnosis. He and his wife, Katherine Romney Warner, served a medical mission together to western Europe. They are the parents of six children, the grandparents of twenty-three, and the great-grandparents of five.

Breakfast on the House

EGGS, PANCAKES, WAFFLES, AND DELICIOUS BRUNCH IDEAS

Flora Benson's Eggs-à-la-Goldenrod

BARBARA BENSON WALKER

Mother always made this for our special family breakfasts, brunches, and birthdays; and whenever General Authorities stayed overnight with us in Washington, D. C., or Idaho. I have continued this tradition with family, friends, and General Authorities who visited our home in Calgary, Alberta, Canada.

White sauce (made with real butter)

Eggs (1 per person)

Toast (1 or 2 slices per person)

Butter

Bacon slices, cooked

Make a basic white sauce (you will need about ½ to 1 cup of white sauce per person). Boil as many eggs as needed; cool. Peel eggs and cut in half, separating yolks and whites into separate bowls. Finely chop egg whites and mix in the white sauce. Make toast, butter it, and place on serving dishes. Immediately pour a scoopful of sauce over toast; then put egg yolks in sieve and push some through onto white sauce. Top with slice of bacon, if desired.

Servings vary.

The oldest daughter of President Ezra Taft and Flora Benson, Barbara Benson Walker attended the University of Utah and Brigham Young University, where she studied home economics and music. A highly trained coloratura soprano, one of her singing teachers was Anna Kaskas of the Metropolitan Opera. Barbara has sung solos in many countries, on television, and for presidents of the United States. One of her favorite singing moments happened when she sang a solo of "O Divine Redeemer" for her father, President Benson, in the Tabernacle Solemn Assembly, April 1986. She and her deceased husband, Dr. Robert Harris Walker, are the parents of five children, the grandparents of thirty, and the great-grandparents of one.

Eggs Benedict

RICHARD AND LINDA EYRE

You have to be careful when you start a tradition in a family. Once a tradition is firmly established, there is almost nothing you can do to stop it! When our children were small we decided that we wanted to have a special breakfast on Christmas morning, rather than spending the day cooking a huge holiday dinner. Since our favorite breakfast was Eggs Benedict, which we had enjoyed only in nice restaurants previously, we decided to give it a try at home. After a couple of entertaining failures, we finally found a recipe that was pretty hard to mess up, so we proceeded.

There have been years when the sauce was too thick or too thin, or we ran out of asparagus or forgot the Canadian bacon, but we have faithfully managed to pull off the cholesterol extravaganza almost every year. The assembly line is one of our most treasured holiday memories—with grandma cutting grapefruit, one child cracking eggs into muffin tins, another toasting English muffins, another warming Canadian bacon, and still another heating asparagus; and Mom trying to get everyone out of the way so the hollandaise sauce could be prepared before everything got cold.

As our children began to leave home and were away from us at Christmas on missions, their attempts to carry on the Eggs Benedict tradition in Bulgaria, Romania, England, Spain, Brazil, and Chile have been quite hilarious. Toasted Bulgarian bread has been used for English muffins, strange bacon cuts substituted for Canadian bacon, sour orange juice used instead of lemon juice, fried eggs exchanged for poached, and green beans have filled in for asparagus. But their version of our Christmas tradition was an absolute must!

On her mission, one of our daughters and her companion had been teaching a poverty-stricken woman living in a hovel. They somehow managed to make Eggs Benedict for her on Christmas morning. The woman was overcome with gratitude, saying that she had heard of Eggs Benedict but had thought that it was something she would never be able to taste. She had no table, so they ate sitting on the floor.

One Christmas we decided to do a humanitarian service project in Bolivia rather than have our traditional Christmas celebration at home. Our flight left at 7 A.M. on Christmas morning; and, since we had to check in two hours early, I insisted that there would be no Eggs Benedict that Christmas. Like true Santa's elves, the kids got up at 4 A.M. to surprise us with their rendition of Eggs Benedict a la Kids.

Note: The basic sauce recipe serves about three. With our Christmas crowd, we usually multiply it by six. If you want to poach more than six eggs, we have found it easier to spray a muffin tin with cooking spray, add about a tablespoon of water and an egg, lightly salted, to each cup. Put a pan of water in the bottom of the oven to create humidity, and cook at 350° F.

for 8 to 10 minutes, according to preference for doneness. It results in a close resemblance to a poached egg. We usually serve half a grapefruit with a maraschino cherry on top for an appetizer.

6 eggs, poached

6 halves of toasted English muffins

6 slices of Canadian bacon

1 sm. can asparagus (use fresh if available)

Poach the eggs, warm the asparagus, and toast the muffins. Place a slice of Canadian bacon on each muffin half. Next add a poached egg and several stalks of asparagus (at the side or on the egg); top with hollandaise sauce.

ALMOST-NEVER-FAIL HOLLANDAISE SAUCE

3 egg yolks

1 Tbs. lemon juice

Pinch of salt

½ c. butter

To prepare hollandaise sauce, put egg yolks, lemon juice, and salt in blender. Turn on and off. Heat butter until just boiling. (This heat is what cooks the eggs.) Turn blender on high and slowly pour the very hot butter into the egg yolks and lemon mixture, until it becomes thick and fluffy (about 30 seconds). Makes about ⅔ cups.

Serves 3.

Richard and Linda Eyre are nationally and internationally recognized as the authors of the *New York Times* number one best-seller *Teaching Your Children Values.* The Eyres are widely respected for their Values Parenting (www.valuesparenting.com) program and regularly promote the importance of family and the joys of parenting on national and local television and radio shows. Together and individually they have authored more than thirty books. Richard and Linda are the parents of nine children and the grandparents of one. They reside in Salt Lake City, Utah.

Sourdough Hot Cakes

ROBERT K. AND MARY JAYNE DELLENBACH

Having lived in Alaska for many years, we became enamored with sourdough cooking. No one knows exactly where sourdough originated; but wherever it did, it is a lively and tasty treat for the whole family. Legends abound regarding the use of sourdough. In the early days of Alaska, pioneering supplies would arrive only once a year. Those settlers relied heavily on the sourdough for sustenance. Perhaps that is how they got the nickname *Sourdoughs*. "Sour on Alaska, and no dough to get out" was a common joke.

To make these delicious pancakes, you'll have to plan ahead. The project begins the night before when you set the starter and the batter. You can make your own starter and batter with this recipe. Please note: The recipe is courtesy of the University of Alaska Extension Services.

SOURDOUGH STARTER

1 pkg. dry yeast

2 cups warm water

2 cups flour

To make your starter, dissolve yeast in ¼ cup of the warm water. In a medium mixing bowl, add remaining water and flour and mix all three ingredients well. Lightly cover and let stand in warm place or cupboard overnight. In the morning, the batter will have gained half again its bulk and will be covered with air bubbles. It will have a pleasant, yeasty odor. Put ½ cup of the starter in a scalded pint jar, cover and store in the refrigerator (or a cool place) to use in the future in place of the dry yeast. Leave room for expansion in the container, or set the lid on without tightening it. This is the sourdough starter. Starter will keep almost indefinitely in a clean, covered glass contained in the refrigerator. Never use a metal container or leave a metal spoon in the starter or batter. If unused for several weeks, the starter may need to sit out an extra night before adding flour and water.

SOURDOUGH HOT CAKE BATTER

1 tsp. baking soda

1 Tbs. water

1 to 2 eggs

1 Tbs. oil

1 tsp. salt

1 Tbs. sugar

Now you are ready to complete the sourdough hot cake batter.

Dissolve soda in water and set aside. In a large bowl, beat the remaining sourdough batter (you should have about 2 cups left). Add eggs, oil, salt, and sugar to batter and blend well. Add soda-water mixture just before baking. The batter for sourdough hot cakes should be the same consistency as the batter for other hot cakes. Pour scoops of batter onto hot griddle, turning once and cooking until golden brown. Serve with favorite toppings.

To make sourdough waffles, use the basic hot cake recipe, but add two extra tablespoons of oil. Add the oil, then the soda-water mixture, and bake at once according to the directions that come with your waffle iron.

Makes 9 to 10 6-inch hot cakes.

Elder Robert K. Dellenbach was sustained as a General Authority of The Church of Jesus Christ of Latter-day Saints on March 31, 1990, at the age of fifty-two. He currently serves in the Pacific Islands Area Presidency. He has also served in Area Presidencies in the United States and Europe and as general Young Men president. Prior to his call, Elder Dellenbach was an administrator in universities and businesses, including president of Alaska Methodist University. At the Salk Institute, he was an assistant to Dr. Jonas Salk. He directed a co-operative advanced technology project with the former Soviet Union. Throughout Elder Dellenbach's professional career and Church assignments, he and his wife, Mary-Jayne (Broadbent) Dellenbach have been assigned to live and serve in many cities and countries of the world. They were married in the Manti Temple August 17, 1962. They are parents of three sons and have eight grandchildren.

Kelly's Pancakes

STEVE HARMSEN

Steve's wife, Kelly, explains why this recipe is so delicious: "Separated eggs, stiff egg whites, and a hot, buttered griddle (the first pancake will not be the best one)."

4 eggs, separated

4 c. buttermilk

8 Tbs. salad oil or melted shortening

4 c. flour

4 Tbs. sugar

4 tsp. baking powder

2 tsp. salt

2 tsp. baking soda

In small mixing bowl, beat egg whites until stiff and glossy peaks form. In large mixing bowl, mix egg yolks, buttermilk, and oil. Stir in dry ingredients. Fold in egg whites—and the batter is ready for the hot, buttered griddle.

Steve and Kelly Harmsen met in Los Angeles, where Steve moved after graduating from the George Washington Law School in Washington, D.C. The Harmsens then moved to Salt Lake City, where Kelly taught English at Viewmont High School and Steve practiced law. Steve worked as a Salt Lake City prosecutor, president of the American Public Works Association (Utah chapter), and Republican State Finance chairman. He is the owner of the Steve Regan Company, a farm and rancher supplier and was recently elected an at-large member of the Salt Lake County Council. Steve and Kelly have six children and three grandchildren and are looking forward to having more of the latter.

Hootenanny Pancakes

MICHAEL MCLEAN

Hootenanny Pancakes can and should be eaten most anytime: Christmas morning, New Year's Day, birthday mornings, special occasions, late nights after the game or show when you're not yet ready to call it a night.

The greatest part about this pancake is that it "poofs" while it's cooking and has all this glorious butter swirling around it. When you see that the poofie edges are golden brown, bring it out of the oven and do this—I'm serious, if you don't do this, you'll not have the Hootenanny Pancake Experience—chant with all those who will be eating: "Hootenanny, Hootenanny, Hoot, Hoot, Hoot." Once, in a foolish moment, we did not do the chant and were miserable. Since then we have followed the true path of the Hootenanny, and joy has been ours. This pancake is so delicious that it is impossible to not be friends with the folks you share this experience with. When I served my mission in Southern Africa, I shared the Hootenannies and found that it's impossible to argue or have contention over them; even atheists believe the scriptures are true while they're eating Hootenanny Pancakes.

We like to heat up several different syrups to serve with the pancakes. It's also delicious to slice up some lemons and squeeze them over the hallowed Hoot and sprinkle with powdered sugar. Add some herb tea or cocoa and a side of fresh fruit, and you'll have to check to see if you're still living on planet earth and not in some celestial sphere.

6 eggs

1 c. milk

1 c. flour

Pinch of salt

Stick of butter

Preheat oven to 450° F. Mix the eggs, milk, flour, and salt into a creamy, frothy batter. Melt the stick of butter in a nine-inch dripper pan in the oven until it bubbles. Pour the batter into the pan of melted butter, but don't stir it. Place the pan back in the oven for about 15 minutes. Don't open the oven door while it is baking.

Michael McLean has written music and lyrics for twenty-one albums, including the popular *Forgotten Carols*, which have been performed in front of sell-out crowds throughout the western United States every Christmas for the last nine years. Michael has also written, produced, and directed *Nora's Christmas Gift*, starring Celeste Holm, and *Mr. Krueger's Christmas*, starring Jimmy Stewart. Michael and his wife, Lynne, are the parents of three children and live in Heber City, Utah.

Ralph's Swedish Pancakes

SHARON G. LARSEN

Ralph's two Swedish grandmothers passed this recipe down to his mother, who served it many times to her children. His grandmothers taught that the Swedes do not add baking powder like the French do in their crêpes. Swedes serve these pancakes with *The Queen's Cream* (a mixture of raspberry and blueberry jam). While our own children were growing up, Ralph would make these pancakes every Sunday night. Invariably friends would just *happen to drop by* while he was serving pancakes. (We usually multiply the recipe several times.)

2 eggs, well beaten

2 Tbs. sugar

2 c. milk

2 Tbs. vegetable oil

1½ c. flour

½ tsp. salt

Choice of toppings: Powdered sugar, butter, syrup, fresh fruit, whipping cream

Heat crêpe pan or skillet with small amount of oil over medium heat. In a large bowl, mix together the beaten eggs, sugar, milk, oil, flour, and salt. Batter should be very thin. Ralph's mother always says, "If you think the batter is too thin, add more milk!"

Drop a scoopful of the batter (¼ to ⅓ cup) onto hot crêpe pan and cook only until lightly browned, and flip over. Serve with powdered sugar, butter, syrup, or other choice of toppings.

Serves 4.

Sharon Greene Larsen attended the University of Alberta and graduated from Brigham Young University with a bachelor of science degree. She taught in elementary schools in Utah and Missouri. She wrote, produced, and starred in programs for the Utah Network for Instructional Television. She has twice served on the Young Women general board and in the Young Women general presidency and served as the national president of Lambda Delta Sigma. Sister Larsen taught institute at two colleges. She and her husband, Dr. Ralph T. Larsen, are the parents of two children and three grandchildren.

Brinton Family's Light and Crispy Waffles

SALLY BRINTON

Every Sunday evening, our family carries on a tradition passed down from our parents of eating these light and crispy waffles.

2 eggs, separated

2 c. milk

2 c. all-purpose flour

1 Tbs. baking powder

½ tsp. salt

⅓ c. oil

Syrup or fruit topping, as desired.

Separate eggs and beat egg whites until stiff peaks form. Set aside. Preheat waffle-maker. Put all ingredients except egg whites in a large mixing bowl and beat on low until moistened. Increase to medium speed; mix until smooth. By hand, gently fold in beaten egg whites. Pour ½ cup batter over waffle grid; close lid and bake until golden, 2½ to 3 minutes. Serve warm waffles with choice of syrup or topping.

Makes 8 waffles.

Sally Peterson Brinton first performed as a piano soloist with the Utah Symphony at age eleven. She has since been featured nine times with the symphony, including the world premiere of the Ramiro Cortes Piano Concerto. Sally was named Miss Utah in 1972 and went on to compete in the Miss America pageant, where she won the Talent Award and was named Miss Congeniality. She has a master's of music degree from the Juilliard School of Music in New York City and is a member of the Mormon Tabernacle Choir. Sally's husband, Dr. Gregory S. Brinton, is a retina specialist in private practice, a clinical professor of ophthalmology at the University of Utah, chair of the Division of Ophthalmology at LDS Hospital, and a past president of the Utah Ophthalmological Society. They are the parents of seven children and reside in Salt Lake City.

Daddy's French Toast

LLOYD D. NEWELL

Nearly every Saturday morning, I delight my children with a favorite family tradition—homemade French toast, hot off the griddle. I always make more than enough so that we can enjoy the leftovers for days. Sometimes the children will make sandwiches with them for lunch or as an after school snack. Daddy's French Toast has even been the entrée of choice for special birthday dinners. While the recipe is not particularly unique, no one gets tired of it, because we keep inventing new, creative toppings. Along with the traditional maple syrup, a few of our favorites include: yogurt and kiwi (or strawberry or banana) slices, chocolate sauce and whipped cream, pineapple tidbits and mandarin oranges, and whatever we may decide to try next Saturday morning.

2 Tbs. butter or margarine

1 doz. eggs

½ c. milk

Dash of vanilla

Dash of cinnamon

Loaf of bread (white or wheat, thicker
   is better, like Texas Toast)

Powdered sugar

Toppings of choice

Melt the butter in a frying pan or griddle. Beat eggs, milk, vanilla, and cinnamon together. Dip bread into egg mixture; fry until light brown and egg is cooked. Remove from pan; sprinkle with powdered sugar, if desired, and serve at once.

Lloyd D. Newell has been the voice of *Music and the Spoken Word* since 1990. He travels throughout the world with the Mormon Tabernacle Choir and contributes writings to the weekly *Spoken Word* broadcast. He has worked as a television news anchor for a CBS affiliate in Pennsylvania and for *CNN Headline News* in Atlanta. He has spoken in forty-five states and thirteen countries as a professional speaker and now teaches religion and family life at Brigham Young University. He is the author or co-author of several books. He and his wife, Karmel, are the parents of four children: Hayley, McKay, Abigail, and Jacob.

Jericho Road Breakfast Cake

JERICHO ROAD

This cake comes from the recipe box of our manager's mother. If you prepare it the night before, you have a quick—and delicious—breakfast on hectic mornings. For a little extra nutrition, add a cup of blueberries to the batter.

2½ c. flour

½ c. sugar

2 Tbs. baking powder

Pinch salt

½ c. shortening

1⅓ c. milk

2 eggs

FOR TOPPING:

1½ c. flour

2 c. sugar

2¼ tsp. cinnamon

1¾ sticks margarine (approx. 14 Tbs.)

Sift dry ingredients. Cut in shortening. Add milk and eggs. Mixture should not be lumpy. Set aside. Prepare topping by combining dry ingredients and cutting in margarine. Grease 9x13-inch pan. Pour in half the cake mixture. Top with half the cinnamon topping. Pour in remainder of cake mixture and top with the remainder of the cinnamon topping. Bake at 400° F. for 25 minutes. (You can bake this the night before and keep it in the fridge until morning).

Serves 12 to 15.

Justin Smith (Parma, ID), Abe Mills (St. Louis, MO), Bret Bryce (Knoxville, TN), Dave Kimball (Sandy, UT) are Jericho Road. The four returned missionaries met while attending Brigham Young University. After performing for two years as the a cappella group VOX, the group made a change in genre and launched into the Christian music scene with a best-selling, self-titled debut CD. Their second CD, *True North*, hit stores in the fall of 2002 along with their DVD documentary, *Backstage Pass*.

Bill's Classic French Quiche

ELAINE CANNON

Many years ago, I asked my brother-in-law, Bill Robinson, for this classic French quiche recipe that he learned to make while in chef's school. When he served it, he was ahead of his time. Now it is a popular dish with many variations. I have found it to be a success no matter what combination of vegetables or meat I choose. The secret touch is the French sauce—the clam juice adds an exotic flavor. Instead of bacon in the basic quiche, you may substitute crab, shrimp, or ham. Zucchini or artichoke hearts may also be added.

Baked 9-inch pastry shell (recipe follows)

6 strips cooked bacon, drained and crumbled

½ c. mushrooms (optional)

¼ c. onion, diced (or sprinkle of onion flakes)

4 eggs (less 1 egg white)

1 c. heavy cream

½ c. milk

½ tsp. salt

1 c. Swiss cheese, shredded

Dash of pepper

Pinch of nutmeg

Clam sauce topping (recipe follows)

Lightly sauté mushrooms and onion, if desired. Beat 3 eggs and the extra yolk (reserving extra egg white for another use). Add cream, milk, and salt, mixing thoroughly. Sprinkle bottom of lightly baked pie shell with crumbled bacon, mushrooms, onions, and grated Swiss cheese. Pour cream mixture over bacon-cheese layer. Bake at 350° F. for 25 to 30 minutes, until knife inserted in center comes out clean. Serve warm with clam sauce topping.

Serves 8.

PASTRY SHELL

2 c. flour

½ tsp. salt

4 Tbs. soft butter

4 Tbs. shortening or lard

1 egg yolk

4 to 6 Tbs. ice water

CLAM SAUCE TOPPING

3 Tbs. butter

3 Tbs. flour

1 c. heavy cream

¾ c. bottled clam juice

1 c. clear chicken broth

To make the pastry shell, combine dry ingredients in a medium bowl. Cut in soft butter and shortening until dough is mealy. Stir ice water into egg yolk; add to dry ingredients a little at a time until dough is the right consistency. Form into a ball and chill for 1 hour. Roll out on floured surface and shape to fit a 9-inch pie plate. Line the crust with foil and fill with beans or rice to prevent crust from puffing. (Beans used should be reserved for this purpose only.) Bake at 350° F. for about 10 minutes, until very light brown.

For clam sauce, melt butter in a small saucepan. Add flour to make a paste, then stir in liquids. Cook, stirring constantly until thickened. Serve as a topping for freshly-baked quiche.

Elaine Cannon has published seventy books in her long career as a writer and editor. A former general president of the Young Women organization, Sister Cannon also lectured for BYU's continuing education program for thirty years and served as associate editor for several Church magazines. Elaine is wife of the late D. James Cannon and lives in Salt Lake City, Utah. She currently serves as the Relief Society president of the Salt Lake Emigration stake.

Ebleskivers (Danish Pancakes)

MICHAEL BALLAM

In 1901, my great-grandfather heard a congregation singing through closed doors in Randers, Denmark. The spirit within the music touched his soul so deeply that he determined to discover who the people were on the other side of the doors. Much to his surprise, they were members of The Church of Jesus Christ of Latter-day Saints. This was not the first time he had been acquainted with the Mormons; but previously he had taunted and tried to confound the young missionaries who had attempted to bring him to a new understanding of the gospel. This time the Spirit witnessed to him to listen. He and his wife, Marianne, converted and immigrated to the United States to be near the Saints, settling in Benson, Utah. They brought with them many traditions from their Danish heritage; the most delicious was their recipe for Ebleskivers. My grandfather had a deep testimony of the gospel and told me to lean on his till I had one of my own. I did, and though I now have a deep and abiding testimony of my own, I still hearken to his faith and think of him and my Danish heritage whenever I prepare and enjoy these delectable confections. (To make these Danish pancakes, you will need an ebleskiver pan. They are available at most kitchenware stores and are well worth purchasing.)

3 c. flour

1½ tsp. baking soda

½ tsp. baking powder

½ tsp. salt

3 eggs

2 Tbs. sugar

3 c. buttermilk

6 Tbs. melted shortening or vegetable oil

Combine dry ingredients in medium bowl and set aside. In a large mixing bowl, beat together eggs and sugar. Stir in buttermilk and shortening; then add the dry ingredients, gently stirring until blended.

Heat ebleskiver pan on stovetop. Thoroughly coat each cup with shortening. Fill each cup three-quarters full with batter. As it begins to bubble around the edges, turn gradually with a skewer or chopstick. Cook until golden brown all around.

Serves 6 to 8.

Michael Ballam is the founder and director of the Utah Festival Opera Company. Michael has performed in concert halls throughout America, Asia, and Europe, with command performances at the White House and the Vatican. He has shared the stage with the world's greatest singers, including Joan Sutherland, Kiri Te Kanawa, Birgit Nilsson, and Placido Domingo. At the age of twenty-four, Dr. Ballam became the youngest recipient of the degree of Doctor of Music with Distinction in the history of Indiana University. He is a professor of music at Utah State University and an accomplished pianist and oboist. Michael and his wife, Laurie, are the parents of six children and reside in Logan, Utah.

All the Fish in the Sea

DELECTABLE
FISH AND
SHELLFISH DISHES

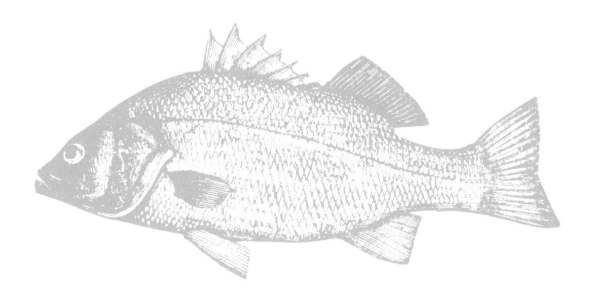

Angel Hair Pasta with Shrimp

JANET LEE CHAMBERLAIN

12 oz. fresh or frozen shrimp, peeled and deveined

1 c. chopped onion

2 cloves garlic, minced

1 Tbs. olive oil or cooking oil

¼ c. white cooking wine or water

1 Tbs. snipped fresh basil

1½ tsp. snipped fresh oregano

1 tsp. instant chicken bouillon granules

1 tsp. cornstarch

⅛ tsp. pepper

6 oz. dried angel hair pasta, cooked

2 medium tomatoes, peeled, seeded, and chopped

¼ c. snipped parsley

¼ c. grated Parmesan cheese

Thaw shrimp, if frozen.

In a large saucepan cook the onion and garlic in hot oil until onion is tender. Combine the cooking wine or water, basil, oregano, bouillon granules, cornstarch, and pepper. Add to saucepan. Cook and stir until bubbly.

Add shrimp to liquid mixture in saucepan. Cover and simmer about 3 minutes or until shrimp turn pink.

Meanwhile, cook pasta in boiling water for 2 minutes, until it is al dente. Stir tomatoes into shrimp mixture and heat through. To serve, toss pasta with parsley. Spoon shrimp mixture over pasta. Sprinkle with Parmesan cheese.

Serves 4.

Janet Lee Chamberlain earned her bachelor of science degree in education from Brigham Young University. She is a frequent and popular speaker at firesides, women's conferences, and BYU devotionals. She and her late husband, Rex E. Lee, the former president of Brigham Young University, are the parents of seven children. Janet has served as a member of the Young Women general board. She is married to Wayne Chamberlain.

Shrimp Curry

HEIDI S. SWINTON

When I was a little girl and we had company for dinner or for my mother's church study group, we always had shrimp curry for the main course. As Mother cooked the curry, the house filled with the aroma of exotic spices. I was in charge of putting the toppings—coconut, raisins, olives, green onions, peanuts, chutney, and watermelon pickles in dishes. As I got older, I advanced to chopping peanuts and watermelon pickles. My mother would taste and stir and add seasonings and taste again. She would ladle the curry into an English bone china tureen she had bought on Vancouver Island on our way home from Alaska when I was five. I learned to cook watching my mother make shrimp curry.

Today, when I have people over, we have shrimp curry, and Mother has let the tureen take up residence at my home. This curry dish is great served with a tossed salad that has oranges in it.

⅔ c. butter

6 Tbs. flour

1 tsp. salt

2 tsp. grated onion (not dried)

½ tsp. paprika

Dash nutmeg

4 Tbs. curry

4 c. half-and-half (not milk)

Dash white Worcestershire sauce

2 Tbs. candied ginger, chopped

2 Tbs. fresh lemon juice

6 c. small shrimp, well-drained (or large shrimp with tails removed)

Saffron or white rice

Orange zest (optional)

Prepare garnishes or condiments and put in bowls of appropriate size. Set aside.

In a heavy saucepan, melt the butter on low and stir in the flour. After the mixture bubbles, add the salt, grated onion, paprika, nutmeg, and curry. Adding the seasonings early in the preparation ensures that the spices will blend. Also, it is important that your spices are fresh. Don't use ones that have been on the shelf for months or years—especially the curry.

Let the mixture cook for several minutes. Add the half-and-half, stirring continuously as it thickens. Add Worcestershire sauce, candied ginger, and lemon juice. When you are nearly ready to serve, add the shrimp.

CONDIMENTS:

Chutney (I buy Major Grey's, or you can make your own)

Coconut

Green onions, chopped (you can also use French's French-fried onion rings)

Olives, sliced

Peanuts or cashews, chopped

Raisins

Watermelon pickles, chopped

Serve the curry over white rice, saffron rice, or rice with a touch of orange zest. Let your guests select the garnishes—tell them to be brave.

Heidi S. Swinton is an award-winning author and screenwriter. Her work includes *Sacred Stone: The Temple at Nauvoo*, which is the companion book to the PBS documentary *Sacred Stone: Temple on the Mississippi, American Prophet: The Story of Joseph Smith, and Trail of Hope: The Story of the Mormon Trail*. Heidi graduated from the University of Utah and attended Northwestern's Graduate School of Journalism. She and her husband, Jeffrey, have five sons.

Shrimp Newburg

ELAINE JACK

This is my all-time favorite—easy and deliciously rich. Everyone loves it. I got it from Marian Boyer when she was serving as a counselor to Barbara Smith in the general Relief Society presidency, and have used it for years.

2 Tbs. onion, finely chopped

Butter

½ tsp. curry powder (to taste)

1 (10.75-oz.) can cream of shrimp soup

1 c. sour cream

1 c. cooked shrimp

¼ c. lemon juice

In a 2-quart saucepan, sauté onions in a little butter until transparent. Add curry powder to taste. Stir in canned soup and sour cream and cook gently over medium heat. Add shrimp and heat through, but do NOT let boil. Add lemon juice to taste.

Serves 4 to 6.

Elaine's Variation: Cream of shrimp soup is difficult to find. You may substitute cream of chicken soup then add a drop of red food coloring and slightly more lemon juice. Lemon juice is the key to this recipe's delicious flavor. I also like to cook my own shrimp in seasoned water until barely done. It has more flavor than purchased cooked shrimp.

Elaine L. Jack grew up in Cardston, Alberta, Canada, where she recently served as matron of the Cardston Alberta Temple. Sister Jack has also served as general president of the Relief Society, as a counselor in the Young Women general presidency, and has a great love for the women of the Church of all ages. She's involved in community service in the areas of education and children's literacy. She and her husband, Joseph E. Jack, are the parents of four sons and the grandparents of fifteen children.

Mobile Shrimp and Green Noodle Casserole

JESIKA JEAN HENDERSON

I had the incredible experience of representing young women around the nation as America's Junior Miss 2000. During my year holding this title, I was privileged to travel all around this great country and experience food that was unique and delicious. I particularly enjoyed my trips to Mobile, Alabama, where America's Junior Miss program originates. I have had the chance to spend several weeks there each of the past two summers, where I was treated to the great Southern hospitality of the people in Mobile, and where I enjoyed many unique tastes of the South. I found that they have wonderful seafood there, though I didn't care much for the oysters. I also experienced many first tastes . . . boiled peanuts, cheese straws, hush puppies, and shrimp casserole.

1 (10- to 12-oz.) pkg. green noodles

1 bunch green onions, chopped

3 lbs. shrimp, cooked and cleaned

1 c. mayonnaise

1 c. sour cream

1 (10¾-oz.) can cream of mushroom soup

2 Tbs. prepared mustard

2 eggs, beaten

1 c. sharp cheese, grated

½ c. butter, melted

Cook noodles according to package directions and drain. While noodles are still hot, toss with green onions; place in a buttered casserole dish and top with the shrimp. In a separate bowl, combine mayonnaise, sour cream, soup, mustard, and eggs. Cover shrimp with sauce mixture. Combine cheese and melted butter and pour over sauce. Bake in a 350° F. oven for 30 minutes. Serve with a good salad and bread.

Serves 6 to 8.

Jesika Henderson was America's Junior Miss during the 2000–2001 year where she promoted the message "Be Your Best Self" to young people across the country. Jesika works each summer as a counselor at a camp that helps young girls develop self-esteem. She has also served as an emergency room volunteer and has organized a number of fundraisers for the needy and elderly. She had the opportunity to spend time in Lusaka, Zambia, where she worked with orphaned and abandoned children. Jesika can be seen Saturday mornings on HealthSouth's *Go for It!* television show. She is currently an honor student at Brigham Young University, studying English and dance, and performing with the BYU Dancers' Company.

Sandra's Shrimp-Noodle Salad

STEPHEN AND SANDRA COVEY

We have a large family that gets together often for parties, birthdays, holidays, and other special occasions. We also frequently entertain large groups of friends, which requires great quantities of food. This recipe is tried and true—used and enjoyed often.

1 (24-oz.) pkg. American Beauty® shell-roni noodles (small)

2 to 3 (6-oz.) cans medium or large shrimp, drained (or use fresh shrimp)

1 can crab meat, drained (optional)

4 to 5 green onions, diced

1 (5-oz.) bottle stuffed green olives, drained

1 pkg. sliced or slivered almonds (optional)

1 c. celery, diced

1 (8-oz.) can sliced water chestnuts

Mayonnaise (or light mayo), to taste

Cook noodles according to package directions and drain. Pour noodles into large bowl and gently fold in shrimp and crab meat, green onions and olives, almonds, celery, and water chestnuts. Add mayonnaise, stirring just until blended. Refrigerate until ready to serve. Serve on lettuce bed.

Serves 25.

Stephen R. Covey is co-founder/co-chairman of FranklinCovey Company, the largest management and leadership development organization in the world. His book, *The 7 Habits of Highly Effective People,* is a *New York Times* number-one bestseller and has sold more than 14 million copies in thirty-three languages and seventy-five countries throughout the world. Dr. Covey and his wife, Sandra Merrill Covey, have a lifelong legacy of service to the Church and community. Together they presided over the Irish Mission for The Church of Jesus Christ of Latter-day Saints. Dr. Covey has also served as a regional representative of the Twelve and on several general Church leadership committees. The Coveys are the parents of nine children and the grandparents of thirty-eight. They reside in Provo, Utah.

Weilenmann's Halibut au Gratin

MILTON WEILENMANN

2 lbs. fresh or frozen halibut

¾ c. fresh mushrooms (or canned)

¼ c. butter

5 Tbs. flour

2 c. cheddar cheese, grated

1 qt. half and half, light cream, or milk

1 tsp. salt

½ tsp. white pepper

½ tsp. dry mustard

Grated cheese to top

Poach halibut, covered, in boiling water for 15 minutes, or until fish flakes easily. Drain. Wash, slice, and sauté fresh mushrooms; combine with flaked halibut. Make a roux by melting butter and blending in flour; set aside. Grate cheese and set aside. In large, heavy saucepan, scald cream or milk. Add seasonings and stir in roux mixture, cooking and stirring until smooth and thickened. Cool about 5 minutes, then stir in grated cheese, continuing to stir until cheese is melted. Coat bottom of large casserole or baking dish with a cup of the cheese sauce. Spread with half of the halibut-mushroom mixture; cover with half of remaining cheese sauce. Make another layer with remaining halibut pieces and cheese sauce. Sprinkle top with additional grated cheese. Bake at 350° F. for 20 minutes.

Serves 8.

Milton L. Weilenmann is best known for his popular Bratten's Grotto chain of restaurants. Milt's fresh fish bar, gourmet side dishes, best-ever chowder, and hot cocktail sauce made Bratten's a success for more than thirty years (1953–1988). He also developed Della Fontana, a popular Italian restaurant in Salt Lake City between 1967 and 1994. Milton has also served as chairman of the Utah State Democratic party and was the first director of the Utah Department of Economic Development. He and his wife, Diane, are the parents of seventeen and the grandparents of forty-eight.

Low Country Boil

GERRY AVANT

This one-pot meal of shrimp, sausages, potatoes, and corn-on-the-cob gets its name from the 175-mile coastal region between Savannah, Georgia, and Charleston, South Carolina. Locals call this area the *low country*. It's an apt description since most of this stretch of land lies at or slightly above sea level; a few places are below sea level.

Some South Carolinians call this meal *Beaufort Stew* or *Frogmore Stew*. There is deception in these names, however; this isn't a *stew*. After being cooked by boiling, the ingredients are removed from the water and served *dry*. The stew or broth is discarded; don't bother setting the table with soup spoons. When I was growing up in South Georgia, I never saw *Low Country Boil, Beaufort Stew,* or *Frogmore Stew* on any restaurant menu. During the 1980s, on frequent visits and stays at my home in Georgia, I began to notice this meal as a menu item, mostly in small coastal restaurants. By the 1990s, it had become the in-thing to serve at special, even fancy, occasions, such as company Christmas parties and wedding suppers. It came to the point that if we wanted to serve good food while impressing our guests, we served Low Country Boil.

This is a flexible meal, as easily prepared for a large crowd as for a small family. Appetites determine the amount of ingredients. If your guests include lots of people or some folks who have hearty appetites, add more of each ingredient. Plan for about ¼ pound of sausage and ¼ pound shrimp per person. If shrimp is too expensive, keep the portions small and add more of all the other ingredients. Decrease all ingredients if you're cooking for a few people or those with dainty appetites. I've seen Low Country Boil prepared in huge kettles over fires outdoors and in large or medium pots on kitchen stove tops. If you're using an outdoor kettle or other extremely large pot and are more than doubling ingredients, add an additional bag of the seasoning. For a large crowd, use quarter- or half-ear corncobs. The partial ears fit better in the pot when you've increased the amount of ingredients. For a small group, whole ears are fine.

I don't have any particular talent for cooking, but I've discovered that people think I'm a good cook when I serve Low Country Boil. If you can boil water, you can cook this meal. I've never seen a printed recipe; other folks just told me how they prepare it.

1 packet of crab/shrimp boil seasoning

8 medium potatoes (red or new potatoes), skins on, washed

To a large pot (20- to 30-quart size), add water until about three-quarters full. There should be enough water to cover all the ingredients that will be placed in the pot. Drop in crab/shrimp boil seasoning packet. Add potatoes; bring to a boil and cook about 10 minutes (depending on size), or until potatoes start to

2 lbs. sausage of choice (smoked beef, kielbasa, pork, or turkey), cut into 3-inch pieces

8 ears of corn on the cob (see tips below)

3 to 4 medium yellow onions, whole, peeled (optional)

2 lbs. medium raw shrimp, in shells

Fresh lemon wedges

Shrimp cocktail sauce

cook but are still firm. Add sausage; let water return to near boiling. Add corn; let water return to near boiling. Add onions; let water return to near boiling. Clean the shrimp while other ingredients are cooking; leave in shells. Test corn and potatoes for doneness. Using a slotted spoon or wire scoop, remove all ingredients from water, except the seasoning bag. Add washed shrimp to water. The shrimp will turn pink and rise to the top almost immediately. Without letting the water boil, cook the shrimp for about 3 minutes; but *do not overcook*. Use a wire scoop, strainer, or large slotted spoon to remove shrimp from water immediately.

Serves 8.

TO SERVE:

Serving Low Country Boil is part of the fun. Be creative. Folks used to dump it onto newspapers, but now they use butcher paper, waxed paper, or foil. For a more refined presentation, serve on round platters, with the potatoes, corn, and lemon wedges around the outside edges, and the sausage, shrimp, and onions piled in the center.

However it is served, provide plenty of napkins. Better still, provide paper towels or terry-cloth hand towels. This isn't a mind-your-manners meal; you'll have to dig in with your hands to peel the shrimp. Set out several empty bowls so everyone will have something in which to put the shrimp shells and corncobs. No salt or pepper will be needed. Low Country Boil can be served as is, but some people like cocktail sauce with the shrimp.

After Gerry Avant graduated from Brigham Young University in 1969, she returned to her home state of Georgia and taught high school English for two years. After completing her graduate work at BYU, she joined the *Church News* staff of the *Deseret News* in 1972. As a writer, photographer, and associate editor, she has traveled extensively throughout the world, reporting on news and events of The Church of Jesus Christ of Latter-day Saints. She was appointed *Church News* editor in 1999.

Halibut Casserole

DALE AND BEVERLY JOHNSON

This is a favorite dish of Dale's; he loves fish of all kinds. Asparagus goes well with this recipe.

1 lb. halibut

1 c. cheddar cheese, grated

Bread crumbs, buttered, seasoned

SAUCE

¼ c. butter

½ c. onion, chopped

½ c. green bell pepper, chopped

½ c. sweet red pepper, chopped

2 Tsp. flour

1 c. milk

Wrap halibut in foil and steam for 20 minutes in a covered pan with a little water. Put chunks of fish in a 9x13-inch casserole. Sprinkle with grated cheese.

To prepare sauce, melt butter in a medium saucepan. Sauté onion and peppers in butter; stir in flour. Gradually add milk and stir continuously until mixture is thick and bubbly. Pour sauce over the fish and cheese.

Top with buttered, seasoned bread crumbs.

Bake at 400° F. for 20 minutes.

Serves 6.

Dale Johnson is a professor of surgery and pediatrics at the University of Utah School of Medicine. He recently retired as surgeon-in-chief at Primary Children's Medical Center in Salt Lake City, Utah. Dale served a mission in South Africa and has performed humanitarian service throughout the world, including Guatemala, Viet Nam, Peru, and a ten-year relationship with the Institute of Pediatrics in Krakow, Poland. Beverly currently serves as a supervisor of organists in the Salt Lake Temple. She has been active with the Utah Symphony Guild and a variety of community volunteer endeavors. Dale and Beverly both enjoyed many years of singing with the Tabernacle Choir. They have been married fifty years and have four children, thirteen grandchildren, and five great-grandchildren.

Seafood Casserole

KANAKO NAKAMOTO

Tip: Japanese mayonnaise has a little more vinegar and salt, and less oil than American mayonnaise. You can get Japanese mayonnaise in most Asian food stores; if not, substitute with sour cream and American mayonnaise mixed.

2 c. fresh halibut

1 c. scallops

1 c. shrimp, shelled and deveined, with tails removed

½ tsp. salt

¼ tsp. pepper

1 c. fresh cream

1 c. Japanese mayonnaise

1 Tbs. snipped parsley

Rinse and pat seafood dry with paper towel. Cut halibut into 3 portions. Place seafood in a single layer on a baking pan. Season with salt and pepper. Combine fresh cream and Japanese mayonnaise. Spread over the seafood; sprinkle with parsley. Bake, uncovered in a 400° F. oven for 20 to 25 minutes.

Serves 4 to 5.

Kanako Nakamoto is a well-respected and well-known member of the Church in her native land of Japan. In 1978, at age nineteen, Kanako gave the opening prayer in the first Young Women meeting to which all Relief Society sisters and Young Women were invited. Kanako was too frightened to pray in English, so in her formal Japanese robe, she prayed in her native tongue. A wonderful spirit filled the Tabernacle and spread across the television broadcast of the conference. Today, Kanako holds three callings in her ward and stake and continues to share the gospel. She and her husband, Chikashi, are the parents of two daughters and four sons and reside in Yokohama, Japan.

Gill's Teton Two-Forks
Dutch-Oven Trout Dinner

GILL SANDERS

The preparation for this tasty recipe begins in the early hours of a crisp Teton morning. All willing participants can load the ingredients into a cooler and onto the boat, as they get ready for the day's catch! After a wonderful day of fly-fishing, our family pulls over at the bank of our favorite spot along the Teton River called Two Forks, where two beautiful sections of the river intertwine. This recipe has been the source of a few Personal Progress Awards and merit badges, as the family cooks together. Don't forget to bring a camera and allow enough time to fall asleep in the willows after a very hearty meal!

Occasionally for this recipe, someone slyly purchases a few trout from the town market and slips them into the cooler—just in case the fish in the river are feeling a little fickle about our fishing flies. If you ignore this precaution and have a difficult day on the river, simply enjoy the recipe as a vegetarian delight! (Don't forget the Dutch oven—we use a twelve-inch pot. You'll also need plenty of aluminum foil.)

12 long carrots, peeled and cut lengthwise

4 Idaho potatoes, cut into large chunks

3 sweet potatoes, cut into large chunks

2 sweet onions, cut into large chunks

2 Tbs. vegetable oil

Dash of salt & pepper

1 to 2 tsp. dried dill weed

1 Tbs. dried parsley

4 or 5 ears of corn

2 pats of butter

4 or 5 8- to 10-inch trout (cleaned)

Prepare a hot fire from dried pieces of river wood and let it burn until there is a good supply of hot coals. Find and cut a 2- to 3-inch green, forked willow branch to use as a lifter for the lid of the Dutch oven, and for adjusting it on the hot coals.

Place the cut vegetables in two large pieces of aluminum foil, crossed and formed into a bowl shape. Drizzle vegetables with oil and sprinkle with salt, pepper, dill, and parsley. Bring the sides of the foil together and twist around to close. Put the vegetables in the Dutch oven. Place ears of corn in two pieces of foil, similar to the vegetable mixture. Add 2 pats of butter and a dash of salt. Close the foil and put in the pan with the other vegetables. Place oven over the coals to cook the vegetables for 15 minutes.

5 pats of butter

5 slices bacon

1 to 2 Tbs. lemon pepper seasoning, or to taste

½ tsp. salt

¼ tsp. pepper

1 Tbs. dried parsley (or 2 Tbs. fresh)

Juice of 2 lemons

While the vegetables cook, prepare the trout. (Cut the heads and tails off, clean out, and scrape off the scales.) Place cleaned fish on two large pieces of aluminum foil. Put a pat of butter and piece of bacon inside each trout. Sprinkle inside and out with lemon pepper seasoning, salt and pepper, and parsley. Squeeze lemon juice over the trout fillets. Bring both sides of foil up; fold and press closed. Poke a few holes in the foil bag with a fork; add fish to the Dutch oven to cook with the vegetables for 15 to 20 more minutes. Carefully remove the Dutch oven from the fire and open the foil bags. Drizzle leftover lemon juice over everything and enjoy your riverside feast. The fish should be tender enough to eat off the bone (like corn on the cob); or dig in with *two forks,* and the juicy meat will fall easily away from the bones.

Gill Sanders, a retired pediatrician and neonatologist, runs a very successful business doing work that relaxes and soothes. He carefully hand carves hundreds of beautiful, authentic-looking trout every year. His lifelike creations have been sold in galleries throughout the country, including Tiffany's on Rodeo Drive, and garner anywhere from $400 to $5,000 apiece. His shop in Yellowstone is a busy hub for tourists and locals to visit, shop, and admire Gill's work. His Web site is just as active (www.gillsfish.com). Gill and his wife, Virginia Cook Sanders, are the parents of six children and the grandparents of eleven.

Cultured Crab

ELAINE CANNON

When I was a little girl, I learned a great deal about cooking when my mother had parties. I especially loved her small dishes that were shaped like the Shell Gasoline logo. She used them only when serving her baked crab or deviled shrimp entrée for Sunday night suppers or luncheon groups. She would oil the shells and place them on a big cookie sheet for filling and baking. I used to pray for leftovers! Sometimes she would let me use the extra shell dish if one of her friends could not come to the luncheon. In those days, it was hard to get fresh fish at the supermarket so we used canned crab and shrimp. With today's fresh fish availability—crab meat or imitation crab—the recipe is even more delicious. I inherited the shell dishes along with the recipe!

1 c. crabmeat, fresh or imitation

Juice of ½ a large lemon (and a bit of grated zest)

1 c. dry bread crumbs

1 c. heavy whipping cream (or whole milk, or half and half)

1½ c. Best Foods® Real mayonnaise

6 hard-cooked eggs, sliced

1 Tbs. fresh parsley, chopped

½ c. onion, chopped (or 1 Tbs. dried onion flakes)

¼ c. celery, chopped

½ tsp. salt

Dash white pepper

½ c. dry bread crumbs for topping

1 Tbs. butter, melted

Paprika sprinkle

Fresh parsley sprigs

Green olives, pimiento-stuffed

Preheat oven to 350° F. Lightly blend together the crabmeat, lemon juice, 1 c. dry bread crumbs, cream, mayonnaise, sliced eggs, parsley, onion, celery, and seasoning. Spoon into buttered shells or baking dishes. Mix the ½ cup bread crumbs and melted butter; sprinkle over top, adding a dash of paprika. Place on baking sheet and bake in oven for 20 minutes. Garnish with fresh parsley sprigs or large pimiento-stuffed green olives, if desired.

Serves 6.

Elaine Cannon has published seventy books in her long career as a writer and editor. A former general president of the Young Women organization, Sister Cannon also lectured for BYU's continuing education program for thirty years and served as associate editor for several Church magazines. Elaine is wife of the late D. James Cannon and lives in Salt Lake City, Utah. She currently serves as the Relief Society president of the Salt Lake Emigration Stake.

Family Feasts

HEARTY BEEF,
CHICKEN,
LAMB, AND
PORK DISHES

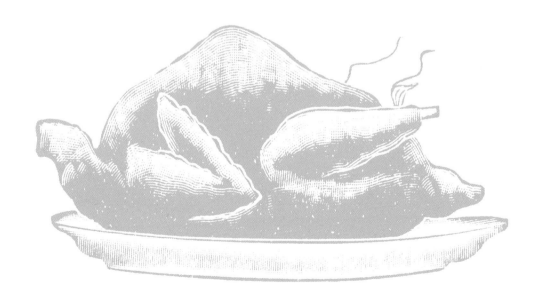

Grandpa's Wowie Meat Loaf

RON CARTER

When Grandpa Carter doubled this recipe and whipped it up for a family gathering, one of the grandkids jumped right in with his fork, raised his head, and exclaimed, "Wowie!" So, if someone at your table doesn't say, "Wowie," you probably didn't do it right. (Some of the recipe is found in an old Betty Crocker cookbook, and some of it is the result of long experience.)

1½ lbs. ground beef

3 slices soft white bread

1 c. milk

1 egg, beaten

¼ c. minced onion

¾ tsp. salt

¼ tsp. sage

¼ tsp. celery salt

¼ tsp. pepper

¼ tsp. garlic salt

1 Tbs. Worcestershire sauce

1 Tbs. mustard

5 Tbs. ketchup

Preheat oven to 350° F. Place meat in large mixing bowl. Tear slices of bread in small pieces and add to meat. Pour in milk, beaten egg, and remaining ingredients, reserving 3 tablespoons of the ketchup. Mix thoroughly. (Seeing the result, you'll conclude that someone's lost his mind!) Place mixture in an 8x9-inch baking pan or a large loaf pan. Add reserved 3 tablespoons ketchup on top to add flavor and keep it moist. Bake at 350° F. for 90 minutes.

Serves 8.

Ron Carter, author of the acclaimed Revolutionary War series *Prelude to Glory*, has a remarkable ability to tell stories—both historical and fictional—and has thus captivated hundreds of thousands of readers. He received a juris doctor degree in 1962 after attending the law schools at George Washington University and the University of Utah and has been a research and writing director for the Superior Court system of Los Angeles County, California. He and his wife, La Rae Dunn Carter, of Boise, Idaho, are the parents of nine children. The family resides in Park City, Utah.

Don's Dutch Oven Favorite

DON BUSATH

The outdoors have been important in my life since early childhood, when a good run outside following each meal was necessary to restore me to life and energy. As a portrait photographer, I experienced the same need to break out of the routine and began using outdoor photo sessions, under whatever pretence. The result was that our studio became a pioneer in portraying families, couples, and kids in outdoor settings.

When our kids were growing up, camping was a natural lifestyle for our family. We regularly used our experienced tent and didn't know a car without a rack on top. We had fun tailgate cooking in our Jeep Wagoneer, but our favorite form of cooking out gradually became the good old black pot over charcoal. What I liked best besides the great flavor imparted by the Dutch oven was the fact that it was slow! After getting things started, we could relax, ponder nature, read, or (my favorite) scan the area for scenic photo-ops. Also lovely is the community nature of gathering around the simmering pots and building anticipation while enjoying the fantastic fragrances that go with this kind of camp cooking. The recipe I offer here is a variation on one I received from a member of a super cooking family. Craig Ruesch is a school administrator, friend, and great cook. He called it: Western Dutch Oven Chili (without beans). It earned cook-off awards.

2 Tbs. vegetable oil

3 lbs. pork loin, diced small

3 lbs. beef sirloin, diced small (¼-inch chunks)

5 onions, minced

4 cloves garlic, minced

3 bell peppers, diced

I Tbs. dry oregano

2 bay leaves

2 Tbs. cumin powder

6 Tbs. chili powder

I Tbs. paprika

¼ tsp. cinnamon

Prepare a good hot bed of coals to brown the meat. Preheat the pan. Gently brown the meat in oil. Remove from the pot, but leave the drippings. Add the vegetables and sauté until transparent. Reduce the heat, with coals on top and underneath. Return the meat and remaining ingredients and slow cook until the sauce is thick. The aroma will draw a crowd. Serve over pasta or alone.

Over pasta, will serve 15 plus.

3 Tbs. beef base

1 (1 lb.) can tomato sauce

1 (7-oz.) can green chilies, diced

3 Tbs. vinegar

1 c. water

Don Busath has been taking award-winning photographs for more than four decades. He is one of only six people worldwide who hold fellowships in both the American Society of Photographers and the British Institute of Photography. He is the past president of the Intermountain Professional Photographer's Association. His work has been exhibited in the Photographic Arts and Sciences Hall of Fame and the EPCOT Center in Orlando, Florida, and a collection of his photographs hangs in the Maurice Abravanel Hall in Salt Lake City. He has photographed Church presidents since David O. McKay and the last five governors of Utah. His work has been published in several books, including *Temple Square: In the Light of Its Seasons* and *Salt Lake City: In a Different Light*. Don and his wife, Donna, are the parents of five children and reside in Salt Lake City.

Korean-Style BBQ

VICTOR CLINE

One summer during the break between college semesters, our daughter Robyn decided to go to Hawaii to work and have an experience away from home. She is an adventurous kind of girl, and what more beautiful place could she choose for a wonderful adventure! Robyn has always had a flare for the exotic, something with a little more oomph than the ordinary. This includes her taste in food. She would always open the spice cupboard and reach for something zesty to add to whatever Lois had cooked for dinner. There in that lovely island in the Pacific she found many exciting adventures, friends, and new foods. When Robyn came home she delighted us when she shared her newly found recipes for two of her favorite dishes she had been served at the home of a friend. The recipes have become favorites of our family and friends who have requested them after tasting them at family reunions and dinner parties. (See Banana Cream Dessert recipe on page 203.)

2 to 4 lbs. rib-eye or Delmonico steaks, or short ribs

1 c. soy sauce

⅔ c. sugar

1 Tbs. sesame seeds

Dash Accent® seasoning salt

3 green onions, chopped

3 cloves garlic, crushed

2 tsp. pepper

2 Tbs. sesame oil

Salt

Place meat in a shallow container. Combine remaining ingredients and pour over meat. Cover with airtight lid and marinate meat for several hours (up to 6 hours). Broil the meat over charcoal grill. The longer the marinating time, the more tender the meat will be.

Serves 4 to 8.

Dr. Victor Cline graduated from the University of California, Berkeley with a Ph.D. in psychology. He has been a research scientist with George Washington University's Human Resources Research Office and is an emeritus professor in psychology at the University of Utah. He is in private practice in Salt Lake City. Victor and his wife, Lois, are presidents of Marriage and Family Enrichment, a seminar group that teaches communication and marital skills nationwide. He has written a number of books on marriage, parenting, and the media. Lois is a passionate, creative, gourmet cook who has a talent for turning the ordinary into a sumptuous creation. They are the parents of nine children and the grandparents of twenty-eight.

BBQ Brisket

JEROLD AND JOANN OTTLEY

During the LDS Church's Sesquicentennial celebration, we were invited to do some guest work for the Church members in Long Island, New York. We stayed with Brother and Sister Donovan and Nonie Larsen. She is a gourmet cook, with enough cookbooks and cooking magazines to fill a fair-sized room. She prepared this recipe for us while we were there, and it was one of *those* food moments. She was generous enough to share the recipe, and we have served it (and given the recipe) many times since.

5 to 6-lb. beef brisket

2 tsp. salt

Dash cayenne pepper

2 large onions, chopped

4 Tbs. butter

1½ c. water

2 c. ketchup

½ c. lemon juice

4 Tbs. brown sugar

6 Tbs. Worcestershire sauce

4 Tbs. vinegar

3 Tbs. dry mustard

Preheat oven to 275° F. Place meat in roasting pan (large enough to accommodate the generous amount of sauce to be added later) and season with salt and pepper. Cover and bake at 275° F. for 5 hours.

After the roast has cooked for 4½ hours, combine other ingredients in saucepan and simmer for 30 minutes. Pour fat from meat. Add sauce, cover, and bake one hour longer. Slice thinly, across grain. Serve with rice.

Serves 10 to 12.

Jerold Ottley directed the Mormon Tabernacle Choir for twenty-five years and is now the director of the new Tabernacle Choir Training School. His wife, JoAnn South Ottley, is a soprano vocalist, recording artist, and former vocal coach for the Tabernacle Choir; she now teaches vocals at the training school. Brother Ottley is currently serving on the high council of the South Cottonwood Stake and Sister Ottley as Gospel Doctrine leader and ward organist. They are the parents of two children and the grandparents of one grandson.

Tomato Beef Stir Fry

ED AND PATRICIA PINEGAR

This recipe comes from a Chinese cooking class that my mother took when we lived in Hawaii. It has become one of our family's favorite recipes.

1 lb. beef, cut in thin slices

1 Tbs. soy sauce

1 Tbs. cornstarch

1 Tbs. sugar

2 Tbs. vegetable oil

1 to 2 cloves garlic, crushed

1 slice fresh ginger

1 round onion, cubed

1 c. celery, sliced

1 green bell pepper, sliced

3 tomatoes, sliced in wedges

Soy Glaze (recipe follows)

3 stalks green onions, sliced in 1-inch lengths

Cooked rice, kept warm for serving

SOY GLAZE

½ c. water

1 Tbs. cornstarch

1 Tbs. soy sauce

2 Tbs. sugar

Mix together beef, soy sauce, cornstarch, and sugar and let stand while cutting up vegetables. Heat oil in wok or cooking pan. Add garlic and ginger, then marinated beef strips, and brown slightly. Remove meat chunks and set aside. Add more oil; then add onions, celery, and green pepper. Cook quickly. Add tomatoes then pour Soy Glaze over vegetables. Cook just to thicken glaze. Add meat and green onions. Stir while cooking until heated throughout. Pour over cooked rice to serve.

Serves 6 to 8.

For soy glaze, mix all ingredients in small bowl until smooth.

With Patricia at his side, Ed Pinegar has presided over the Provo Missionary Training Center and the London South Mission. Sister Pinegar has served as general president of the Primary and in the general presidency of the Young Women. Both are popular speakers and beloved leaders by Church members throughout the world. Brother Pinegar also runs an inspirational Web site: www.thoughts.com. The Pinegars are the parents of eight children, thirty-two grandchildren, and two great-grandchildren.

Cornell Chicken

BRAD ROCK

This is a family recipe of sorts. My wife says it came from the Ithaca, New York, newspaper and was passed on by her brother. We often use it at family gatherings. I understand this recipe is named after the university. As far as I can tell, Cornell's chicken is a lot better than its football team. If not big enough to handle an entire team, it's at least a large enough recipe to handle an average offensive line.

1 egg

1 c. cooking oil

1 pt. cider vinegar

3 Tbs. salt

1 Tbs. poultry seasoning

1 tsp. pepper

10 to 12 chicken breasts, split (for a total of 20 to 22 pieces)

Beat the egg, add oil and beat again. Add remaining ingredients, except the chicken, and stir. Baste chicken lightly at first and heavier near the end of the cooking period. Place breasts bone side down on a hot grill. Baste often, but don't turn for 30 minutes. Flip over, use more sauce, and finish cooking—10 minutes, or until red disappears in meat and the meat splits easily.

Serves 10 to 15.

Brad Rock is a sports columnist for the Salt Lake City *Deseret News*. A graduate of the University of Utah, he has won over fifty local, regional, and national writing awards, including placing among the top ten nationally three times. He is a three-time Utah Sportswriter of the Year and winner of the Dan S. Blumenthal writing award. He has written two books and is currently working on a third. He has served as elder's quorum president, Young Men president, and as a member of the bishopric and high council. He and his wife, Julie, are parents of six children and live in Sandy, Utah.

Jake's Favorite Bar-B-Q with Secret Dry Rub and Anne's Bar-B-Q Sauce

CHAD HAWKINS

I never fully realized how American it is to barbecue until I served my mission in Frankfurt, Germany. The many United States military bases in that region of Germany provided a wonderful opportunity to teach the gospel to people of both cultures. As my companions and I went door to door, it was easy to identify American homes because there were always U.S. license plates on the cars parked out front and barbecue grills on the front stoops. On the military bases, it was common to see rows of ten grills or more by the servicemen barracks. The pleasure Americans take in cooking meat over coals or a fire further enhances their cowboy image.

I love to cook, and it does not get much better than preparing a meal and slowly cooking it over a smoky fire. Cooking and camping by our backyard barbecue pit is one of my family's summer highlights. Whether cooking breakfast, lunch, or dinner, the meal always tastes better if it is cooked over the flames of our pit. When we really want to rough it, we pitch our tent, throw logs on the fire, and watch a favorite movie on our portable VCR/TV. The recipes here are named after two of my children, Jake and Anne, because they make cooking—and life in general— so much fun. After the barbecued chicken dinner, try a dessert of grilled pineapple (see recipe on page 62).

Make the barbecue sauce about an hour ahead of grilling and prepare the meat and the rub at least one half hour before grilling. Two essentials of real barbecue are a low cooking temperature and a cloud of wood smoke.

6 skinless, boneless chicken breasts, pounded lightly

Anne's Bar-B-Q Sauce (recipe follows)

Dry rub (recipe follows)

Wash chicken breasts and pat dry. Pound meat lightly between waxed paper; discard paper. Coat chicken pieces with dry rub and place in glass casserole; cover and let stand at room temperature for 20 minutes before grilling.

When ready to grill, drizzle the chicken with one-third of the barbecue sauce. Transfer chicken pieces to grill or smoker. While grilling, baste meat with additional sauce. Turn chicken pieces only once, cooking through. Baste with remaining sauce for a final glaze before serving.

Serves 4 to 6.

ANNE'S BAR-B-Q SAUCE

¼ c. butter

¼ c. canola or corn oil

2 medium onions, minced

1 c. ketchup

½ c. cider vinegar

¾ c. fresh orange juice

¼ c. pure maple syrup

⅓ c. unsulphured dark molasses

2 Tbs. Worcestershire sauce

½ tsp. freshly ground black pepper

½ tsp. salt

To prepare barbecue sauce, melt butter with oil in a saucepan over medium heat. Add onions and sauté for about 5 minutes, or until they begin to turn golden. Mix in remaining ingredients, reduce heat to low; cook, stirring frequently, until sauce thickens, approximately 40 minutes.

Makes about 3 cups.

DRY RUB

1 Tbs. paprika

1 tsp. salt

1 tsp. sugar

½ tsp. freshly ground black pepper

½ tsp. onion powder

To prepare dry rub, combine ingredients together in small bowl.

Chad Spencer Hawkins began creating his unique series of temple prints in 1989, at age seventeen, to support his mission. Upon returning from the Germany Frankfurt Mission, Chad pursued an education in fine art at Weber State University. His paintings hang in galleries and private collections throughout the world, and his original work of the Vernal Utah Temple is on permanent display inside that edifice. His artwork has been selected for placement in twelve of the cornerstones of the Church's temples. Chad is the author of the bestselling book *The First 100 Temples* and *Youth and the Temple*. He and his wife, Stephanie, live in Layton, Utah, with their children.

Chicken and Rice Casserole

KARL BROOKS

This recipe was given to us by Helen Lee Goates, President Harold B. Lee's daughter. According to Helen, it was his favorite. And we love it too. Whenever we serve the casserole, everyone loves it.

2 c. water

1 (10.75-oz.) can cream of mushroom soup

1 (10.75-oz.) can cream of chicken soup

1 (10.75-oz.) can cream of celery soup

1 c. uncooked rice

1 chicken, cut up—or 8 chicken breasts, skinned

½ c. butter (optional)

Mix the water, soups, and rice thoroughly in saucepan and cook until evenly heated. Pour into casserole dish. Top with chicken pieces (and butter, if desired); cover, and bake at 350° F. for 2 hours. Uncover for the last 10 minutes.

Serves 8.

Karl Brooks served as mayor of St. George, Utah, for twelve years, and was honored with the opportunity to light the Olympic cauldron when the torch passed through St. George on the way to the Salt Lake 2002 Winter Games. He also served as vice president of Dixie College and on the Utah League of Cities and Towns. His wife, Carla, taught English at Dixie High and served on the National Board of Directors of the United States Academic Decathlon. The Brooks are the parents of four children and the grandparents of four.

Scalloped Chicken

DAVIS BITTON

I was born and raised in and near Blackfoot, Idaho, graduating from Blackfoot High School in 1948. When I was twelve, my parents moved to a forty-acre farm in Groveland, an adjacent farming community. World War II was on. Food rationing was something everyone was familiar with, but living on a farm had its advantages. We had chickens, cows, all the meat we wanted, and an abundance of fruit trees.

My parents entertained friends quite often; and, because of the abundance of chickens, Mother would often serve a casserole she called Scalloped Chicken.

1 whole chicken

1 loaf of bread

1 (8-oz.) can mushrooms

Put prepared chicken in pot. Cover with water; add salt and boil until tender. Remove chicken from pot and let stock cool. Separate chicken meat from bones and set aside. Break loaf of bread into small pieces and fry in ¼ cup butter or chicken fat. Don't let the bread brown; it should be slightly crunchy. Dice the chicken. In a casserole baking dish, alternately put a layer of chicken, then a layer of bread, and sprinkle with mushrooms. Pour stock over casserole. Bake at 375° F. for 1 hour or more, until stock is absorbed in the casserole.

Serves 6 to 8.

Davis Bitton is an award-winning author and Church historian. His book *George Q. Cannon: A Biography* was the winner of the 1999 Evans Biography Award. He served as assistant Church historian for ten years, during which time he had many remarkable and faith-affirming experiences. His writings include a number of significant historical works, such as *The Mormon Experience: A History of the Latter-day Saints*, which he co-authored with Leonard Arrington, and *Images of the Prophet Joseph Smith*. Brother Bitton is married to JoAn Borg Bitton, and they reside in Salt Lake City.

Geri's Glazed Chicken

DOUGLAS E. BRINLEY

From 1968 to 1972, our family had the opportunity to live in Hawaii, where I was teaching at the LDS Institute at the University of Hawaii in Honolulu. While living there, my wife became acquainted with some military wives living in our neighborhood, and they often shared child-rearing techniques and recipes over the backyard fence. One day, while visiting with a neighbor, my wife mentioned she had some rather important company coming for dinner in a few days and was racking her brain to come up with an elegant but simple menu. This particular neighbor described a chicken dish she had prepared recently. My wife immediately went into the house and wrote down what she remembered, and created the following recipe.

NOTE: The dinner party was a success, and everyone raved about the chicken dish. Several weeks later my wife happened to see a paragraph in the daily newspaper about a chicken cooking contest sponsored by the DelMarva Poultry Industry. On a whim, she entered this recipe. After dropping her entry in the mail, she immediately forgot about it until weeks later, when she got a call from Maryland, informing her that she had won the contest, and was invited to come and represent the state of Hawaii in a cook-off to be held in Ocean City, Maryland. Wow! They mailed her a check to cover the cost of the trip. Another Wow! It cost a lot to fly from Honolulu to Maryland! Her first thought was to keep the money and forget the contest; but instead, I bought a ticket too, and we both went. What a great time! She competed against forty-nine other state winners. One of the judges was the famous chef James Beard. Although she didn't win the grand prize, it was a great experience, and we went home with a silver tray, $100, and some great memories. (Incidentally, the grand prize winner was a woman from Connecticut who entered a chicken appetizer she called Chicken Delight Bites. I'm sure that McDonald's bought the recipe and it became Chicken McNuggets.)

1 c. flour

1 tsp. curry powder

1 tsp. ground nutmeg

½ tsp. salt

¼ tsp. pepper

4 whole chicken breasts, skinned and boned

3 Tbs. oil

Mix flour with curry powder, nutmeg, salt, and pepper. Dip chicken breasts into seasoned flour, coating evenly. Heat oil in a large heavy skillet over medium heat. Add chicken and then brown, turning as needed. Reduce heat and continue cooking about 20 minutes until tender. Just before serving, pour in the sherry (red wine vinegar), adjust heat, and simmer

3 Tbs. cooking sherry (substitute red wine vinegar)

1 (8¼-oz.) can seedless grapes, drained—or use fresh green grapes

4 Tbs. orange marmalade

several minutes. Push chicken to one side of skillet and warm the grapes. Add marmalade and toss gently.

Serves 8.

Douglas E. Brinley is the co-author of the runaway best-seller *Between Husband and Wife*. A professor at Brigham Young University, Brother Brinley is a popular speaker and writer, his emphasis being on marriage and family and family relationships. His newest book, *First Comes Love* (co-authored with Mark Ogletree), is a follow-up to *Between Husband and Wife* and is geared to couples who are dating or engaged. He and his wife, Geri Rosine, are the parents of six children and live in Provo, Utah.

Sweet and Sour Chicken

MARY ELLEN SMOOT

An excellent recipe from a friend in Cleveland, Ohio.

Chicken pieces (enough for each serving)

1 bottle Wishbone® Russian dressing

1 pkg. onion soup mix (or more, as desired)

1 (8- to 10-oz.) jar apricot preserves

Skin chicken pieces, if desired, to reduce fat content. Place chicken in baking dish; combine remaining ingredients. Depending on number of people eating, add ½ to 1 c. water to sauce. Mix well. Pour over chicken. Bake at 325° F. for 2½ hours (or for 1½ hours at 350° F.; or for 1 hour at 375° F.), or until done. Serve with rice pilaf. Pour sauce from pan over top of rice and chicken.

Serves up to 10.

Mary Ellen Wood Smoot served as general president of the Relief Society from April 1997 to April 2002. She loves family history and has written histories about her parents, grandparents, and their local community. She served with her husband, Stanley M. Smoot, when he was called as a mission president in Ohio, and they later served together as directors of Church Hosting. They are the parents of seven children and the grandparents of fifty.

Lemon Chicken

BRETT RAYMOND

Next to an In-n-Out burger, this is my favorite entrée. (Yes, an In-n-Out burger can be considered an entrée in the music business!) This recipe comes from a cookbook compiled by the Tokyo-English-speaking ward in 1985. We were living in Japan at that time. The recipe was submitted by Mary Kimoto. It has been a favorite of ours through the years and has fed many a visitor to the Raymond house—especially the missionaries. It seems that whenever we're having a dinner with someone new, we serve this. If it doesn't taste delicious to you, Deseret Book will gladly refund your money for this book and give you a gift certificate to the Mandarin, which has the second best lemon chicken. Okay, that's not true . . . but you're gonna love it, baby!

3 lbs. chicken breasts or chicken tenders

1 Tbs. soy sauce

2 eggs, beaten

½ tsp. salt

¼ c. cornstarch

½ tsp. baking soda

2 c. salad oil

Lemon Sauce (recipe follows)

LEMON SAUCE

2 Tbs. cornstarch

⅓ c. sugar

1 c. chicken broth

1 Tbs. lemon juice

1 tsp. salt

2 lemons

2 Tbs. salad oil

Wash and remove fat and bones from chicken. Combine chicken and soy sauce and let marinate for 15 minutes. Beat the eggs in a small bowl, adding the salt, cornstarch, and baking soda until blended. Heat oil in wok to 350° F. Dip chicken pieces in batter; fry until evenly browned. Slice into 1- to 1½-inch pieces.

For lemon sauce, mix cornstarch and sugar in saucepan, stirring until smooth. Add chicken broth, lemon juice, and salt. Cook till thick. Wash and cut lemons into slices. Sauté in salad oil for 3 minutes. Then slowly stir into the sauce. Pour over chicken.

Serves 6.

Brett Raymond is a talented composer, arranger, and performer. Television stations and movie studios throughout the world often use Brett's work for promotions and theme songs. His music can be heard on NBC's *Today Show*, *Oprah*, and ABC's *Wide World of Sports*. His trademark sound on albums such as *A Case of Pop*, *Primarily for Grown-ups*, and *Primarily for Christmas* has won him many fans throughout the world. Brett and his wife, Becky, are the parents of five and reside in Bountiful, Utah.

Chicken Bake

MARGARET D. NADAULD

I got this recipe at a mission presidents' seminar from Sister Rosanna Brough. It is a favorite in our family of missionaries—seven sons! We serve it over rice and accompany the main dish with green salad and French bread.

6 to 8 chicken breasts

1 (14-oz.) bottle ketchup

1 (10¾-oz.) can tomato soup, undiluted

1 green bell pepper, chopped

¼ c. brown sugar

¼ c. vinegar

1 tsp. dry mustard

1 (8-oz.) can pineapple tidbits, with juice

Preheat oven to 375° F. Place chicken pieces in 9x13-inch roasting pan; mix remaining ingredients in bowl and pour over the chicken. Cover and bake at 375° for 1 hour. Uncover and bake an additional 15 minutes.

Serves 6 to 8.

Margaret D. Nadauld is the former general president of the Young Women organization and a former member of the board of trustees of Brigham Young University. She has taught piano lessons as well as high school English and is the author of *Write Back Soon: Letters of Love and Encouragement for Young Women.* She and her husband, Stephen D. Nadauld, a former member of the Second Quorum of the Seventy, are the parents of seven sons and the grandparents of eight.

Chicken Cutlets with Citrus Greens and Pine Nut Pilaf

LIZ LEMON SWINDLE

In 1997 I traveled to Washington, D.C. to speak at a fireside about my Joseph Smith paintings, which were on display in the visitors' center at the Washington, D.C. Temple. While there I stayed with a lovely host couple, the Bentleys. Charlene Bentley served this wonderful dish and kindly gave me the recipe when I requested it. Now it is often on the menu for Sunday dinners at our house.

CITRUS GREENS

⅓ c. olive oil

2 Tbs. fresh cilantro, chopped

2 Tbs. balsamic vinegar

½ tsp. grated lime zest

I Tbs. fresh lime juice

½ tsp. grated orange zest

I Tbs. fresh orange juice

I tsp. fresh ginger, grated

I tsp. salt

I lb. assorted greens: lettuces, arugula, watercress, etc.

Tomatoes, red and yellow (pear, or large tomatoes, chopped)

To prepare greens and citrus dressing, blend first 8 ingredients, whisking thoroughly. Set aside while washing greens and chopping tomatoes. Toss greens with dressing when chicken is ready to serve.

CHICKEN CUTLETS

6 to 8 boneless chicken breasts (serving-sized pieces)

Flour for coating

Salt and pepper seasoning to taste

Butter (for sauté pan)

To prepare chicken cutlets, dip chicken pieces in flour seasoned with salt and pepper. Brown in buttered skillet, turning carefully until browned and cooked through, about 20 minutes.

PINE NUT PILAF

1 small white onion, chopped

1 c. long grain white rice

½ c. pine nuts or slivered almonds

1 Tbs. butter

2 Tbs. olive oil

2½ c. chicken stock (or use canned broth)

¼ tsp. salt

½ tsp. grated lemon zest

2 Tbs. fresh parsley, minced

For Pine Nut Pilaf, lightly brown onion, rice, and nuts in butter and oil. Stir well to maintain even color. Cook until golden brown. Add chicken stock, salt, and lemon zest. Cover and continue cooking for about 20 minutes. Garnish with parsley, and serve with Chicken Cutlets and Citrus Greens on top.

Liz Lemon Swindle's beautiful paintings of the Prophet Joseph Smith are recognized throughout the Church. Her collection of thirty paintings has traveled across the United States for shows in Independence, Missouri; Nauvoo, Illinois; and Washington, D.C. Liz began her artistic career with a focus on wildlife and nature, but turned to religious paintings in an effort to express her spiritual beliefs in a nonthreatening way. Liz's work can be seen in *Joseph Smith: Impressions of a Prophet* and *She Shall Bring Forth a Son*. Liz and her husband, John Swindle, are the parents of five children and reside in Orem, Utah.

Lamb with Egg Sauce
(Abbacchio O Capretto Brodettato)

FRED S. BALL

I have been cooking for most of my life. One of my first jobs was as a fry cook at The Well Cafe in Ogden, Utah, when I was fourteen years old. I later cooked at Rusty's in Ogden, and than at Tige's in Salt Lake City—all while attending school. I attended many cooking classes and schools over the years to increase the enjoyment of this avocation of cooking for family and friends. This particular dish is an adaptation of one that my wife, Joyce, and I enjoyed at the Hotel Villa Serbolini in Belaggio, Lake Como, Italy.

3 lbs. baby lamb loin

Salt

Freshly ground pepper

1½ fresh lemons

4 Tbs. olive oil

2 Tbs. butter

1 c. onions, chopped

2 oz. Parma ham, finely diced

4 tsp. all-purpose flour

2 c. chicken broth

3 egg yolks

1 tsp. grated lemon zest

1 Tbs. fresh parsley leaves, finely
  chopped

½ tsp. fresh marjoram leaves, finely
  chopped

Cut the lamb into 1-inch cubes; season with salt and pepper. Toss the meat with juice from half a lemon.

In a large sauté pan, over medium heat, add the oil and butter. When the oil/butter is hot, add the lamb, onions, and ham; cook until the lamb is brown on all sides, about 6 to 8 minutes. Sprinkle the flour over the lamb and continue to cook for one minute. Stir in the broth and bring to a simmer; cover and cook for 30 minutes.

In a small mixing bowl, beat the egg yolks. Add the lemon zest and the juice from the remaining lemon. Slowly stir the egg mixture into the lamb and cook for 2 minutes, stirring constantly so the eggs won't curdle.

Remove from the heat and stir in the parsley and marjoram. Season with salt and pepper, to taste. Spoon the lamb onto serving plates and serve at once. Suggested accompaniments are diced fried potatoes or rice.

Serves 6.

Fred S. Ball is the senior vice president for Zions Bank and president and CEO emeritus of the Salt Lake Area Chamber of Commerce. During his twenty-five years as head of the Chamber of Commerce, Fred was the widely recognized voice of the Metro Business Report. He returned to radio in 1997 to host the *Fred Ball Speaking on Business* program, which airs every weekday on KSL Radio in Salt Lake City. He has been named a "Giant in Our City" by the Salt Lake Area Chamber of Commerce; Speaker of the Year by Toastmasters International; and Communicator of the Year by the Public Relations Society of America. He has served as a member of the general Sunday School board and as assistant director of Church Hosting. Fred and his wife, Joyce, are the parents of four and the grandparents of fifteen.

Daddy's Ribs and Beans

STEPHEN E. ROBINSON

There are two ways of cooking food: Daddy's way and Momma's way. This dish is usually cooked at our house by Daddy; but for those who cook the other way, instructions are provided.

DADDY'S WAY

Throw a mess of ribs in a baking dish and smush 'em all together. (If all the pans are dirty, you can throw the ribs in a Crock-Pot or whatever.) Then cover 'em up with BBQ sauce, and throw in a little water if you need to. (And you can also throw in a little onion or garlic or whatever else looks good and is handy.) Add a dash of liquid smoke for taste, and cook 'em till the fat melts and the ribs get all to fallin' apart. Then spoon it like a stew over rice (or noodles or even bread; it don't really matter. But it's best served hot and consumed on the spot).

Now, if you're going to have beans with those ribs, and you should, then mix up a couple cans of pork and beans, with a handful of brown sugar, a slug of molasses, a little bit of mustard, and a dash of liquid smoke. Then put 'em in a flat pan lined with bacon and cook 'em with the ribs till the beans on top start to get kinda crusty, and the ones underneath aren't really runny anymore. Good hot or cold and, of course, eaten with Daddy's ribs.

MOMMA'S WAY

3 lbs. lean country-style pork spare ribs, boneless

1 (32-oz.) jar Bullseye® barbecue sauce, or other brand

2 c. water

½ tsp. liquid smoke

1 tsp. minced onions

For ribs, preheat oven to 325° F. Place ribs close together in a large covered casserole at a uniform depth. Combine barbecue sauce with liquid smoke and cover the ribs with mixture; add up to 2 cups water to cover them completely. Sprinkle with minced onions. Cover and bake at 325° F. for 2 hours. Serve on a bed of wild rice, accompanied by beans.

Wild rice, cooked

Pork and Beans (recipe follows)

PORK AND BEANS

2 (28-oz.) cans Bush® baked beans

1 c. brown sugar

2 Tbs. heavy black molasses

1 tsp. yellow mustard

½ tsp. liquid smoke

½ lb. sliced lean bacon

For pork and beans, preheat oven to 325° F. Pour canned baked beans into large mixing bowl. Add brown sugar, molasses, mustard, and liquid smoke. Pour into flat baking dish lined with strips of bacon. Bake, uncovered, at 325° F. for 2½ hours. Serve hot or cold, preferably with ribs.

Serves 8 to 10.

Stephen E. Robinson is the bestselling author of *Believing Christ* and *Following Christ.* Among a long list of his other published books and articles is *Are Mormons Christians?* a book he is eminently qualified to write. Now a professor of ancient scripture at Brigham Young University, Brother Robinson previously taught religion at Hampden-Sydney College (a Presbyterian-related school) and at Duke University and Lycoming College (both Methodist-related schools). During his tenure at Lycoming College, he served simultaneously as chairman of that school's Religion Department and as bishop of the LDS ward in Williamsport, Pennsylvania. Brother Robinson and his wife, Janet Bowen Robinson, are the parents of six children and reside in Provo, Utah.

Pork Tenderloin Roast

MIRIAM FROST ANDERSON

This recipe is simple, yet makes a lovely presentation served with small red potatoes and carrots.

4-lb. pork tenderloin roast

Garlic powder to taste

4 tsp. chili powder

¾ c. currant jelly

4 tsp. vinegar

½ c. ketchup

¾ tsp. chili powder

Mix the desired amount of garlic powder with 4 teaspoons of chili powder and rub over roast. Bake roast for two hours at 325° F., then baste regularly for the next half hour (meat thermometer should register 180° F.).

For basting sauce, combine jelly, vinegar, ketchup, and chili powder in a small pan. Bring to a gentle boil and simmer for 2 minutes. Reserve some of the sauce to pour over sliced meat on the serving platter.

Serves 8.

Miriam Frost Anderson managed for twenty years the popular and inviting Frost's Bookstore in Salt Lake City's Foothill Village. In her family's store she learned to love books—something that will forever be passed down through the Frost-Anderson family. Miriam now spends her time volunteering: for the 2002 Winter Olympics, as a docent at the Church Museum of History and Art, and as a teacher to foreign students learning English as a second language in junior high and at the university level. Miriam and her late husband, Lowell Anderson, are the parents of six children.

George's Sweet and Sour Pork

LAEL LITTKE

My late husband, George Littke, loved to cook. If he ate something that he liked but didn't have a recipe for, he figured out the ingredients and put together a recipe himself. Back in the '60s, when he first tasted sweet and sour pork, he experimented until he matched the taste as closely as he could. The results became one of our favorite family recipes. It's easy and nourishing. (When choosing vegetables for this dish, consider broccoli broken into small florets, carrots cut very small—they add color—and Chinese pea pods, which make the dish pretty.)

3 Tbs. cornstarch

1 lb. pork, cut in 1-inch cubes

2 to 3 Tbs. peanut or vegetable oil

Sliced vegetables

1 (8-oz.) can pineapple tidbits or chunks (reserve liquid)

Water (added to pineapple juice to equal 1 c. liquid)

1 to 3 Tbs. soy sauce, as desired

½ c. rice vinegar

1 to 2 Tbs. ketchup (mostly for color)

2 Tbs. brown sugar

Cornstarch and water, as needed to thicken (1 Tbs. per 1 c. liquid added)

Cooked rice—or couscous

Sprinkle cornstarch on plate or in a soup bowl. Add pork, dredging it well with cornstarch. In a large fry pan or wok, heat oil until very hot, but not smoking. Dump in pork and stir-fry until browned all over. Add sliced vegetables and fry for 2 minutes. Add pineapple juice and water, soy sauce, vinegar, ketchup, and brown sugar. Heat through, then cover and steam for 7 to 8 minutes, so the total cooking time for the pork is 12 to 15 minutes. When pork and vegetables are done, dump in the drained pineapple chunks and heat through. Mix cornstarch with water, stirring until lumps are gone. Add to pork and vegetables; stir until liquid thickens. Remove from heat and serve with rice or couscous.

Serves 4.

As a young girl, Lael Jensen Littke dreamed of becoming a writer. She planned to live in a penthouse in New York City, wear leopard-skin pants, and date Cary Grant for exquisite dinners at fancy restaurants. And while Lael did indeed become a writer—she even lived in New York City for a time—she still hasn't found a good pair of leopard-skin pants. Lael has authored thirty-six books for children and young people and lives in Pasadena, California. Her book include *Lake of Secrets, Haunted Sister, There's a Snake at Girls Camp,* and *Blue Skye.* Her latest venture, *Stories from the Life of Joseph Smith,* which she co-authored with Richard Turley, will be out in May 2003.

Stuffed Pork Chops

BARBARA B. SMITH

My husband's favorite meat! Ask the butcher to cut a pocket in each chop. The chops can also be cooked on the stovetop for an hour in a covered pan.

6 pork chops, 1 inch thick

2 c. bread crumbs

½ tsp. dry sage

1 Tbs. minced parsley

¼ tsp. salt

2 Tbs. onion, diced

2 Tbs. melted butter

1 egg, beaten

2 Tbs. melted fat

1 (10¾-oz.) can mushroom soup

Preheat oven to 325° F. In a medium bowl, combine bread crumbs with seasonings and onion. Stir in melted butter and beaten egg. If too dry, add enough hot water to moisten. Stuff each chop with several heaping spoonfuls of the bread crumb mixture. (The chops should be thick and split, so the stuffing can be put in.) Secure with a toothpick, then sear chops in 2 tablespoons fat until browned. Place chops in a baking pan or roaster, cover with the undiluted soup, and add a small amount of water. Cover and bake at 325° F. for one hour.

Serves 6.

Barbara Bradshaw Smith served as general president of the Relief Society from 1974 to 1984. She has also served as national president of the American Mothers, Inc., and on President Jimmy Carter's White House Advisory Committee for the Conference on Families. She is married to Douglas H. Smith, a former member of the First and Second Quorums of the Seventy and President of the Asia Area. Brother and Sister Smith have sent out thirty-five missionaries from their immediate and extended family. They have served on every continent of the world with the exception of Antarctica, and there is no mission there.

Pantry Pleasers

BEANS, CASSEROLES,
PASTA DISHES,
AND OTHER
THROW-TOGETHER MEALS

Company Potato Bake

STEPHEN AND SANDRA COVEY

This is a wonderful and delicious recipe for large groups or family.

1 onion, diced

½ c. (1 stick) butter

1 (32-oz.) pkg. Ore-Ida® frozen hash browns

1 pt. sour cream

1 lb. bacon, cooked and crumbled

2 c. mild cheddar cheese, grated

½ c. milk, if needed

Sauté diced onion in butter until shiny. Put hash browns in bottom of baking pan to soften and thaw. Spread layer of sour cream over top; then sprinkle with bacon bits and grated cheese. Drizzle melted butter and onion over layers. Add milk if too dry. Bake between 325° and 350° F. for several hours, or time required for size of casserole.

If preparing this for a larger group, multiply the ingredients and repeat the layers. We prefer to use a Magnalite® roasting pan.

Serves 20.

Stephen R. Covey is co-founder/co-chairman of FranklinCovey Company, the largest management and leadership development organization in the world. His book, *The 7 Habits of Highly Effective People*, is a *New York Times* number-one bestseller and has sold more than 14 million copies in thirty-three languages and seventy-five countries throughout the world. Dr. Covey and his wife, Sandra Merrill Covey, have a lifelong legacy of service to the Church and community. Together they presided over the Irish Mission for The Church of Jesus Christ of Latter-day Saints. Dr. Covey has also served as a regional representative of the Twelve and on several general Church leadership committees. The Coveys are the parents of nine children and the grandparents of thirty-eight. They reside in Provo, Utah.

Janette's Chicken Salad

JANETTE BECKHAM

I had never been east of Evanston, Wyoming, when we moved to Texas. So having the Air Force send us to New York was an adventure. We were happy to find family there. Aunt Mary Wilson lived in Westchester, New York, where for many years her husband, David J. Wilson, served as a federal judge. It was a highlight for us to be invited regularly to Aunt Mary's and to eat her wonderful food. We loved reading the names of distinguished guests, such as J. C. Penney, as we added our little family's name to her guest registry. Because I was learning to cook and entertain, Mary would often send me three or four typed carbon-copy sheets for Christmas entitled "Recipes I Have Enjoyed."

Aunt Mary taught me that cooking is also about relationships. It never took her long to become acquainted with people, and when she and Dave returned to Salt Lake City in their later years she thought it would be fun to invite all of her new ward members to dinner—and she did—one tableful at a time. She was known in New York and Utah for her hospitality and good cooking. This recipe has served many guests at showers, luncheons, and neighborhood gatherings.

3 c. cooked chicken breasts, cut in large pieces

1 c. celery, diced

⅔ c. almonds, slivered (lightly toasted)

1 (8-oz.) can water chestnuts, sliced

2 Tbs. onion, finely diced

6 to 8 large stuffed green olives, sliced

3 Tbs. (3-oz. bottle) capers, drained

3 Tbs. apple cider vinegar

Salt

Pepper

Paprika

¾ c. sour cream

¾ c. mayonnaise

Place chicken in a bowl and add celery, almonds, water chestnuts, onion, and olives. Sprinkle with capers, vinegar, and seasonings. Mix lightly. Cover and refrigerate at least 3 hours or overnight. One hour before serving, add sour cream and mayonnaise and stir gently. Refrigerate until serving. Scoop onto red leaf lettuce on salad plates. Garnish with fresh fruit, such as red grapes, melon chunks, and pineapple. Serve with warm, fresh rolls for a light, tasty luncheon. This recipe is easy to double or triple for groups.

Serves 6 to 8.

Janette Hales Beckham has served in the Utah State Legislature, as the Young Women general president, and on the Primary general board. She served at Brigham Young University as a member of the Board of Trustees, Cougar Club Board, Women's Conference Committee, and the advisory committee for BYU-TV. She received the Reed Smoot Citizen of the Year award for her many years of civic and community service. She and her late husband, Robert H. Hales, are the parents of five children and thirteen grandchildren. In 1995, Janette married Raymond E. Beckham who has five children and eighteen grandchildren. Together the Beckhams served four years on the Church's Olympic Coordinating Committee for the Salt Lake 2002 Winter Games.

Aunt Rhoda's Baked Beans

MARILYN ARNOLD

Aunt Rhoda is my mother, but her recipe for baked beans has circulated among family and friends, who call it Aunt Rhoda's Baked Beans. No one knows where the recipe originated, but my memories of enjoying mother's beans are centered in the years I lived in a mountain home south of Provo, Utah. Once a week during summer and fall months, Mother and Dad would drive out for supper. I barbecued pork steaks or hamburger, and Mother brought her baked beans and potato salad.

5 slices bacon, cooked and broken

1 onion, diced and sautéed in bacon grease

1 qt. canned baked beans (We like Bush's®.)

½ c. ketchup

1 Tbs. Worcestershire sauce

½ c. brown sugar

8 oz. crushed pineapple with juice

Mix all ingredients and pour into casserole dish. Bake at 250° F. to warm through. Do not overbake.

Serves 6 to 8.

Marilyn Arnold is an emeritus professor of English at Brigham Young University, where she also served as dean of Graduate Studies, as assistant to former president Dallin H. Oaks, and as director of the Center for the Study of Christian Values in Literature. She was awarded a Ph.D. in American literature from the University of Wisconsin–Madison and went on to receive various research awards, teaching awards, and lectureships. An internationally recognized scholar on the writings of Willa Cather, and a widely published writer and speaker in academic circles, she has also authored several nonacademic books, including three novels that grow out of her spiritual roots and her deep attachment to the desert country of southern Utah.

Beans and More Beans

SUSAN EASTON BLACK

About ten years ago my husband and I concluded that we needed to eat healthier. He became a vegan and I followed suit, except for the Sunday roast. Although we have had friends who have wanted to follow our diet plan, the boredom of lettuce salads has caused them to rethink their decision. We attribute the continuance of our healthy habit to one recipe—our weekly feast of Beans and More Beans. We vary the recipe each week with spices and new vegetables, but through all of the variations we never forget the beans and diced tomatoes. It makes a great addition to any meal. And if you are a vegetarian, a great main course. I have used it in meatless tacos and taco salads, and as a side dish and a soup. Start with our simple recipe, then be creative.

1 (16-oz.) can black beans, drained

1 (16-oz.) can garbanzo beans, drained

1 (16-oz.) can kidney beans, drained

1 (16-oz.) can spiced chili beans, undrained

1 (16-oz.) can Mexican corn, drained

1 large onion, diced and sautéed

2 Tbs. jalapeños, chopped

Spices to taste

1 (32-oz.) can diced tomatoes, undrained

Stir it all together and serve it hot or cold.

Serves 15.

Susan Easton Black is a professor of church history and doctrine and a past associate dean of general education and honors at Brigham Young University. Dr. Black has received many university awards and fellowships for her research and writing over the past twenty-five years, including the Karl G. Maeser Distinguished Faculty Lecturer Award in 2000, the highest award given a professor at Brigham Young University. She has authored, edited, and compiled more than ninety books and as many articles. Her most recent book is *The Nauvoo Temple, Jewel of the Mississippi*. She is married to Harvey B. Black, and they are the parents of eight children.

Calypso Black Beans and Rice

CLAUDIA BUSHMAN

Now that we live in the smallest space ever—a New York City apartment—we have the most company. We have space to entertain, which many do not, so we frequently have groups over—our Columbia students, our ward members, committees, groups of friends. I present here an excellent, delicious, and simple vegetarian casserole, which all groups have enjoyed. It can be made mostly in advance, finished easily, doubled and tripled, and looks pretty on the table.

1 c. peppers (various colors), diced

1 c. onions, chopped

2 Tbs. prepared garlic

Half a dozen good shakes of hot pepper sauce

2 (16-oz.) cans black beans, drained

⅔ c. water

Salt and pepper, to taste

1 (10-oz.) pkg. yellow rice mix

1 tomato, diced

2 limes, cut in wedges

In an olive-oil-sprayed skillet, sauté peppers and onions over medium-high heat until somewhat cooked. Add prepared garlic and half a dozen good shakes of hot pepper sauce. Add black beans and water. Cook for 6 minutes. Add salt and pepper to taste. Cook yellow rice mix according to package directions. Put rice on a platter and spoon bean mixture over rice. Squeeze on the juice of 1 lime. Top with diced tomatoes and the other lime, cut in wedges on the side.

Serves 4 generously.

Claudia L. Bushman holds degrees in literature and American studies from Wellesley College, Brigham Young University and Boston University and teaches history and American studies at Columbia University. She is the author and editor of nine books and is currently writing a contemporary study of the LDS Church. She is married to scholar Richard Lyman Bushman, and they have lived in New York City for fifteen years. They have six children and sixteen grandchildren. Claudia Bushman was named New York State Mother of the Year in 2000.

Lasagne a la ragu Bolognese
(Lasagna as you would find in Bologna)

MICHAEL BALLAM

Since I chose to be an opera singer and to catapult myself into the passionate association with Italian culture, one might think that my adoration of things Italian would be limited to Rossini, Bellini, and Puccini. I am equally passionate about other members of the "ini" family—linguini, tortellini, fettuccini! Perhaps my affection for the heritage of sunny Italy comes as much through the cuisine as it does the music. If the wonders of this great land have eluded you through your sense of hearing, perhaps they can touch you through your sense of taste.

1 onion, diced

1 stalk celery, chopped

1 carrot, sliced

1 Tbs. butter

1 lb. lean ground beef

1 onion, chopped

1 c. tomato sauce

1 c. ketchup

½ tsp. garlic salt

2 c. beef bouillon

1 (8-oz.) can sliced mushrooms, with juice

1 (16-oz.) pkg. lasagna noodles

2 Tbs. olive oil

Salt

In small pan, slowly sauté onion, celery, and carrot in butter over low heat. Brown beef with other onion in a large skillet. Add onion, celery, and carrot mixture to skillet. Stir in tomato sauce, ketchup, garlic salt, and beef bouillon. Simmer for 3 hours. Add mushrooms with juice.

Cook lasagna noodles in 8 quarts water with olive oil and salt. Drain and rinse. Blend ricotta cheese with egg and sour cream; add chopped green onions. Mix mozzarella and Swiss cheeses together. Put 3 to 4 tablespoons of sauce on bottom of oblong casserole (9x13-inch) dish. Place half of the noodles lengthwise on bottom of pan; cover with sauce, grated cheese, ricotta mixture, and Parmesan sprinkle.

Make the next layer with noodles set crosswise,

2 c. Ricotta or cottage cheese

1 egg

1 c. sour cream

1 bunch green onions, chopped

1 (8-oz.) pkg. mozzarella cheese,
    grated

1 (8-oz.) pkg. Swiss cheese, grated

1 (4-oz.) can Parmesan cheese

repeating other ingredients. Sprinkle Parmesan cheese abundantly on top. Bake at 350° F. for 30 minutes. Let stand 10 minutes before serving.

Serves 9 to 12.

Michael Ballam is the founder and director of the Utah Festival Opera Company. Michael has performed in concert halls throughout America, Asia, Europe, and the Soviet Union, with command performances at the White House and the Vatican. He has shared the stage with the world's greatest singers, including Joan Sutherland, Kiri Te Kanawa, Birgit Nilsson, and Placido Domingo. At the age of twenty-four, Dr. Ballam became the youngest recipient of the degree of Doctor of Music with Distinction in the history of Indiana University. He is a professor of music at Utah State University and an accomplished pianist and oboist. Michael and his wife, Laurie, are the parents of six children and reside in Logan, Utah.

Spaghetti with Fresh Herbs and Garlic

KORY KATSEANES

This is a favorite pasta recipe we found several years ago in a vegetarian cookbook of Linda McCartney's. It is so easy; all you need to go with it is a green salad and some crusty French bread.

3 cloves garlic, minced

4 to 5 Tbs. olive oil

Black pepper, freshly ground

12 oz. spaghetti noodles

Parmesan cheese, grated

2 c. fresh herbs, chopped (parsley, basil, oregano, etc.)

Stir the minced garlic into the olive oil and add lots of freshly ground black pepper. Cook the spaghetti until al dente; drain well. Mix the garlicky oil into the hot spaghetti. Sprinkle with the desired amount of fresh herbs and Parmesan cheese; toss thoroughly. Serve immediately.

Kory Katseanes is the director of orchestras at the Brigham Young University School of Music, where he conducts the Philharmonic and Chamber orchestras in Utah and on their regular tours throughout the world. From 1987 to 2002 he was the assistant conductor of the Utah Symphony, collaborating with guest artists such as the King's Singers, the Chieftans, Nancy Griffiths, Riders in the Sky, Kathy Mattea, Michael Martin Murphy, Judy Collins, Art Garfunkel, Maureen McGovern, and Marvin Hamlisch. He played violin with the Utah Symphony for twenty-six years and teaches private violin lessons and coaches chamber music. He and his wife, Carolyn, are the parents of four children.

Ravioli with Spinach

CLAUDIA BUSHMAN

This recipe is a favorite for large Bushman events because it can be adapted for crowds very easily, is colorful, and tastes good. Meat can be added to the sauce, if desired. The dish is assembled in a large casserole from three items: cooked bowtie pasta, store-bought spaghetti sauce of any kind, and a filling. A pound of pasta, two big jars of sauce, and the filling makes a generous amount.

1 lb. bowtie pasta

2 (10-oz.) boxes chopped frozen spinach

1 c. parsley, chopped

1 c. fine, dry, prepared bread crumbs

1 c. grated Parmesan cheese

2 cloves garlic, minced (or use prepared garlic or a powder)

4 Tbs. olive oil

6 beaten eggs

1 lb. Italian sausage or ground beef (optional)

2 (30-oz.) jars spaghetti sauce (any kind)

Cook bowtie pasta according to package directions; drain and set aside. Thaw, cook, and drain spinach; add remaining ingredients, except sauce and meat, to spinach and mix; set aside. If using meat, brown and stir into sauce. Spread a layer of sauce in a 4-quart baking dish, then some macaroni mixed with enough sauce to keep pieces separate, then more sauce, some filling, and pasta; repeat layers until the filling is used up. Finish with a layer of pasta and sauce and sprinkle with additional Parmesan cheese. Bake, uncovered, at 350° F. for about 30 minutes. Leftovers taste good, too.

Serves 20.

Claudia L. Bushman holds degrees in literature and American studies from Wellesley College, Brigham Young University and teaches history and American studies at Columbia University. She is the author and editor of nine books and is currently writing a contemporary study of the LDS Church. She is married to scholar Richard Lyman Bushman, and they have lived in New York City for fifteen years. They have six children and sixteen grandchildren. Claudia Bushman was named New York State Mother of the Year in 2000.

Macaroni and Cheese

RODNEY H. BRADY

From the time I was a young child many years ago, my mother, Jessie Madsen Brady, would ask me as my birthday approached, "What would you like for your birthday dinner?" Always my answer was, "maca-roni and cheese." To this day, over sixty years later, there are few dishes I enjoy more than a plate full of my mother's macaroni and cheese served from a large baking dish and seasoned with freshly ground pepper.

1 (8-oz.) pkg. macaroni (2 c. cooked)

2 Tbs. butter

1¼ c. (⅓ lb.) sharp cheddar cheese, cut in ½-inch cubes or strips

¾ tsp. salt

¼ tsp. pepper

2 c. milk

Paprika

Cook macaroni according to package directions. Drain macaroni and layer with cheese in a 12x7½x2-inch casserole dish. Dot with butter; sprinkle with seasonings; then pour milk over the top. Bake at 350° F. for 40 minutes—or until crust is golden brown. Sprinkle the casserole with paprika to serve.

Serves 6 to 8.

Rodney H. Brady is president and CEO of Deseret Management Corporation, the holding company that oversees the commercial businesses of The Church of Jesus Christ of Latter-day Saints. He previously served as president and CEO of Bonneville International Corporation, president of Weber State University, as a member of the Sub-cabinet of the President of the United States, and as assistant secretary of the U.S. Department of Health, Education, and Welfare. He holds a doctor of business administration degree from Harvard University. He has served in many community and church assignments including local and national leadership appointments in the Boy Scouts of America. He served as a missionary to Great Britain and as president of the Los Angeles California Stake. He and his wife, Carolyn "Mitzi" Hansen, are the parents of three sons.

© Busath Photography

One-Crust Chicken Pot Pie

ROGER AND MELANIE HOFFMAN

This recipe comes from a book compiled by wonderful cooks in Melanie's hometown, Richfield, Utah. Although we do not know Julie Christensen, we thank her every time we make this marvelous comfort food! It is our family's favorite dinner and a perfect dish to take to anyone in need of good food. Our oldest son said he used to think fondly about chicken pot pie when he was serving his mission in England.

⅓ c. butter

½ c. Bisquick®

⅓ c. onion, chopped

¼ tsp. pepper

2 c. chicken broth

⅔ c. milk

2 c. cooked chicken, cubed

1 (10-oz.) pkg. frozen peas and carrots

1½ c. Bisquick®

3 Tbs. hot water

3 Tbs. butter, softened

Preheat oven to 425° F. Heat butter in a 2-quart saucepan over low heat until melted. Stir in ½ cup Bisquick, onion, and pepper. Cook over low heat until bubbly. Stir in broth and milk. Heat to boiling, stirring constantly. Boil, stirring, for 1 minute. Stir in chicken and frozen vegetables; heat through. Keep warm over low heat.

In a separate bowl, combine remaining ingredients to form a dough ball. Roll dough out until it's large enough to fit casserole dish (such as a 9x13-inch Pyrex). Place chicken mixture into casserole dish and cover with dough. Cut several slits on top to allow steam to escape while baking. (With a 9x13-inch pan, the dough will barely reach the edges—so there is no need to slit the crust.) Bake for 20 to 25 minutes, until crust is deep golden brown.

Note: For the chicken, I use chicken breasts, sprinkled with lemon pepper seasoning, placed in a shallow baking dish, uncovered, and baked at 400° F. for 25 minutes or until juices run clear.

Serves 6 to 8.

Roger and Melanie Hoffman have been writing and performing LDS music since 1980. Their works include *Scripture Scouts* and *Alexander's Amazing Adventures* for children, and *Consider the Lilies*, the title song for the Tabernacle Choir's new CD, as well as six CDs of their own. The Hoffmans love singing together and have performed throughout the United States. Roger's long and extensive vocal career has ranged from singing under the baton of Leonard Bernstein as a young man to soloing with the Tabernacle Choir on *Music and the Spoken Word*. The Hoffmans have four sons.

"Thou Shalt Not Want" Shepherd's Pie

JANE CLAYSON

Nothing says comfort food like my mom's shepherd pie. Whether it's a family buffet or a Sunday feast, this creation is simply delicious and a beautiful conversation starter for your table. When we were kids, Mom would place a festive ceramic blackbird in the middle of the pie just a few minutes after it came out of the oven. And every time she served this dish, we would take turns ceremoniously removing the bird and placing it next to our plate during dinner. It's still a tradition.

8 lbs. bottom round

1 (5-oz.) bottle Worcestershire sauce

1 (5-oz.) bottle A-1® sauce

Lawry's® seasoning salt

White pepper

1 envelope Lipton® onion soup

½ c. red wine vinegar

Bay leaves

1 onion, quartered

1 oven bag

1 bag frozen peas

1 (1-lb.) bag baby carrots

1 (14½-oz.) can beef bouillon soup

1 box Hungry Jack® instant potatoes

1 c. (2 sticks) butter

Lawry's® seasoning salt, to taste

White pepper, to taste

2 eggs, beaten

1 pint sour cream

Onion powder, to taste

¼ c. cheddar cheese, grated

The night before serving the pie, place the roast, sauces, seasoning salt, white pepper, onion soup, red wine vinegar, bay leaves, and quartered onion in a clear oven bag. Poke several holes in the bag and place it in a roaster pan. Bake overnight at 225°F. for approximately 8 hours.

After roast is done, pour off juice and reserve it. Shred meat into bite-sized pieces and remove fat. Set aside meat. Pour juice into roasting pan and add frozen peas, baby, carrots, and beef bouillon soup. Soup should partially cover vegetables. Simmer for 5 to 10 minutes. Add meat and simmer for an additional 15 minutes. Pour vegetables and meat in a large Shepherd's Pie dish or another deep round dish (at least 4 quarts).

For topping, bring to a boil the amount of water needed to make 1½ quarts of potatoes (see back of box for measurement). <u>Do not add the milk called for on the box.</u> Add 2 sticks of butter, seasoning salt, and white pepper. Remove from heat and add beaten eggs, sour cream, onion powder, and instant potato flakes. Spread potatoes over meat and vegetables, just to the edge of the pan. Sprinkle cheese on top. Bake until warmed through and cheese is melted. Place an artificial ceramic bird in the center.

Serves 10.

As an anchor and correspondent for CBS News, Jane Clayson provides in-depth, original reporting for *48 Hours* and the "Eye on America" segments of the *CBS Evening News*. Previously, Jane co-anchored, with Bryant Gumbel, *The Early Show* on CBS. She has also been a correspondent for *ABC Network News* in Los Angeles (1996–99), reporting for *World News Tonight* and *Good Morning America* network broadcasts. Between 1990 and 1996 she anchored and reported for KSL-TV in Salt Lake City. Her work has received numerous awards from the Society of Professional Journalists, as well as an Emmy and the prestigious Edward R. Murrow Award from the Radio and Television News Directors Association.

Holiday Turketti

ALAN AND KAREN ASHTON

Last Thanksgiving I roasted seventy-five pounds of turkey, mashed twenty pounds of potatoes, and cried over tons of chopped onions. My kitchen looked like the local soup kitchen. We had a wonderful Thanksgiving dinner. Somehow, there was some leftover turkey. Imagine that! "Oh, what do you do in the wintertime with all that frozen fowl?" Make turkey casserole. I even make up several at one time and keep them in the freezer as compassionate casseroles.

½ lb. spaghetti, broken into 2-inch pieces

3 to 4 c. roasted turkey, cubed

1 c. cooked ham, cubed (optional)

½ c. canned pimientos, minced

½ c. green peppers, diced

2 (10¾-oz.) cans Campbell's® condensed cream of chicken soup

1 c. chicken or turkey broth

¼ tsp. celery salt

¼ tsp. pepper

2 Tbs. onions, diced

2 c. sharp American cheese, grated

Cook the spaghetti pieces according to package directions. Drain, rinse, and set aside. Preheat oven to 350°F. Combine meat and the remaining ingredients; then stir in the cooked noodles. Pour into a 3-quart casserole and bake, covered, for about 40 minutes.

Serves 8 to 10.

Hawaiian Haystacks

ALAN AND KAREN ASHTON

Also known by this mother as Food Storage Haystacks, this is an adaptation of one of our family favorites. The original recipe was labor intensive—but there's seldom time for that. I never can tell when married children and their families will drop by. Do I stress? Never! I keep the basic ingredients for this dish in my storage. That way, I can summon up smiles all around the table at any time. This recipe will satisfy eight to ten hungry relatives. I have even been known to quadruple this recipe for a big family gathering.

½ c. instant rice (per person)

3 (10¾-oz.) cans Campbell's® condensed cream of chicken soup

1 (14½-oz.) can chicken broth

2 (10-oz.) cans premium chunk white chicken with broth

½ c. sour cream

2 (20-oz.) cans pineapple tidbits

1 (6-oz.) large can of pitted olives, sliced

2 (15-oz.) small cans mandarin oranges

1 (5-oz.) can dry Chinese noodles

2 (8-oz.) cans water chestnuts, sliced

1 (14½-oz.) can diced tomatoes (or use fresh tomatoes)

⅓ c. green onions, diced

1 c. green bell pepper, chopped

1 c. celery, chopped

1 c. cheddar cheese, grated

Prepare rice and place it in a serving bowl. Combine the soup, chicken broth, chicken chunks, and sour cream in a kettle, separating the chicken chunks while stirring. Cook over medium heat until heated throughout and pour into a bowl next to the rice. Guests help themselves to rice and sauce, and then top with their preferred condiments.

Serves 8 to 10.

Sloppy Joes for Fifty

ALAN AND KAREN ASHTON

Stop! You probably think this recipe is not for you. Twelve pounds of ground beef? You are thinking: "When would I ever use that much Sloppy Joe?" Well, this recipe has saved me over and over. It has been the mainstay at numerous PTA carnivals, Young Women and Young Men activities, family reunions, Relief Society service projects, and now, with our family numbers reaching forty-two, monthly family birthday parties. You're going to love this recipe. Start with your largest pan. I use a big roaster pan. Sometimes I make a batch and then freeze bags for future use. At our house you never can tell who will drop by and how many of them will need to eat.

12 lbs. lean ground beef

3 c. ketchup

6 c. tomato juice

2 Tbs. dry mustard

4 Tbs. vinegar

2 Tbs. salt

4 Tbs. Worcestershire sauce

4 large onions, chopped

1 Tbs. pepper

3 c. brown sugar

Brown the ground beef in a very large roasting pan. (This can give your arm a workout, so keep a teenage boy or a husband handy.) Drain off any fat. Add the remaining ingredients. Simmer, uncovered, for at least 1 hour.

If you have surprise dinner guests, you can take out a freezer bag of this mix, add it to Prego Mushroom Spaghetti Sauce, and serve it over noodles for a simple and satisfying meal with a perfect blend of flavors.

Serves 50.

Alan and Karen Ashton are the parents of eleven children and twenty-one grandchildren. Alan is the cofounder of WordPerfect corporation and past president and CEO. He is a director of Deseret Book Company, Candesa, and eRooms Systems Inc. Karen is the founder of the popular Timpanogos Storytelling Festival and has served on the boards of Governors for the Utah Shakespearean Festival, the Brigham Young University Museum of Art, and the Foundation of Primary Children's Medical Center. The Ashtons are the founders and owners of Thanksgiving Point in Lehi, Utah.

Pizza Siddoway

RICHARD M. SIDDOWAY

Over thirty years ago, my wife and I signed contracts to teach school in the middle of the Navajo Nation. One Friday, near the end of August, we loaded a U-Haul truck and headed for Arizona. The next morning as we were unloading our fairly meager belongings and carrying them into a small cinder-block apartment owned by the school district, the assistant principal of the school drove up to help us. I was surprised to see that it was an old friend whom I hadn't seen for a half dozen years. He greeted us warmly, helped us move in, and then asked if we'd like to come to their double-wide trailer for dinner. "We're going to have pizza," he told us. My wife and I eagerly accepted the offer, although our experience with homemade pizza began and ended with Chef Boyardee. That night, we drove to our friend's trailer and knocked on the door. We could already smell the tangy cheese, basil, oregano, and garlic through an open window. Although the pizza craze of today had not yet permeated America, we had eaten enough pizza to know that the pizza we had that night was good—really good!

As we were leaving, I said, "I've got to have that recipe."

"Oh, I've got it down at school," was the reply.

Two days later school began. On my preparation period I wandered down to the office and accosted my friend. "I've come for the pizza recipe," I said.

He hemmed and hawed a little, then said, "Oh, I took it home, since I knew you wanted it."

Over the next month I found that the elusive recipe was at home when I was at school, and at school when I was at their trailer. Finally I cornered my friend, "What's the deal with the pizza recipe? If you don't want to give it to me, just say so."

"Well," he said, looking down at his hands, "actually, I used to run a commercial pizza palace in the town we moved from. When you franchise with them they bring a chef in who makes several different kinds of crust and sauce and let's you sample them. When you decide which one you're going to use, he gives you the recipe and makes you sign a non-disclosure agreement."

"Meaning?"

"Meaning I can't tell you the recipe."

"Why didn't you just say so?" I inquired.

"Well, I didn't want to hurt your feelings." Then a smile came over his face. "Next week I'm making pizza for a fund-raiser for the student-body officers."

"So?" I asked.

"How would you like to help? I didn't say I wouldn't let anyone see how I made the pizza."

I immediately agreed to help, and that Saturday we made three hundred crusts, baked them off, to kill the yeast, and froze them. The following Friday we mixed the sauce and, using the school's ovens, baked and sold all three hundred pizzas in less than an hour and-a-half. The only problem with the recipe I wrote down was that it made about fifty pizza crusts. However, over the years, my wife and I found a way to reduce the amounts, alter them slightly, and create a ten-crust recipe.

PIZZA DOUGH

4 lbs. flour

¼ c. sugar

1 oz. salt

1 oz. oil

1 oz. yeast

1 qt. water

PIZZA SAUCE AND TWO-CHEESE TOPPING

1 (10½-oz.) can tomato soup

1 (6-oz.) can tomato paste

½ tsp. basil

½ tsp. oregano

Garlic salt, to taste

¼ lb. mozzarella cheese, grated

¼ lb. cheddar cheese, grated

To prepare crusts, mix flour, sugar, and salt thoroughly in large mixing bowl. Stir in oil, yeast, and water and knead together for about 5 minutes. Place the mixture in a bowl and let it rise for 1 hour. Punch down and let it rise again for 1 hour. Roll crust on floured surface; place on pizza baking pan and prick with fork. Bake at 400° F. for 3 to 5 minutes, until crust browns slightly. This will kill the yeast and allow storage of crusts in freezer for up to two months.

Makes 10 14-inch crusts—2 for now, 8 for the freezer.

To prepare sauce, mix can of tomato soup and can of tomato paste in bowl. When thoroughly blended, add basil and oregano. Sprinkle with garlic salt to taste (it doesn't take much). Grate cheeses together in separate bowl, mixing to blend. Spread half of the sauce on one pizza; top with half of the cheese, and sprinkle a little bit of basil and oregano in the cheese. Top with any ingredients you'd like. Repeat process for second pizza. Bake in a hot oven (450° to 500° F.) until the cheese is melted.

Richard M. Siddoway is the best-selling author of *The Christmas Wish*, which was produced as a made-for-TV movie starring Debbie Reynolds and Neil Patrick Harris. A professional educator for more than forty years, Richard is currently the director of the Electronic High School for the State of Utah and a three-term member of the Utah State Legislature. He is the author of several memorable and touching books, including *Christmas Quest*, *Christmas of the Cherry Snow*, and *Twelve Tales of Christmas*. He and his wife, Janice, are the parents of eight children and the grandparents of sixteen plus. They reside in Bountiful, Utah.

Paul's Cougarito Burgerito

PAUL JAMES

I love creating new dishes. As you might guess, this is a combination of a hamburger and a burrito—strips of grilled ground beef patty with garnishes of sour cream, chopped tomatoes, avocados, and onions, all wrapped in a warm flour tortilla. The essential part is a plastic sandwich bag to hold the creation together. Other garnishes could be added to suit individual preferences. Add your own flair to the preparation.

2 lbs. lean ground beef

Salt and pepper

6 large flour tortillas, warmed

1 pt. sour cream

1 to 2 bunches green onions, chopped (white included)

2 to 3 tomatoes, cut into ½-inch cubes

1 to 2 avocados, peeled, pitted, diced

6 plastic sandwich bags (a must)

OPTIONAL CONDIMENTS

Salsa

Grated cheddar cheese or blue cheese

Diced green chilies

Jalapeños

Chopped olives

Tomatillo sauce

Pickle relish

Diced cucumbers

Bacon bits

Form the ground beef into meat patties rather thickly so they will remain juicy after grilling or frying. After cooking, season the meat with salt and pepper and cut lengthwise into 3- or 4-inch strips. Warm the tortillas so that they will roll easily and not tear during the rolling. They can be heated one at a time on an ungreased fry pan, or wrapped in foil and placed in a warm oven for 5 to 6 minutes (or microwaved briefly on waxed paper).

Spread the tortilla with sour cream, overlap strips of meat down one side, sprinkle with generous amounts of onion, tomato, and avocado. Roll snugly, place one end in a plastic sandwich bag and wrap the excess bag firmly around it. Top the other end with an additional dollop of sour cream. Serve immediately.

Serves 6.

156 Five-Star Recipes

For thirty-seven years Paul James was the voice of the BYU Cougars, calling plays for KSL radio in Salt Lake City. Paul retired with Coach LaVell Edwards at the end of the 2000 season. With Bob Welti and Dick Nourse, Paul James formed a noteworthy trio of broadcasters that Utahns will remember for years to come. Paul now spends his time painting, caring for the orchids in his greenhouse, and learning to play the piano. He and his wife, Annette, are the parents of four children and reside in Salt Lake City.

Turkey and Dressing Casserole

MARY ELLEN SMOOT

This makes a delicious entrée for the day or two after your big turkey dinner. Chicken can be used instead of turkey.

Turkey scraps

4 c. turkey dressing

WHITE SAUCE

½ c. butter

⅓ c. flour

3 Tbs. minced onion

Pepper, to taste

2 to 3 c. milk

Preheat oven to 350° F. Lightly butter a 9x13-inch casserole dish. Alternate layers of cooked turkey and turkey dressing. Pour white sauce over top and bake for 30 minutes. Serve with cranberry sauce and other condiments, as desired.

For white sauce, melt butter and sauté onions over medium heat in a medium saucepan. Stir in flour; cook until bubbly. Add onion and pepper. Stir in milk. Cook, stirring constantly, until sauce thickens and bubbles

Serves 4 to 6.

Mary Ellen Wood Smoot served as general president of the Relief Society from April 1997 to April 2002. She loves family history and has written histories about her parents, grandparents, and their local community. She served with her husband, Stanley M. Smoot, when he was called as a mission president in Ohio, and they later served together as directors of Church Hosting. They are the parents of seven children and the grandparents of fifty.

Rosemary's Chicken Enchiladas

ALBERT AND MARILYN JEPPSON CHOULES

This recipe belonged to Rosemary, Albert's late wife. Albert and Rosemary's extended families, friends in Phoenix, and missionaries in New York City all loved it. When I married Albert, the recipe was passed on to me (as were many other blessings because of Rosemary). We continue to serve it often; and during our three-year assignment in Germany found many creative ways to improvise with some of the ingredients while living in the German economy.

4 chicken breasts (or 1 large chicken), cooked and cubed

1 bunch green onions, chopped

¾ lb. Monterey Jack cheese, grated

¾ lb. cheddar cheese, grated

1 small can diced green chilies, drained

1 pt. sour cream

2 (10¾-oz.) cans cream of chicken soup

12 corn tortillas

Heat a small amount of oil in sauté pan over low heat for one minute; then turn off burner. Set out three mixing bowls. In one, mix chicken pieces with chopped onions. In another bowl, mix the cheeses together and set aside. In the third bowl, mix green chilies, sour cream, and soup. Dip corn tortillas into warm oil to soften; drain on paper towels. Preheat oven to 325° F.

To assemble: place spoonful of chicken mixture on tortilla; top with spoonful of sauce; sprinkle with grated cheese. Roll up and place with seam down in 9x13-inch baking pan. Continue in the same manner for all tortillas. Top with remaining sauce and sprinkle with remaining cheese. Bake for 30 minutes or until bubbly.

Makes 12 enchiladas.

Albert Choules, Jr., has been a member of the Second Quorum of the Seventy, a Regional Representative, and president of the New York, New York City Mission. He is the senior vice president of Coltrin and Associates, a New York City-based public relations firm. He was married to the former Rosemary Phillips, who passed away in 1984. Albert married Marilyn Jeppson in 1987. Marilyn has a Ph.D. from BYU and is a counselor in private practice in Salt Lake City. Together, the Choules have twenty-two grandchildren.

Foreign Flavors

A VARIETY OF
DISHES AND
DESSERTS
FROM ALL OVER
THE WORLD

Danish Sweet Soup

RODNEY H. BRADY

During the first eighteen years of my life, our family of two parents and four children made frequent trips to the home of my grandmother, Rozena Fechser Madsen, first in Mt. Pleasant, Utah, and later in Sandy, Utah. Grandma Madsen's heritage was a combination of Scandinavian and German, her husband being Danish, her father being German, and her mother being Norwegian. She seemed to have a never-ending variety of recipes from the Old Country. One of the most unusual yet delicious dishes she served was hot Danish Sweet Soup, a dish absolutely worth trying.

1 qt. plum juice

½ c. tapioca

1 c. pitted prunes

1 c. raisins

Oyster crackers (optional)

Mix juice and tapioca in saucepan and let stand 5 minutes. Cook over medium heat 20 minutes, stirring constantly until it comes to a full boil. Add prunes and raisins and cook over low heat an additional 5 minutes. If too thick, add more juice or water. Serve hot with oyster crackers.

Serves 8 to 10.

Rodney H. Brady is president and CEO of Deseret Management Corporation, the holding company that oversees the commercial businesses of The Church of Jesus Christ of Latter-day Saints. He previously served as president and CEO of Bonneville International Corporation, president of Weber State University, as a member of the Sub-cabinet of the President of the United States, and as assistant secretary of the U.S. Department of Health, Education, and Welfare. He holds a doctor of business administration degree from Harvard University. He has served in many community and church assignments including local and national leadership appointments in the Boy Scouts of America. He served as a missionary to Great Britain and as president of the Los Angeles California Stake. He and his wife, Carolyn "Mitzi" Hansen, are the parents of three sons.

© Busath Photography

Russian Borscht Soup

HOWARD SHARP

Galena Efimova, our Russian mission president's wife in Ekaterineburg, Russia, was an excellent cook. Her authentic Russian borscht is served hot, unlike the cold borscht that was served years ago at the Hotel Utah. With a loaf of crusty bread, this soup makes a delicious meal.

1 beef brisket, breastbone

2 medium beets, cut into 3 or 4 pieces

4 to 5 carrots, diced

2 onions, diced

3 small potatoes, diced

1 tomato, quartered

8 peppercorns

Salt to taste

2 bay leaves

1 to 2 Tbs. apple cider vinegar

3 Tbs. tomato sauce

Small cabbage, shredded (don't use the heart)

Parsley

Sour cream

Boil meat an hour, or until tender. Remove and cut into pieces. Clean and skin beets and cut into 3 or 4 pieces. Boil beets in beef broth from meat for 15 to 20 minutes. Dice carrots, onions, and potatoes and add to broth. Remove beets and cool. Add quartered tomato. Grate cooled beets and add to soup. Add peppercorns, salt, bay leaves, vinegar, and tomato sauce. Simmer 20 minutes; then stir in shredded cabbage. Sprinkle with cut fresh parsley. Stir again and simmer 5 to 10 minutes. Serve with dollop of sour cream.

Serves 8 to 10.

Howard Sharp serves in the temple presidency of the Salt Lake Temple with his wife, Marjorie, at his side as an assistant matron. Howard's medical career includes twenty-five years at the Bryner Clinic in obstetrics and gynecology. In 1983 he joined the faculty of the OB-GYN Department at the University of Utah, specializing in pelvic surgery. He is a member of the Church's Missionary Medical Advisory Committee and took his wife on an eighteen-month humanitarian mission to Russia for their fiftieth wedding anniversary. The Sharps are the parents of seven children and the grandparents of twenty-five.

Sam Gae Tang (Chicken Soup)

WON YONG KO

As part of my calling, my wife and I host many guests of the Church in our home and have often discussed how we can treat our guests well but spend less effort and time preparing a meal. Sam Gae Tang is one such meal because it is nutritious, tasty, and does not need a lot of other dishes as accompaniments. We need only Kimchi and salt. Additionally, one of the ingredients is ginseng, which Koreans believe promotes good health. Our Korean guests enjoy Sam Gae Tang because they want to become healthier.

Now even foreign missionaries like this soup—at first out of curiosity but later because of the taste. It has become one of my wife's trademarks. The challenge is to know exactly how many people will come so that each person can have a bowl. My wife has begun preparing extra bowls; and now some people are lucky enough to enjoy two servings.

Ginseng is available throughout the year, but summer is the best time to enjoy this food. If you cannot get ginseng, make the soup without it—it will still be tasty.

2 fresh ginseng roots

½ c. sweet rice (Chap Sal)

4 chestnuts, peeled

2 Cornish game hens (2 servings)

4 red jujubes (Chinese dates), seeds removed

4 whole garlic cloves

Small piece of ginger, thinly diced

2 green onions, chopped

8 c. water

Salt & ground black pepper to taste

If ginseng roots are dried, soak in water until soft (at least 1 hour). Cut out small roots. Rinse the rice and soak in water for an hour. Wash Cornish game hens and pat dry. Combine ginseng, rice, chestnuts, jujubes, and garlic. Stuff hens with rice mixture.

Make a vertical cut on inner part of one drumstick and pull the other leg through the cut. By doing this, the drumstick helps keep the dressing inside the hen. Place hens in a pot with water; add green onion and ginger. Bring soup to a boil over high heat; reduce heat to medium and boil about 1 hour, covered. With straining spoon, skim fat off the soup. Season soup with salt and black pepper before serving. Serve soup with game hens.

Serves 2.

Won Yong Ko is president of Hanjin Information Systems and Telecommunications (HIST). Previously, he was managing director of IBM Korea. He studied electrical engineering at Seoul National University. He has served as an area authority seventy since 1997. He was born in Pusan, Korea, on October 15, 1945, and is married to Eun Hee Kim. They are the parents of one daughter and one son.

Moroccan Lamb Stew

JAMES WELCH

I was a bachelor for a long time—I finally got married at age forty-six and now have a beautiful wife and two fine sons. During all my single years I got pretty good at cooking for myself and friends. While most of it was simple but tasty fare, I did find some excellent recipes for dinner parties. The trick was to find something that was exceptionally easy to make but, when served, gave the impression of being complicated—of having slaved over a hot stove all day to prepare. It's sort of like finding a piece of music that is impressive and audience-pleasing but isn't nearly as hard to play as it sounds!

That is why my vote for Best Party Dish Ever is Moroccan Lamb Stew, which I was first served in Santa Barbara by my friends Lillian and Denis Stevens in their villa overlooking the ocean. This dish is rather exotic, with turmeric, cinnamon, and dried fruits. It's wonderfully aromatic and gets the guests' mouths watering as soon as they come in the door. But the greatest thing is how fast and easy it is: You put everything in the pot and let it cook. You don't even have to brown the meat!

1 to 2 lbs. boneless lamb stew meat

⅓ c. honey

1 large onion, chopped

3 to 4 large cloves garlic, pressed

2 cinnamon sticks (or 1 tsp. ground cinnamon)

2 to 3 Tbs. lemon juice

2 to 3 tsp. turmeric

3 carrots, peeled and chopped at an angle

1 c. dried apricots, chopped or whole (California apricots have better flavor and are softer than Turkish variety)

For stew, cut off fat from lamb and slice in small pieces. Don't brown meat. Combine all ingredients in Dutch oven or covered pot and bake at 350° F. for 1½ hours. If you prefer, add some liquid or broth, but for thicker stew don't add any liquid. Stir occasionally. Serve over couscous or rice with a dish of minted yogurt for spooning on top. Accompany with spinach salad, French or sourdough bread, and a tart beverage. Dinner's a success!

Note: You can improvise greatly on the proportions in this stew. I like more turmeric and apricots; you may prefer less.

Serves 6.

1 c. dried prunes, chopped or whole

½ c. raisins (regular and/or golden)

Salt and pepper to taste

Couscous or saffron rice (cooked
according to package)

MINTED YOGURT SAUCE

2 c. plain yogurt

2 Tbs. lemon juice

Fresh mint leaves, crushed (or 1 tsp.
mint jelly)

Fresh dill

1 English cucumber, diced

Pinch of white pepper

Salt, to taste

Sprinkle of garlic

To prepare yogurt sauce, combine all ingredients until blended well.

James Welch, University Organist at Santa Clara University in the San Francisco Bay Area, is a frequent performer at guest recitals on Temple Square. His musical career has taken him around the world, where he has performed in concerts at Notre Dame Cathedral, Paris, and in the cathedrals of Würzburg, Germany; Lausanne, Switzerland; Salzburg, Austria; Wellington, New Zealand; Olomouc, Czechoslovakia; and Beijing, China. He is the composer of "Bless Our Fast, We Pray" (*Hymns,* no. 138). James and his wife, Deanne, are the parents of two sons and reside in Palo Alto, California.

Spanakopitas

JACALYN S. LEAVITT

This Leavitt family favorite came from the governor's mother, Anne. The succulent little sandwiches were served at our wedding reception. These multilayered pastries filled with spinach and cheese can be made, refrigerated or frozen, then baked just before serving. The secret to their triangular shape is to fold the strips of dough as one would fold a flag: *a triangle here, a triangle there.*

2 eggs

1 medium onion, quartered

½ lb. Greek feta cheese, crumbled

1 (8-oz.) pkg. cream cheese

1 (10-oz.) pkg. frozen chopped spinach, thawed

2 Tbs. chopped parsley

1 tsp. dill weed

Dash pepper

1 (1-lb.) pkg. phyllo dough or strudel leaves

1 c. butter or margarine (2 sticks), melted

Combine eggs, onion, and feta cheese in electric blender. Whirl at medium speed until smooth; add cream cheese, whirl again a few seconds until smooth. Squeeze spinach with hands to remove as much liquid as possible. Add to cheese mixture along with parsley, dill, and pepper; blend just until combined. Refrigerate at least 1 hour.

For each pastry sandwich you will need 2 sheets of phyllo dough, each cut into a 2-inch-wide strip (sheets should already be about 16 inches long) and stacked, one on top of the other. To cut the sheets into strips, stack them and cut all at once. Separate large stack of strips into piles of 2 sheets each. Work with one 2-sheet-strip at a time. Keep remaining sheets covered with plastic wrap to prevent drying. Brush top sheet with melted butter or margarine.

Place a rounded teaspoon of filling on one end of the strip. Fold the top corner of that end down to the opposite side, forming a triangle. Fold triangle over onto strip, and then fold the square corner down to the opposite side. Each time you fold, the strip will get shorter and the triangular shape at that end will be maintained. Continue folding, in triangle pattern, to the other end. Repeat with each 2-sheet strip.

Place pastries on an ungreased baking pan. Bake at 375° F. for 15 to 20 minutes or until golden brown. Serve hot.

Makes 43 appetizers.

As First Lady of Utah, Jacalyn Smith Leavitt is a champion for children. She has developed, led, or promoted a number of programs designed to protect and educate Utah's children. Among them are the "Read to Me" Campaign, which encourages literacy and provides every new parent in the state of Utah a book to read to their child; the Children's Health Insurance Program (CHIP), which provides health benefits for uninsured children; the "Every Child by Two" Immunization Task Force, which works to inform parents of the importance of immunizations; and Baby Watch, a program for early detection of developmental delays in children. She is a former second grade teacher and the mother of five children.

Swedish Kaka Bread Dough

CHARLOTTE GARFF JACOBSEN

This recipe came from my maternal grandmother, Charlotte Critchlow Ryberg, who married a young man from Logan born of Swedish parents. Charlotte Ryberg's mother-in-law taught her how to make this Swedish kaka bread, which is a flat bread with fork holes poked in it. My own mom, Gertrude Ryberg Garff, also used the recipe to make sweet rolls, hamburger buns, and the world's best scones. Whenever we had special guests at our cabin in Montana, my mom would mix up a batch of this dough at night in our old hand mixer (we all took turns stirring the paddle), let it raise overnight in the cold mountain air, and serve hot scones the next morning at breakfast.

2 c. milk, scalded

¼ c. butter

1 Tbs. shortening

1 Tbs. salt

¼ c. sugar

1 c. cold water

2 eggs, beaten

1 pkg. yeast

6 to 7 c. flour

Pour milk into bread mixer; then add butter and shortening, stirring to melt. Mix in the salt, sugar, and cold water. Add beaten eggs and yeast, and mix until blended. Add flour by cups, mixing until dough looks smooth and the dough pulls away from sides of bowl. Allow dough to rise until doubled. Punch down and pour onto floured rolling board.

To make kaka bread, roll into 2- or 3½-inch thick 10x5-inch rectangles. Place on greased baking sheets. Let raise until doubled. When ready to bake, puncture all over top with fork tines; then bake at 350° F. until golden brown, 10 to 15 minutes.

Makes 2 to 3 loaves kaka bread.

SCONES

To make scones, roll dough into ½-inch thick rectangle and let rise on breadboard, covered to keep warm, until doubled. To cook, cut dough into strips about 3 inches long by 1½ inches wide. Drop strips in hot shortening, turning once as scones brown. Drain on paper towels and serve hot with honey butter or jam.

Makes 2 dozen scones.

SWEET ROLLS

To make sweet rolls, roll dough into an 8x12-inch rectangle, slightly less than ½-inch thick Cover with melted butter, brown sugar, cinnamon, chopped nuts, and raisins (if desired). Roll from 12-inch side to form a log. Cut log into 1-inch slices and place on greased baking sheet or in muffin tins. Let rise until doubled, then bake at 375° F. for 10 to 15 minutes. Immediately invert onto a cooling rack. When cool, frost with a simple powdered sugar and milk frosting, flavored with vanilla.

Makes 12 cinnamon rolls.

Note: Mom always doubled this recipe. That way we had scones for breakfast, sweet rolls to eat on the way to the beach, and kaka bread for sandwiches later in the day. We were living good!

Charlotte Jacobsen graduated from the University of Utah in 1964. She served as editor of the *Daily Utah Chronicle* and as president of Kappa Kappa Gamma. She has continued to be involved with the University as a member of Friends of the Libraries Board, Kappa Advisory Board, Red Butte Garden Board, and the Alumni Board. She currently serves on the University of Utah Publications Council, Community Advisory Committee for International Students, and as chair of the Lowell Bennion Community Service Center Advisory Board. Charlotte has served as president of her ward Young Women and Primary organizations, as stake Relief Society president, and in numerous teaching positions. Married to Ted M. Jacobsen, they are the parents of seven children and grandparents to eleven.

Kartoffel Puffer
(German Potato Pancakes)

DIETER AND HARRIET UCHTDORF

Frying these pancakes on the stove for the whole family was Elder Uchtdorf's job. We would all sit around the kitchen table waiting for the next batch until everyone was satiated and happy. Then it was his turn—he was always the last to eat and afterwards he always smelled like a pancake himself.

We like to eat the potato pancakes with applesauce; they are also great with meat and gravy.

2 eggs

1 medium onion, quartered

2 lbs. russet potatoes, peeled and cubed

2 tsp. salt

⅓ c. flour

Vegetable oil

Blend the eggs, onion, and part of the cubed potatoes until no lumps remain. Repeat with remaining cubed potatoes. Add salt and flour and blend shortly to mix. For a coarser consistency, use a grater for the potatoes and onions and stir in the other ingredients.

Heat vegetable oil in a heavy pan. Put pancake mixture in pan by spoonfuls, flattening each cake. Fry on both sides until brown and crisp. Remove from pan and drain on paper towel. The pancakes are best when fresh out of the frying pan.

Makes 20 pancakes.

Elder Dieter F. Uchtdorf was sustained as a General Authority on April 6, 1994. He was senior vice president for flight operations and chief pilot for Lufthansa German Airlines, and check and training captain for Boeing 747s. He and his wife, Harriet Uchtdorf, grew up in Frankfurt, Germany. Harriet enjoys sports and the arts and most of all being with her family. She loves to entertain guests, trying out new international recipes. Brother and Sister Uchtdorf are the parents of two children and the grandparents of five.

Norwegian Pancakes

JON SCHMIDT

Both my wife and I served missions in Norway, where we discovered these delicious pancakes. (We did not meet on our missions, by the way.) It has become a tradition in our family to make these on Saturday mornings. They are our kids' favorite! One Saturday as the children were eagerly gathering to get their pancakes, I thought about the far-reaching blessings of serving a mission. This wonderful recipe is definitely one of those.

4 eggs

½ c. warm water

1 tsp. vanilla

⅓ c. sugar

⅓ c. melted butter

1¼ c. flour

1 c. milk

Toppings: powdered sugar, butter, jam, syrup, or fruit topping

Butter a sauté pan or griddle. Beat eggs, water, and vanilla. Beat in sugar; then butter, flour, and milk, beating after each addition. Heat pan to medium; then pour batter by scoopfuls onto griddle (or single scoop for sauté or crêpe pan). Turn quickly and do not overcook. Stack the crêpe-like pancakes and keep in warm place until serving. Serve, buttered and rolled with topping like a crêpe—or serve flat and sprinkled with powdered sugar, allowing individual choice of toppings.

Pianist and composer Jon Schmidt has quickly become well known in the Salt Lake City area, where he consistently performs to sold-out audiences in major performance venues along the Wasatch Front. Jon's credits include five albums, three popular volumes of his original piano scores, performances and radio play all over the country, several top forty songs at mp3.com, a Pearl Award, a televised concert on a local PBS station, and "A Jon Schmidt Christmas," which has fast become a successful yearly Christmas tradition in Salt Lake. Jon and his wife, Michelle, are the parents of two children.

Swiss Birchermuesli

RICHARD H. CRACROFT

Birchermuesli is a Swiss national dish created in 1897 by Dr. R. Bircher-Benner, a pioneering nutritionist. Nutritionally, Birchermuesli is a "perfect" meal. The delicious dish is still served at every meal to patients at the Bircher-Benner Clinic in Zürich and in every restaurant in Switzerland. Usually served with whole wheat or other dark breads, Birchermuesli makes a fine main dish at breakfast or supper, or as the featured refreshment at any social gathering.

I first savored Birchermuesli in Linz, Austria, in July 1956, as a brand-new missionary. Before riding our bicycles out to the Linz branch house and MIA, my companion, Elder Gary O'Brien, pocketing an orange, mysteriously ordered me to put an apple in my satchel "for later." "Later" turned out to be a weekly dinner gathering of the eight Swiss-Austrian elders laboring in Linz. Each extracted from his briefcase an apple, orange, a sack of nuts, and a jar of yogurt, and proffered them to Elder Oswald Schwemmer. I was amazed as I watched Elder Schwemmer slice, dice, and chop our offerings into a large bowl, mix in some dry oatmeal, and, "ach du lieber!," spoon into our bowls a delicious, refreshing, and wonderfully nutritious feast—a meal that my family, friends, and several generations of Swiss missionaries have been enjoying ever since. "Es lebe [long live] die Mormonen Missionare! Es lebe die Schweiz! Es lebe Birchermuesli!"

1 (10-oz.) carton flavored yogurt

1 large apple, peeled and diced

½ c. raisins

½ c. slivered almonds, or chopped nuts

1 banana, sliced

Fruits as desired in any combination: sliced oranges, fresh berries, dried cranberries, mandarin oranges, or drained fruit cocktail

½ c. dry quick-cooking oatmeal (not instant)

Mix all ingredients, adding oatmeal gradually until the muesli reaches a thick, creamy consistency. (Flavored yogurt sweetens sufficiently; Bircher-Benner's recipe calls for sweetened or honied condensed milk instead, but yogurt is much better!) Chill for about 1 hour, to allow flavors to blend. Serve as a breakfast dish; or, with whipped cream topping, as dessert (while yodeling or blowing Alphorn).

Serves 4 to 6.

Richard H. Cracroft has been a professor of English at Brigham Young University and department chair, dean, and director of the Center for the Study of Christian Values in Literature at the same institution. He holds a Ph.D. in English and American Literature from the University of Wisconsin–Madison. He has served as MTC branch president, bishop, stake president, and president of the Switzerland Zürich Mission. He was a founding member and president of the Association for Mormon Letters. He's listed in *Who's Who in Education, Who's Who in the West,* and *Who's Who in the United States.* He and his wife, Janice, live in Orem, Utah, and are the parents of three children and grandparents of six.

Scottish Breakfast

ANNE PERRY

Try this delicious Scottish breakfast of herrings and toast with Seville Marmalade. I learned how to prepare the herrings in Scotland, and the marmalade recipe comes from my mother, who always made the best marmalade I have ever tasted. Enjoy this breakfast with whatever type of hot tea you like—made with water straight off the boil. Take your teapot to the kettle, not the other way around. Have a great breakfast and a good day.

HERRINGS IN OATMEAL

Fresh herrings, one or two per person.

Oatmeal—or rolled oats, if preferred

Yolk of eggs, as required

Olive oil

SEVILLE MARMALADE

6 lbs. Seville oranges

1 lemon

12 c. sugar

12 c. water

To prepare the herrings, clean and gut them, then take off heads and tails. Fillet, if wished, but whole is better. Beat yolks of eggs, dip herring in egg yolk, then coat in oatmeal and fry in oil 7 to 10 minutes, until cooked through. Serve hot, with buttered brown-bread toast served crisp and topped with Seville Marmalade.

Simmer unpeeled oranges in water until the fruit is soft; remove oranges, saving water. When cool, slice fruit coarsely. Save all the seeds in a muslin or cheesecloth bag. Place cut fruit in pan with the water you saved, enough additional water to total 12 cups, and the sugar. Boil fast until the syrup threads when tested. (Pour a little onto a saucer, wait till cool; then test with finger. If the liquid hangs in a thread, it is ready.) When mixture is cool enough, pour into jars. The marmalade will be pungent and tart—gorgeous on crisp toast!

Note: Seville oranges are often available only in January.

Anne Perry is a critically acclaimed writer of Victorian mysteries, having sold more than ten million copies of her books worldwide. The *New York Times* bestselling author is a native of London, England, but resides in Portmahomack, Scotland.

Falafels with Tahini Dressing

BRENT AND BONNIE BEESLEY

We have traveled to the Middle East many times. One moment in our journey stands out: the night of the change of the millennium. As the calendar turned on 31 December 2000, we stood on the shore of the Red Sea at the base of a holy mountain on the sands of ancient Egypt.

Back at home, a good friend, Khaled Salem, an Arab-Christian born in Jerusalem, raised in Amman, and now living in Salt Lake City, taught us how to make falafels—one of our favorite dishes and a delicious reminder of our time in that sacred land.

1 (1-lb.) bag garbanzo beans

1 (1-lb.) bag fava beans, peeled

2 bunches of parsley (stems removed)

1 bunch cilantro

½ of a small hot pepper

1 whole garlic

2 onions, peeled

Spice packet (recipe follows)

Baking powder

Fresh Pita bread

Chopped tomatoes (optional)

Shredded lettuce (optional)

Cucumber slices (optional)

Tahini Dressing (recipe follows)

Soak garbanzo and fava beans in cold water for 24 hours.

When ready to make falafels, process the parsley, cilantro, hot pepper, garlic, soaked garbanzo and fava beans, and onions in food processor. Add spice packet ingredients to taste. This recipe makes 24 servings, so you may want to remove part of the mixture and freeze for later use, depending on the number of people you plan to serve.

Place mixture in a medium-sized bowl; add 1 tablespoon baking powder for every third of the mixture and mix thoroughly. Form small balls of dough and fry in olive oil until brown, about 2 minutes. Place about 4 balls in pita bread with chopped tomatoes, lettuce, and cucumber for garnishes. Add Tahini dressing, if desired.

SPICE PACKET

1½ Tbs. salt, or to taste

1 Tbs. black pepper

1 Tbs. allspice

2 Tbs. cumin

2 Tbs. coriander

To prepare spice packet, mix ingredients thoroughly. Use only the amount needed for flavor.

TAHINI DRESSING

1 tomato, chopped

1 to 2 Tbs. parsley, chopped

Tahini sauce

Juice of ½ lemon

Salt

Water, as needed

To prepare Tahini Dressing, mix ingredients in small bowl, adding water only as needed for consistency. Tahini sauce is sesame paste in a can and can be purchased at Granatos in Salt Lake City or at other specialty stores.

Serves 24.

Brent Beesley is chairman and CEO of Heritage Bank, in St George, Utah. He holds a BA from BYU and an MBA and JD from Harvard University. During the savings and loan crisis in the early 1980s, Mr. Beesley was the director of the Office of the Federal Savings and Loan Insurance Corporation, Washington, D.C. He has been the president and CEO of the Farm Credit Corporation of America, in Denver, Colorado, which was the central entity of the nationwide Federal Farm Credit System. He served a mission in Argentina and now teaches the Gospel Doctrine class in his ward. He is married to the former Bonnie Jean Matheson. They have seven children.

Cornish Pasty

RICHARD AND MAGGIE TOPHAM

In this part of England the traditional meal is the pasty. Deep mining was a chief occupation of people in Cornwall for hundreds of years. In recent centuries, Cornish miners carried their skills and machinery to the prospering shafts of Lake Superior in the United States; and they rescued flooded mines in Grass Valley, California, with their ingenious pumps. Miners carried a food tradition of a potato-meat turnover, called a pasty, that was carried into the pits each day and heated on the miner's shovel held over a candle. The traditional meat pie in Cornwall consisted of "mayt" (meat), "turnits," (turnips), "tatys" (potatoes), and "honyons" (onions). Sealed in a pastry crust, the ingredients would stay fresh until consumed much later in the day.

It was said that the devil wouldn't come into Cornwall because Cornish women would put everything and anything into a pasty—so Lucifer was afraid he would be put into a pie. Looking over a few kinds of pasties, it's easy to see why: Apple pasty, broccoli pasty, chicken pasty, eggy pasty, herby pasty, jam pasty, mackerel pasty, meat and potato pasty, parsley pasty, pork pasty, rabbitty pasty, rice pasty, sour sauce pasty, star gazing pasty, turnip pasty, and windy pasty, Lammy Pies, Tatty Pies, Pilchard Pies, Curlew Pies, Giblet Pies, Squab Pies, Leek Pies—to name a few!

2 c. flour

Pinch of salt

½ c. lard or shortening

½ c. butter or margarine

Small amount of cold water, as needed

Preheat oven to 400° F.

Prepare the pastry, by combining flour and salt; cut in lard and butter until the mixture is mealy. Add a small amount of water to make the dough stick together and come to the proper consistency. Divide dough into 4 equal pieces. Roll each piece of pastry into a round approximately 7 inches in diameter.

1 lb. potatoes, thinly sliced

1 lb. turnips, thinly sliced

1 onion, thinly sliced

Salt & pepper to taste

2 Tbs. butter or margarine

1 lb. high-quality, lean beef, cut into
    ½-inch cubes

On each pastry round, place one-fourth of the vegetables and sprinkle on salt and pepper to taste. Add one-fourth of the meat and a pat of butter.

Dampen the edges of the pastry and bring up from both sides with floured hands to envelop the filling. Pinch the edges firmly together and crimp lightly with fork. Cook on a floured baking sheet for about 45 minutes.

The recipe is very much according to taste. Maggie always uses a lot of onion.

Makes 4 pasties.

Maggie and Richard Topham live on St. Michael's Mount in Cornwall, England. Maggie is the director of the Church Family History Center at Helston Ward. Richard works as a tour guide on St. Michael's Mount, meeting visitors from all over the world. He is involved with the humanitarian program and travels to the Balkans each year with aid. He is also involved locally with future developments at a home for the disabled where he works as a volunteer driver. The couple likes to spend as much time as possible working in the London Temple. They are the parents of four children and the grandparents of seven.

Rulltårta (Swiss Roll)

BIRGITTA KARLFELDT

When my youngest son, Michael, still lived at home, he was the expert on making this Swiss roll. He always got it just right—so he got to make it often!

2 eggs

⅔ c. sugar

1 c. flour

1½ tsp. baking powder

1 Tbs. cold water

Chocolate Butter Cream Filling
(recipe follows)

CHOCOLATE BUTTER CREAM FILLING

⅓ c. butter or margarine

1 c. powdered sugar

2 tsp. vanilla-flavored sugar

2 Tbs. orange peel marmalade
(optional)

1½ Tbs. cocoa (or more)

Line a 10x14x2-inch jelly-roll pan with waxed paper and preheat oven to 450° F. (You may want to lightly coat the paper with cooking spray to make turning out the cake easier.) Whip eggs and sugar until light and foamy. In large mixing bowl, stir flour and baking powder together; then add tablespoon of cold water and blend. Fold in egg mixture and spread batter evenly in pan. Bake for about 5 minutes or until cake bounces back when touched. Immediately turn pan upside down, releasing cake onto sugared waxed-paper or damp cloth. Remove waxed paper from top of cake. Cool. Spread with Chocolate Butter Cream Filling, then roll up the cake, starting from the long side.

Serves 15 to 20.

To make filling, stir butter until smooth. Add remaining ingredients and cream to spreading consistency.

Birgitta Karlfeldt is a prominent member of the Church in Sweden, where she serves as the editor of the Swedish *Liahona*. She has a master's degree in the English and Nordic languages and in Swedish literature and has taught at a senior high school for thirty years. She is the mother of three children and the grandmother of four.

Ruhrkuchen aus Sachsen (Saxony's Family Cake, Glazed)

DIETER AND HARRIET UCHTDORF

Elder Uchtdorf loves this cake with raisins. He can still remember when his grandmother made it in Zwickau, East Germany almost every weekend. Our children love it with chocolate chips and a very thick glaze. We eat this cake—which has been passed from one generation to the next—with a glass of milk, hot chocolate, or a cup of Pero. To make everybody happy, you can make one half of this cake with raisins and the other half with chocolate chips.

10 oz. (2½ sticks) unsalted butter, at room temperature

1 c. sugar

7 eggs

Grated zest of 1 lemon

½ tsp. salt

2 Tbs. vanilla

3 c. all-purpose flour

3 tsp. baking powder

2 c. raisins or 2 c. semi-sweet chocolate chips

Lemon Glaze (recipe follows)

LEMON GLAZE

2½ c. powdered sugar

Juice of one lemon

Preheat oven to 325° F.

Cream butter, using electric mixer on high speed. Gradually add sugar. Continue to beat until the mixture is light and fluffy. Add the eggs as you beat, one at a time. Mix in lemon zest, salt, and vanilla.

In a separate bowl, combine flour and baking powder. Add dry mixture, spoon by spoon, to wet mixture at medium speed. Lightly coat the raisins with flour (this keeps them from sinking to the bottom of the cake pan during baking). Stir in the raisins or chocolate chips. Transfer the mixture to a greased Bundt pan. Bake approximately 50 minutes. Let cake cool slightly before brushing with Lemon Glaze.

For lemon glaze, add juice to powdered sugar and mix well. Brush over warm cake.

Serves 12.

Elder Dieter F. Uchtdorf was sustained as a General Authority on April 6, 1994. He was senior vice president for flight operations and chief pilot for Lufthansa German Airlines, and check and training captain for Boeing 747s. He and his wife, Harriet Uchtdorf, grew up in Frankfurt, Germany. Harriet enjoys sports and the arts and most of all being with her family. She loves to entertain guests, trying out new international recipes. Brother and Sister Uchtdorf are the parents of two children and the grandparents of five.

Cherry Ripe

MARV WALLIN

We served this Australian cookie in the mission home every Thursday evening at the mission open house. There were normally about fifty-five missionaries and guests in attendance, and the word was out that the refreshments were worth the effort. A slush beverage was also served, consisting of frozen fruit juices mixed with soda. Former missionaries still ask us for the recipe.

1 (1-lb.) box graham crackers

½ lb. coconut, shredded or flaked

1 (4-oz.) pkg. candied cherries, chopped

1 (14-oz.) can sweetened condensed milk

Vanilla and red food coloring, as desired

4 oz. melted palmin

Chocolate topping (recipe follows)

CHOCOLATE TOPPING

⅔ c. powdered sugar

¼ c. cocoa

4 oz. palmin, melted

Place biscuits in bottom of a 9x13-inch baking pan. In large mixing bowl, stir together coconut, candied cherries, condensed milk, vanilla, food coloring, and melted palmin. Press down firmly on the biscuits. Pour warm Chocolate Topping over the top. Refrigerate until chilled. Cut into squares to serve.

Note: Palmin is available along the Wasatch Front at Seigfried's Deli and other food specialty stores.

Makes 40 cookies.

To make Chocolate Topping, mix powdered sugar and cocoa together. Add palmin very slowly, and beat well.

Marvin W. Wallin was co-owner and CEO of Bookcraft Publishers for thirty-seven years, overseeing the publication of LDS classics such as *Mormon Doctrine* and *The Miracle of Forgiveness*. He and his wife, Dorothy, presided over the Adelaide Australia Mission from 1977 to 1980. They are the parents of eight children and have thirty-eight grandchildren. He has been an avid antique car collector for many years and can be seen driving his 1931 Model A roadster from time to time. His long time goal . . . to be a publisher in the next world.

Home for the Holidays

RECIPES TO REMEMBER
FOR YOUR
HOLIDAY CELEBRATIONS

Christmas Eggs

RICHARD AND BARBARA WINDER

This recipe for Christmas Eggs has long been a family tradition for Christmas brunch. We have found it to be versatile enough to use for many other occasions, and it has followed us around the world doing just that! Christmas Eggs became the heart of a luncheon menu while we presided over the California San Diego Mission. When we served in the Czech and Slovak Republics, it was the center of a welcome breakfast for new missionaries. We found two-pound canned hams, which we used in place of the sausage. Whether served for breakfast with fruit and muffins, or for lunch with a spinach, apple, and craisin salad, it was always a sturdy, dependable recipe, for which we could find ingredients or substitutes. And it's always good accompanied by orange juice or hot chocolate.

6 slices of bread

2 lbs. sausage, cooked and drained

2 green onions, chopped

½ lb. cheddar cheese, grated

8 eggs

2 c. milk, divided

½ tsp. salt

Dash of pepper

1 (10¾-oz.) can mushroom soup

Prepare a 9x13-inch casserole with cooking spray. Line bottom of casserole with bread slices. Sprinkle with cooked sausage, then with onions and cheese. Beat eggs well; add 1½ cups of the milk, salt, and pepper. Pour mixture over all. Cover and refrigerate overnight to set.

About an hour before serving, preheat oven to 325° F. Mix the mushroom soup with ½ cup milk and pour over the chilled casserole. Bake at 325° F. for about 45 minutes.

Serves 12.

Richard W. Winder is the retired owner of Winder Dairy and Valley View Memorial Park and Funeral Home in Salt Lake City, Utah. He served as mission president over the California San Diego and Czechoslovakia Prague Missions and as a counselor in the Jordan River Temple presidency. His wife, Barbara Woodhead Winder, served at his side in each of these callings. And now serves with him as the first president and matron of the new Nauvoo Temple in Illinois. Sister Winder is a former Relief Society general president, serving from 1984 to 1990. The Winders are the parents of four children.

Ebleskivers

MAC CHRISTENSEN

Every Christmas morning our children and grandchildren gather at Grandmother's for a breakfast of sausage, bacon, eggs, hash browns, fruit, and the featured attraction—ebleskivers. The most popular spot is around the kitchen stove, where everyone lines up to get the light, rich balls as they come hot from the ebleskiver griddle. This tradition is so popular that new brides joining the family usually receive one or more cast iron ebleskiver pans as wedding gifts. (Ebleskiver pans are available at fine kitchen stores and most department stores.)

2 eggs (separated, with whites beaten until stiff)

½ tsp. salt

2 Tbs. sugar

1 tsp. baking powder

⅓ tsp. baking soda

1½ c. flour

½ c. cream

1 c. buttermilk

Shortening, as needed in griddle

Powdered sugar, syrup, honey, jam, fruit, as desired

Mix dry ingredients and stir in egg yolks, cream, and buttermilk. Fold in egg whites. Heat ebleskiver pan to a medium temperature, adding about ¼ to ½ teaspoon shortening to each cup. When griddle is hot, fill cup almost to the top; let cook a few minutes, and turn with a toothpick or other pointed tool. Cook until golden brown. Serve hot with choice of syrup, butter, honey, or jam. You can drop applesauce or a small slice of cooked fruit in center of each ebleskiver before turning. Ebleskivers may also be dusted with powdered sugar while warm.

Makes 2 dozen pancake balls.

Mac Christensen is best known as "Mr. Mac," the founder of the Mr. Mac chain of men's clothing stores. He is currently serving as president of the Tabernacle Choir and has previously served as director of the Church's visitors' center in Washington, D.C. He and his wife, Joan Graham, are the parents of eight children, the grandparents of thirty-five, and the great-grandparents of one.

Oma's Christmas Eve Baked Beans

HARRIS SIMMONS

For the past half century, one of our great family traditions has been to gather on Christmas Eve at the home of George and Oma Wilcox in Layton, Utah, with aunts, uncles, cousins, and other descendants of my grandfather, L. E. Ellison. Uncle George and Aunt Oma are gone now, but we continue to gather each year to hear the children tell stories and sing songs celebrating the birth of our Savior. There's always a wonderful but simple buffet, the center-piece of which is Oma's Christmas Eve Baked Beans. Aunt Oma had a way of turning run-of-the-mill pork and beans into something extraordinary. Served with baked ham, rolls, and salads, this makes for an easy, great meal for a crowd—whether during the holidays or for a tailgate party.

4 c. canned pork & beans

1 lb. bacon, cooked, drained, broken

1 c. brown sugar

1 c. ketchup

2 medium onions, chopped

2 large green peppers, chopped

2 tsp. Worcestershire sauce

Gently mix ingredients together in large bowl; pour into 2-quart baking dish or casserole. Bake at 325° F. for 2½ hours covered; uncover and bake another ½ hour. Serve hot. You can serve a crowd (40 to 50) by using 1 gallon pork and beans and multiplying the rest of the ingredients by 4.

Serves 10 to 12.

Harris Simmons is chairman, president, and CEO of Zions Bancorporation, a banking organization with over four hundred offices throughout the western United States. Under his leadership, Zions Bancorporation was named the nation's top performing bank in 1997. He is the recipient of the 2002 Distinguished Banker Award from the Utah Bankers Association. He and his wife, Amanda, are the parents of three children and live in Salt Lake City.

© Busath Photography

Corn Pudding (A Dinner Soufflé)

ORRIN HATCH

Orrin's wife, Elaine, writes: "This is a recipe Orrin's mother tore out of a magazine over thirty years ago. She used to make it for just Thanksgiving dinner. Then we talked her into making it for Christmas also. Through the years our whole family has insisted that this dish be included for all holiday meals.

"When I started making it for our own family, the kids and their father would have loved to have eaten it every Sunday. So it became a staple in our immediate family.

"After the children were married, whenever I would go to visit them, I would have to make Corn Pudding for their family. Now, all of our daughters and some of our son's wives make this favorite dish quite often; in fact, one grandson tries to get us to double the recipe so that he can graze on it for several days.

"Here it is: The Orrin Hatch Family Favorite—Corn Pudding (this is what it has always been called, and it was the name on the original recipe, but it is really a corn soufflé.)"

2 c. milk (don't use anything less than 1%)

4 eggs, beaten

1 c. soda cracker crumbs

1 (10½-oz.) can whole kernel corn, drained

1 c. sharp cheese, grated

Butter

Salt

Pepper

Paprika

Preheat oven to 350° F. Combine the milk and beaten eggs. Grease a round 2-quart baking dish, then layer the ingredients in the following order:

Half the cracker crumbs, half the drained corn, half the cheese. Dot with a little butter and sprinkle some salt and pepper on top, to taste. Pour half of the milk-egg mixture over the top.

Repeat the preceding steps, then sprinkle a little paprika over the top—just enough to look nice.

Bake 30 to 40 minutes. The soufflé should be high and slightly browned on top. This falls a little after taking out of the oven; but don't worry, it still tastes delicious!

Serves 8 to 12.

Orrin G. Hatch has been a United States senator (R-Utah) since 1976, passing legislation covering everything from tough criminal laws to AIDS research, from reducing costs of prescription drugs to child care. In his spare time, he enjoys writing lyrics for several songwriters. He and his wife, Elaine, are the parents of six children and the grandparents of twenty. Elaine spends much of her time serving as an ordinance worker in the Washington, D.C. Temple, of which Senator Hatch often says, "You get to work in heaven. I have to work in that other place."

Uppy's Sweet Potato Soufflé

JOHN AND LISA ADAMS

As with most American families, Thanksgiving is an important tradition for us. And because John is from a family of twelve children, Thanksgiving is a huge event. Often, more than forty of us gather for a midday meal. John's grandfather, J. Arza Adams, was a noted turkey rancher in Utah County, so the turkey is always wonderful and is the focal point of the meal. Delicious rolls, salads, and a family favorite, riced potatoes, as well as a variety of pies, are all part of the dinner. This is a fairly informal and relaxed meal, with little children abounding. Because of our vast numbers, everyone brings something. Early in our marriage, I was stymied about what I could contribute. My father, T. Upton Ramsey, is a Cordon Bleu-trained chef, so I called him for ideas. He suggested a sweet potato soufflé. It was an instant hit and has become a fixture at our Thanksgiving table. Nieces and nephews have requested the recipe as they have moved away and held their own dinners.

6 baked sweet potatoes, or 4 baked yams

¾ c. sugar

1 tsp. baking powder

1 tsp. cinnamon

½ c. butter, softened at room temp.

¾ c. buttermilk

2 eggs

1 tsp. vanilla

¾ c. whole pecans

½ c. crushed ginger snaps

1 Tbs. melted butter

Bake the sweet potatoes in a 400° F. oven for 1 hour, or until soft to the touch. While still hot, peel, slice, and mash into a large mixing bowl. Combine with sugar, baking powder, cinnamon, butter, buttermilk, eggs, and vanilla. Fold in pecans. Pour into a 2-quart baking dish. Mix the ginger snaps with 1 tablespoon melted butter and sprinkle on top. Bake at 350° F. for 30 minutes.

Serves 16.

John A. Adams, a shareholder in the law firm of Ray, Quinney, and Nebeker in Salt Lake City, is the president of the Utah State Bar for the 2002–2003 year. Both his undergraduate and law degrees are from Brigham Young University. He is a member of the Racial and Ethnic Fairness Commission and on the board of "Friends for Sight." John served a mission in Germany and has served in a variety of callings, ranging from bishop to Blazer leader. His wife, Lisa Ramsey Adams, holds a law degree from the University of Utah. Lisa has served on the board of the Children's Dance Theatre and as a volunteer for Utah's Foster Care Citizen Review Board. She was also an Olympic Winter Games volunteer. They are the parents of four children.

Pumpkin Pie

BETTY JEANNE CHIPMAN

This recipe is from my great-grandmother Eliza Edwards Stevens, who joined the LDS Church in England. I remember my grandmother and mother making it for Thanksgiving. To make it smooth and creamy, they put the squash through a potato ricer. When it was all blended with the other ingredients, they strained it into the pie shells. It is much easier to make now using a blender and it is nearly as creamy and buttery. Even those who don't like pumpkin pie like this recipe. It really should be called squash pie, but somehow that doesn't sound as traditional or appetizing. (For two pies, double the recipe.)

2 c. squash (preferably Hubbard), cooked

2 c. milk, divided

1 c. sugar

1 tsp. salt

1 tsp. cinnamon

1 tsp. ginger

2 eggs

1 9-inch pie crust

Preheat the oven to 375° F. Put the cooked squash and a cup of the milk in blender and blend until smooth. Mix sugar, salt, and spices in a separate bowl. Stir into the squash mixture. Add eggs and remaining milk, blending until thoroughly mixed. Pour into uncooked pie shell and bake at 375° F. for 10 minutes; then reduce heat to 325° F. and cook for about 1 hour. Test by putting knife into center of filling—if it comes out clean it is done. Top with whipped cream to serve.

Serves 8.

Betty Jeanne Chipman is an accomplished musician and teacher. She has been a lecturer, presenter, and clinician for several universities throughout the country and has taught at the University of Utah for more than thirty years. Many of her former students have gone on to successful careers with opera companies across the nation, including the Metropolitan Opera. She has performed with the Utah Opera Company and the Tabernacle Choir on many occasions. Betty Jeanne and her husband, the late D. LuZell Chipman "Chip," are the parents of five children, the grandparents of twelve, and the great-grandparents of fourteen.

Kleiner

ROBERT T. BARRETT

This is a recipe from my wife's grandmother, who joined the Church in Sweden and immigrated to Salt Lake City. She made these every Christmas, so we make them every Christmas in her honor.

6 eggs

½ c. butter

1½ c. sugar

½ c. canned milk

½ tsp. salt

1 tsp. vanilla

5 c. flour

3 tsp. baking powder

Powdered sugar

Combine eggs, butter, sugar, milk, salt, and vanilla. Then add dry ingredients. Roll dough into a triangle, and cut through dough to make long strips. Cut across strips diagonally to form smaller diamond shapes. Cut a slit in the center of each diamond shape. Pull the bottom corner through the cut in the center to make a twist. Deep fry the twists until light golden brown. Place on paper towels to drain. Sprinkle with powdered sugar, or eat plain.

Robert T. Barrett is a professor of illustration at Brigham Young University and a prolific professional muralist, painter, and illustrator. His paintings have appeared on the covers of numerous books, and he has illustrated several best-selling storybooks, including *The Story of the Walnut Tree* and *The Nauvoo Temple Stone*. His work has been exhibited across the country. Just before the *2002 Winter Olympics,* he completed a large commission for the Church at the North Visitors' Center at Temple Square. Robert and his wife, Vicki, have ten children and live in Provo, Utah.

White Christmas Fruitcake

SCOTT ANDERSON

My mother used to make this fruitcake every Christmas. It was the same that her mother used to make. Now I make it every Christmas to give to my brothers and sister. (It's actually best to make it at Thanksgiving and allow it to age.)

1 lb. butter

2 c. sugar

9 large eggs

Juice from 1 lemon

Grated zest from 1 lemon

1 lb. citron

½ lb. white raisins

1 lb. candied cherries

4 slices candied pineapple

4 c. sifted flour

1 lb. blanched almonds

Line four 4x6-inch loaf pans with 3 thicknesses of parchment paper and preheat oven to 300° F. or 325° F. Cream butter and sugar well. Add eggs 1 at a time and beat well. Add lemon juice and rind. Flour the fruit with ¼ cup of the flour. Add remaining flour to creamed mixture. Fold in fruits and nuts and blend well. Fill lined bread pans and bake for 2 hours. Wrap cooled loaves in aluminum foil and store in cool place until used. The fruitcake improves in flavor as it ages. Best if made by Thanksgiving for Christmas giving.

Makes 4 loaves.

A. Scott Anderson is president and CEO of Zions First National Bank, the lead-banking subsidiary of Zions Bancorporation. Scott has also spent seventeen years with the Bank of America in San Francisco and seven years in Bank of America's Asia Division in Tokyo, Japan. Scott and his wife, Jesselie, are the parents of three children and reside in Salt Lake City.

Rainy Day Gingerbread Boys

JOHN W. WELCH

When I was young, we would spend rainy afternoons rolling out, cutting, decorating, cooking, and, of course, eating these delicious creations. The house was filled with unforgettable sweetness. Our family always makes these cookies around Christmastime. We like to share them with friends and neighbors. Now that we have lots of grandchildren in the extended family, all of my siblings carry on this tradition. Every Christmas, all of the great-grandchildren spend an afternoon at my mother's enjoying a huge gingerbread feast. Everyone brings dough, and the old cookie cutters are spread out all over the place. And run, run, run, as fast as we can, we can't catch enough of the Gingerbread Man!

½ c. shortening or margarine

½ c. brown sugar

½ c. pure molasses

3½ c. flour

1 tsp. baking soda

½ tsp. salt

1 tsp. ground ginger

2 tsp. cinnamon

1 tsp. vinegar

½ c. buttermilk or sour cream

Preheat oven to 350° F. Cream shortening; add sugar gradually and cream thoroughly. Blend in molasses. Sift 1¼ cups of the flour with baking soda, salt, and spices; stir into molasses mixture. Add vinegar and remaining 2¼ cups flour, alternating with buttermilk. Chill dough, then roll out ¼-inch thick on a lightly floured board or pastry cloth. Dip cutters in flour each time before using. Place on baking sheet and bake for 10 to 15 minutes. This is an easy dough to handle, so children love making them.

Note: Be sure that the dough is at room temperature when you roll it out. If it's too cold, it isn't fun to squish around. And put a little flour on the rolling pin. Get the right thickness, too—if the cookies are too thin, they will be too crisp; too thick and . . . well, I like them thick.

Makes 2 dozen cookies.

John W. Welch is a professor of law at the J. Reuben Clark Law School at Brigham Young University, as well as founding director of the Foundation for Ancient Research and Mormon Studies (FARMS), and editor in chief of *BYU Studies*. While serving a mission in South Germany, he discovered chiasmus in the Book of Mormon. His wife, Jeannie Sutton, teaches French and is the director of the Foreign Language Student Residence at BYU. They have four children, all happily married. Currently he is the bishop of his home ward.

Sponge Cake

INGER SANDBERG

This beautiful cake is easy to make and delicious to eat. It lends itself best to a fruit topping and whipped cream. It does fall a little when it is finished, but it is always nice and light.

6 eggs

1 c. sugar

1 c. cake flour

1 tsp. baking powder

1 tsp. vanilla

¼ c. vegetable oil

Preheat oven to 350° F. Prepare two 9-inch cake pans with cooking spray. Beat eggs and sugar until very thick and creamy. Stir in flour, baking powder, and vanilla. Mix in vegetable oil until well incorporated; but do not overbeat. Pour batter in equal amounts into the two pans. Bake at 350° F. for 30 minutes. Turn off oven, leaving the cakes in the oven for about 5 minutes, with the door slightly open. Remove from pan; cool on rack.

Serves 10.

Inger Sandberg, a native of Tjome, Norway, worked for the Underground Resistance during World War II and served as editor of the underground newspaper. After the war, she came to the United States and lived in Long Island, New York, where she joined The Church of Jesus Christ of Latter-day Saints. Inger has been a Relief Society Sunday School teacher in Los Gatos, California.

Rice Pudding

RODNEY H. BRADY

As a young boy growing up in a family of two parents and four children, nothing pleased me more than to arrive home from school and find a very large saucepan of Rice Pudding, with an overabundance of raisins, cooking on my mother's kitchen stove. Within minutes of our arrival home, my sister and two brothers and I could be found seated at our designated places around the kitchen table devouring bowl after bowl of the pudding—sometimes seasoned with some extra cinnamon. Happily, my mother, Jessie Madsen Brady, made a sufficiently large supply of Rice Pudding that there was not only plenty left over for my father, Kenneth A. Brady, when he arrived home from work, but there was usually an ample supply for a late night snack, and perhaps a helping or two for the next day—on a first-come-first-served basis.

3 c. cooked rice

Whole milk

1½ tsp. vanilla

Raisins, amount desired

Cinnamon, to taste

½ c. sugar

2 eggs, well beaten

Nutmeg

Add enough milk to rice to make the mixture soupy; then stir in vanilla, raisins, cinnamon, and sugar, and bring to boiling point. Reduce heat to low. Remove a spoonful of the milk mixture and stir it into the beaten eggs. Slowly pour and stir the egg mixture into the saucepan. Cook 20 minutes on low heat, until thickened. Sprinkle with nutmeg when serving. May serve warm or chilled.

Serves 6 to 8.

Rodney H. Brady is president and CEO of Deseret Management Corporation, the holding company that oversees the commercial businesses of The Church of Jesus Christ of Latter-day Saints. He previously served as president and CEO of Bonneville International Corporation, president of Weber State University, as a member of the Sub-cabinet of the President of the United States, and as assistant secretary of the U.S. Department of Health, Education, and Welfare. He holds a doctor of business administration degree from Harvard University. He has served in many community and church assignments including local and national leadership appointments in the Boy Scouts of America. He served as a missionary to Great Britain and as president of the Los Angeles California Stake. He and his wife, Carolyn "Mitzi" Hansen, are the parents of three sons.

© Busath Photography

Holiday Trifle

JOHN AND KIMBERLY BYTHEWAY

My mother, Diane Loveridge, created this dessert for our annual family Christmas dinner. We have enjoyed it as the pinnacle of our Christmas night celebration ever since I was a small child. Now our children enjoy it as a traditional treat at Grandma's house. It truly is something that we all look forward to as part of the holiday.

To save time when preparing the trifle, you may prefer to buy the angel food cake at the bakery. Use a large, glass, trifle bowl to layer ingredients. Be careful not to spill on the inside of the bowl, or the beautiful layered effect viewed from the outside will be marred.

½ of a baked angel food cake

1 (4¾-oz.) pkg. Junkett® Danish Dessert, raspberry flavor

1 c. frozen raspberries, crushed

1 (5.1-oz.) pkg. vanilla instant pudding

2½ c. milk

1 c. heavy cream, whipped

3 Tbs. sugar

1 tsp. vanilla

3 bananas

Maraschino cherries, well drained and halved

Christmas holly leaves

Cut angel food cake into bite-sized squares and set aside.

Prepare Danish dessert according to for pudding package directions; allow the dessert to cool, then add crushed frozen raspberries and set aside.

In a separate bowl, prepare pudding by pouring milk into the powdered pudding mix and stirring well; set aside. Combine whipped cream, sugar, and vanilla, then fold into pudding. Slice in bananas and stir.

To assemble the trifle, repeat the following three times: (1) Layer a third of the cake pieces in the bottom of the trifle bowl, (2) drizzle a third of the raspberry dessert over the cake, and (3) spoon a third of the vanilla pudding over the raspberry dessert. Decorate the top layer with real holly leaves and halved Maraschino cherries to make holly berry design. (Be sure to drain the cherries well, as they might "bleed" into the pudding.)

Serves 10 to 12.

John Bytheway is a sought-after fireside and motivational speaker. He has written a number of best-selling books for youth and adults. His wife, Kimberly Loveridge, graduated from BYU with a degree in English and co-authored, with John, *What We Wish We'd Known When We Were Newlyweds*. The Bytheways are the parents of three children and live in Salt Lake City, Utah.

Christmas Caramels

BONNIE GOODLIFFE

For many years we have given red cellophane-wrapped cups of these caramels to special friends, neighbors, and coworkers during the Christmas season. It is probably the only culinary accomplishment associated with my name. The recipe came from Blanche Sheffield, whose husband was in the stake presidency of my BYU stake in the late 1960s.

If the candy cooks too long, the caramels will be hard as a rock. If not cooked long enough, the caramels will not be firm enough to cut into pieces, though the flavor will be good. Soft candy can be put back in a heavy saucepan, returned to a boil, cooked to 236° F., and poured out to set again.

1 thin slice butter

2 c. white corn syrup

2 c. granulated sugar

½ can sweetened condensed milk (not evaporated milk)

3 c. heavy whipping cream

1 Tbs. vanilla

1 c. nuts (optional, I don't include them)

Butter a 9x9-inch dish or pan and set aside.

In a heavy 3-quart saucepan, cook corn syrup and sugar over medium-high heat. Meanwhile, pour condensed milk into the top of a double boiler pan; slowly add whipping cream, stirring constantly until smooth. Set pan atop simmering water.

When the sugar mixture is boiling fairly hard and has become golden in color, and when the cream mixture in the double boiler begins to scald, begin adding cream to the boiling sugar mixture. Keep the sugar mixture boiling while adding cream one scoop at a time; stir frequently. At this point you must stay by the stove until caramels are done, stirring every minute or two to prevent burning. After adding the cream, continue to cook until temperature reaches firm-ball stage (about 236° F.). Remove pan from heat; add vanilla, stirring briefly. Pour mixture into buttered 9x9-inch pan. Work fast and be careful—the candy will be very hot. Cover caramel candy pan with foil, and don't disturb it until candy is solid—several hours or overnight. When candy is set, remove foil and cut a long 1-inch-wide strip from the pan. Place strip on prepared cutting surface and cut it into individual pieces. Wrap each piece in waxed paper or cellophane. Repeat until all candy has been divided and wrapped.

Makes 100 pieces.

Bonnie L. Goodliffe studied piano and organ at the San Francisco Conservatory of Music, Brigham Young University, and the Mozarteum in Salzburg, Austria. She holds bachelor's and master's degrees in music theory from BYU. Since 1979 she has been an organist on Temple Square in Salt Lake City where she performs organ recitals and accompanies the Temple Square Chorale and the Mormon Tabernacle Choir. She is a Fellow in the American Guild of Organists and serves on the National Certification Committee of the Guild. She and her husband, Glade P. Goodliffe, have seven children and five grandchildren.

Hot Fudge Topping

SHARON G. LARSEN

This is former Young Women general president Margaret Nadauld's favorite! I make extra and bring it to her in a disposable carton. I also used it to bribe the secretaries in the Young Women office. They liked to dip fresh strawberries in it or drizzle it over Bavarian cream puffs. It is also good in Pears Helene: put a scoop of good ice cream in the center of a pear and drizzle hot fudge sauce over it.

2 c. granulated sugar

4 Tbs. cocoa

4 Tbs. butter

1 (12-oz.) can evaporated milk

2 tsp. vanilla

Heat sugar and cocoa over low heat about 2 minutes, stirring continuously. Add butter and blend in thoroughly. Turn range up to medium heat; add milk slowly, stirring constantly. As mixture boils, continue stirring a full 5 minutes. Remove from heat; add vanilla. Serve warm or refrigerate and reheat later. *Makes 2 cups.*

Sharon Greene Larsen attended the University of Alberta and graduated from Brigham Young University with a bachelor of science degree. She taught in elementary schools in Utah and Missouri. She wrote, produced, and starred in programs for the Utah Network for Instructional Television. She has twice served on the Young Women general board and in the Young Women general presidency and served as the national president of Lambda Delta Sigma. Sister Larsen taught institute at two colleges. She and her husband, Dr. Ralph T. Larsen, are the parents of two children and three grandchildren.

Indulgences

DECADENT DESSERTS, PIES, PUDDINGS, AND ICE CREAM DISHES

Apple Crisp

JEROLD AND JOANN OTTLEY

The man in our house has a lifelong weakness for fruit cobblers (thanks to his mom, of course). The recipe satisfies his craving, is low in sugar (an important item in our family), and much faster to prepare than a traditional cobbler. Simple, nutritious, fast, and delicious. What more can we ask?

2 c. oats

½ c. butter, melted

2 to 3 Tbs. brown sugar (or white sugar or granular fructose)

½ c. chopped pecans

5 to 6 apples

¼ c. water

¾ tsp. cinnamon

½ tsp. salt

Preheat oven to 375° F. Combine oats, melted butter, brown sugar, and chopped pecans; set aside.

Peel, core, and slice apples and place in 9x13-inch pan. Sprinkle with water, cinnamon, and salt. Cover with crumbed oatmeal topping and bake for 30 to 40 minutes. Serve warm with vanilla ice cream or half and half cream.

Serves 10.

Jerold Ottley directed the Mormon Tabernacle Choir for twenty-five years and is now the director of the new Tabernacle Choir Training School. His wife, JoAnn South Ottley, is a soprano vocalist, recording artist, and former vocal coach for the Tabernacle Choir; she now teaches vocals at the training school. Brother Ottley is currently serving on the high council of the South Cottonwood Stake and Sister Ottley as Gospel Doctrine leader and ward organist. They are the parents of two children and the grandparents of one grandson.

Peach-Raspberry Cobbler

JANE CLAYSON

This dessert is a Clayson family favorite. How can you go wrong with peaches and raspberries? (Peaches and blueberries make a great combination too.) I remember this cobbler most fondly as a treat after family home evening on Monday nights.

1½ c. unsifted all-purpose flour

2 Tbs. sugar

1¼ tsp. baking powder

½ tsp. baking soda

½ tsp. salt

½ c. cold, unsalted butter, cut into bits

½ c. cold buttermilk

1 tsp. grated lemon zest

1 Tbs. fresh lemon juice

⅛ tsp. coarsely ground black pepper

3¾ lbs. firm, ripe peaches

1 c. sugar

3 Tbs. cornstarch

¼ tsp. ground cardamom

¼ tsp. ground cinnamon

½ pint raspberries

2 Tbs. unsalted butter

In large bowl, combine flour, sugar, baking powder, baking soda, and salt. Cut in butter until mixture resembles fine crumbs. Add buttermilk, stirring with fork just until dough cleans sides and bottom of bowl, forming clumps. Cover bowl. Refrigerate while preparing fruit filling.

Preheat oven to 350° F. In a large bowl, combine lemon zest, juice, and pepper. Set aside. Place peaches in a pan of boiling water for 30 seconds. Remove peaches with a slotted spoon and place in a bowl of ice water. Remove skins, halve, and pit. Cut peaches into ⅜-inch-thick wedges; add to zest mixture.

In a separate bowl, prepare sugar mixture by combining sugar, cornstarch, cardamom, and cinnamon. Sprinkle over peaches; add raspberries. Transfer to a shallow, 3-quart baking dish. Dot with butter. With floured fingers, drop small, uneven clumps of biscuit dough over top until fruit is covered to within 1¼ inches of edge of baking dish. Bake 48 to 50 minutes, until golden and bubbly. Cool on rack 1 hour, or until warm.

Serves 8.

As an anchor and correspondent for CBS News, Jane Clayson provides in-depth, original reporting for *48 Hours* and the "Eye on America" segments of the *CBS Evening News*. Previously, Jane co-anchored, with Bryant Gumbel, *The Early Show* on CBS. She has also been a correspondent for *ABC Network News* in Los Angeles (1996–99), reporting for *World News Tonight* and *Good Morning America* network broadcasts. Between 1990 and 1996 she anchored and reported for KSL-TV in Salt Lake City. Her work has received numerous awards from the Society of Professional Journalists, as well as an Emmy and the prestigious Edward R. Murrow Award from the Radio and Television News Directors Association.

Mystery Dessert

JANENE WOLSEY BAADSGAARD

This one is quick, easy, and great with your favorite ice cream. This is called Mystery Dessert because you can add one can (any size, any type of fruit) and it will turn out differently each time you prepare it. But it always tastes great.

1 c. sugar

1 c. flour

1 tsp. baking soda

1 tsp. salt

1 egg

1 can mystery fruit (i.e., peaches, spiced apples, cherries, gooseberries)

1 tsp. vanilla

½ c. brown sugar

½ c. mystery topping (i.e., raisins, nuts, chocolate chips)

Mix all ingredients together in a baking dish. Level and top with brown sugar. You can also top with raisins, nuts, chocolate chips, or any other "mystery" topping to add to the "mystery" of this quick, easy, and inexpensive dessert.

Bake at 325° F. for 45 minutes.

Serving amount is a mystery that depends on whether or not you have teenage sons living in your home.

Janene Wolsey Baadsgaard is a homemaker and free-lance writer. She has been a columnist for the *Deseret News* and has taught English and literature classes at Utah Valley State College. Her work ranges from humorous and practical advice for mothers and fathers to clever and hilarious fiction. Her next project is a comprehensive book on mothering called *The LDS Mother's Almanac*, which will be published in April 2003. She and her husband, Ross, are the parents of ten children and the grandparents of three. They live in Spanish Fork, Utah.

Apple Dumplings

WILLIAM SMART

Growing up in Star Valley, Wyoming, Donna always walked home from school for lunch. Her memories of the walk home in the cold, crunchy snow are inextricably entwined with the delicious smell of apple dumplings baking and the rush of warm air at the opening of the front door. Her mother's apple pudding dumplings were "to die for." Imagine our surprise after we were married, to find out we both had fond memories of apple dumplings. Both our mothers cooked mainly without recipes; but this comes as close as possible to the way Donna's mother's dumplings tasted.

2 c. sugar

2 c. water

¼ tsp. cinnamon

¼ tsp. nutmeg

¼ c. butter

6 apples

2 c. enriched flour

1 tsp. salt

2 tsp. baking powder

¾ c. shortening

½ c. milk or cream

Preheat oven to 350° F. Combine sugar, water, cinnamon, and nutmeg in a medium saucepan. Heat mixture until sugar is dissolved and the syrup comes to a boil; remove from heat; Add butter and set aside. Pare and core apples; cut in quarters. For crust, sift flour, salt, and baking powder; cut in shortening. Stir in milk. Roll dough to ¼-inch thick; cut in 5-inch squares. Place 4 pieces of apple on each square, arranging the pieces together again in the shape of an apple. Sprinkle generously with additional sugar, cinnamon, and nutmeg; dot with butter. Fold corners to center, pinching edges together to seal. Place 1 inch apart on greased 9x13-inch baking pan. Pour syrup over the dumplings. Bake for 35 minutes, or until lightly browned. Serve hot with milk or cream, as conscience or diet allows.

Serves 6.

Bill's Quick Version: Use biscuit mix, prepared according to package and rolled out thin. Slice apples into center of rolled dough, sprinkle with sugar, flour, butter, cinnamon, and nutmeg. Pinch the whole thing together, pour syrup over, and bake until browned—and a fork prick signals the apples are done. Mmm, good!

William B. Smart spent forty years with the *Deseret News*, including fourteen years as editor and general manager. He has subsequently served as senior editor at the *Deseret News*, editor of *This People* magazine, and president of the Utah Innovation Foundation. He served twenty-five years on the general boards of the Sunday School and the Young Men's Mutual Improvement Association. He and his wife, the former Donna Toland, live in Salt Lake City.

Banana Cream Dessert

VICTOR CLINE

1 c. flour

2 Tbs. sugar

½ c. nuts

½ c. butter

8 oz. cream cheese, softened

1 c. powdered sugar

1 (12-oz.) tub Cool Whip®, divided

1 tsp. vanilla

2 to 3 bananas, sliced

2 (3.4-oz.) pkg. instant vanilla pudding

3 c. milk

½ tsp. banana extract

Chocolate shavings (optional)

Preheat oven to 400° F. Combine flour, sugar, and nuts. Cut in butter and press mixture into a 9x13-inch baking pan. Bake 8 to 12 minutes or until lightly browned.

Prepare the cream cheese layer by combining cream cheese, powdered sugar, 3 cups of the Cool Whip, and vanilla in a mixing bowl. Mix on medium speed until well blended.

Spread cream cheese mixture on top of baked short-bread; top with 2 to 3 sliced bananas.

Prepare pudding layer by mixing pudding, milk, and banana extract on low speed for 2 minutes. Spread over sliced bananas. Cover with remaining 1½ cups Cool Whip. If desired, sprinkle with milk chocolate shavings.

Serves 12.

Dr. Victor Cline graduated from the University of California, Berkeley with a Ph.D. in psychology. He has been a research scientist with George Washington University's Human Resources Research Office and is an emeritus professor in psychology at the University of Utah. He is in private practice in Salt Lake City. Victor and his wife, Lois, are presidents of Marriage and Family Enrichment, a seminar group that teaches communication and marital skills nationwide. He has written a number of books on marriage, parenting, and the media. Lois is a passionate, creative, gourmet cook who has a talent for turning the ordinary into a sumptuous creation. They are the parents of nine children and the grandparents of twenty-eight.

Raspberry Delight

GORDON SMITH

½ c. margarine, melted

1½ c. flour

8 oz. cream cheese

1 (8 oz.) tub Cool Whip®, thawed

1 c. powdered sugar

1¾ c. granulated sugar

6 Tbs. cornstarch

2 c. water

1 small pkg. raspberry Jell-O®

2 Tbs. butter

½ tsp. almond extract

Whipped cream or Cool Whip®, for topping

Preheat oven to 375° F. Combine margarine and flour and press mixture into bottom of a 9x13-inch baking pan. Bake for 15 minutes. Let cool.

In a large bowl, blend cream cheese, Cool Whip, and powdered sugar. Spread over cooled crust.

Put sugar, cornstarch, water, and raspberry Jell-O in a medium saucepan and cook over medium-high heat until thickened, stirring continuously to dissolve Jell-O. Remove from heat; stir in butter and almond extract. Let mixture cool, then spread over cream cheese mixture. Chill in refrigerator six hours. Top with whipped cream.

Serves 12.

Senator Gordon Harold Smith graduated from Brigham Young University in 1976 and earned a law degree from Southwestern University in 1979. After working as an attorney in private practice, Senator Smith assumed management of his family's frozen vegetable processing company, a position he held until his election to the United States Senate in 1996. He first entered politics in 1992 when he was elected to the Oregon Senate. Senator Smith and his wife, Sharon, have three children and maintain homes in Pendleton, Oregon, and Bethesda, Maryland.

Frozen Raspberry Delight

PETER VIDMAR

2 c. crushed chocolate wafer cookies

⅓ c. butter or margarine, melted

¼ c. sugar

1 c. chocolate fudge sauce, softened

1 qt. vanilla ice cream, slightly softened

1 pt. raspberry sherbet, slightly softened

1 (12-oz.) pkg. frozen raspberries (without syrup)

1 (8-oz.) tub frozen whipped topping, thawed

In a medium bowl, combine chocolate wafers, melted butter, and sugar; mix well. Reserve ¼ cup to use as topping. Press remaining crust into 9x13-inch pan. Refrigerate 15 minutes. Spread chocolate fudge sauce over crust. Spoon vanilla ice cream over chocolate. Place spoonfuls of sherbet randomly over ice cream; use a knife to swirl gently. Top with raspberries gently pressed into ice cream. Spread whipped topping over berries and top with reserved crumbs. Cover; freeze 6 hours or overnight. Let stand at room temperature for 15 to 20 minutes before serving.

Serves 20.

Peter Vidmar captained the U.S. Men's Gymnastics Team to its first-ever Olympic gold medal in 1984. He also captured the gold in the pommel horse, scoring a perfect 10, and he became the first American to take a medal (silver) in the individual all-around men's competition. His winning performances average 9.89, making him the highest-scoring U.S. male gymnast in Olympic history. He now lives in California with his wife, Donna, and their five children. He translates his skills as a leader and motivator into inspirational presentations for Fortune 500 companies looking to benefit from his gold-medal performances.

Frozen Lemon Pie

BRETT RAYMOND

This is one of my favorite desserts, and it has a good story to it that always makes me laugh. Years ago, before I was born, my parents worked for the railroad—my dad for the U.P. (Union Pacific) and my mom for the P.F.E. (Pacific Fruit Express). One hot July she was on her way home from work, walking from the P.F.E. up 24th Street in Ogden to their apartment. It was *so* hot and she was remembering the frozen lemon pie she had made. Oh, how she was looking forward to getting home and biting into that delicious cool, creamy refreshment. Finally she walked through the door of their downstairs apartment; the highly anticipated moment had come, and . . . well, gone. There in the sink was the pie tin, a fork, and some crumbs. As she stood there, wide-eyed with disbelief, she realized that my dad had eaten the whole thing and then had gone off to work. I laugh thinking about how a person can just sit there and eat the whole thing! (Yeah, I know, but Ben & Jerry's Chunky Monkey pints are small, pies are *big*.) She found out later that he had been sitting on the couch listening (no TV then) to the all-star game. Really, girls, what's a man to do? . . . Enjoy this—but leave a little for your wife!

3 egg yolks

Juice of 2 lemons

Grated zest from 1 lemon

½ c. sugar

1 c. whipped cream

3 egg whites, beaten stiff

3 Tbs. sugar

Vanilla wafer crumbs (or graham cracker crumbs)

With a wire whisk, beat the egg yolks, lemon juice, lemon zest, and sugar. Place mixture in top of a double boiler and cook slowly to make a custard, stirring continuously. Remove from heat when thickened, and let cool. Whip the cream, then beat the egg whites until stiff; fold in sugar and whipped cream. Fold this mixture into the cooled custard. Line a glass pie dish with vanilla wafer crumbs; fill with lemon custard. Freeze until firm, then slice and serve. You can also cook the custard in the microwave: Whisk custard ingredients very well in a microwave bowl. Cook in microwave on high power, stirring every 2 minutes twice; then stir every minute until it reaches the desired thickness. Watch it carefully so it does not boil over or get too thick. Let cool. Follow instructions as given above.

Serves 8 (. . . or 1).

Brett Raymond is a talented composer, arranger, and performer. Television stations and movie studios throughout the world often use Brett's work for promotions and theme songs. His music can be heard on NBC's *Today Show*, *Oprah*, and ABC's *Wide World of Sports*. His trademark sound on albums such as *A Case of Pop*, *Primarily for Grown-ups*, and *Primarily for Christmas* has won him many fans throughout the world. Brett and his wife, Becky, are the parents of five and reside in Bountiful, Utah.

Kate's Classic Cheesecake

JOSEPH BRICKEY

Great desserts are like great works of art—they remind us that there's more to life than just rice and beans. They tap into those taste buds that highlight what it means to be human. We who are served the handiwork of the gifted are grateful for our capacity to savor and for the capacity of others to create. I would like to thank Kate Lees for this recipe, and for that magical touch that comes with her passion to not just feed the hungry but to make them wish they could never be filled!

½ c. butter

⅓ c. sugar

1 c. all-purpose flour

½ Tbs. vanilla

⅔ c. pecans, crushed

4 (8-oz.) pkgs. cream cheese

1½ c. sugar

4 large eggs

1 (12-oz.) pkg. milk chocolate morsels

Preheat oven to 350° F. Prepare crust by creaming butter and sugar; gradually mix in the flour. Add vanilla and pecans. Work into a firm ball and spread into bottom of a 9-inch springform pan. Bake for 12 minutes. Meanwhile, beat cream cheese, then gradually add 1½ cups sugar. Add eggs one at a time, mixing after each one. Stir in chocolate chips. Pour batter into baked crust. Bake for 1 hour. Remove and let cool on rack. The cheesecake may be served warm—or after chilling in refrigerator.

Serves 8 to 10.

Joseph Brickey's award-winning paintings have appeared in many Church publications, on the cover of several books, and have been displayed in the Springville Museum of Art and the Joseph Smith Memorial Building. A large number of his paintings hang in temples throughout the Church. His book of paintings, *When Jesus Was Born in Bethlehem*, was an immediate bestseller. Joseph is the fourth of twelve children born to Wayne and Joanne Brickey and resides in Orem, Utah.

Milwaukee Cheesecake

JENNY OAKS BAKER

My mother, June Dixon Oaks, was a fabulous cook, and I have all of her best recipes. However, she was such a great cook that she rarely wrote down precise directions as to how to create a dish, and many of her recipes are also missing some of the ingredients. This didn't affect her cooking, as she knew how to create each dish; but it has made it difficult for me to replicate her cooking. Through trial and error (and lots of phone calls to my sisters, who have good memories), I have been able to recreate many of her dishes. These are two of my favorites.

2½ c. graham cracker crumbs (17 crackers)

⅓ c. sugar

⅔ c. butter, melted

1 (16-oz.) pkg. marshmallows

¾ c. milk

2 (8-oz.) pkgs. cream cheese

2 c. whipped cream

Can of cherry or blueberry pie filling

To make crust, combine cracker crumbs, sugar, and melted butter. Press into a 9x13-inch pan, reserving one-fourth of the mixture for the topping. If you're short on time, as I always am, instead of making the crust from scratch, use 2 store-bought 9-inch graham cracker crumb crusts.

In a heavy pan, melt marshmallows in milk over low heat. In large bowl, combine melted marshmallows with cream cheese. Allow to cool to room temperature. Fold in whipped cream until smooth. Pour filling on top of crumb crust in pan. Top with remaining crumbs. Chill until ready to serve. Top each slice with large spoonful of pie filling.

Serves 12.

Coconut/Banana Cream Pie

JENNY OAKS BAKER

PASTRY SHELL

2½ c. flour

1 c. shortening

¾ tsp. salt

1 egg

6 Tbs. water

1 Tbs. vinegar

To prepare pastry shell: Preheat oven to 350° F. Work together flour, shortening, and salt until crumbly. Mix in egg, water, and vinegar. Roll out pastry and place in a 9-inch pie plate. Prick crust with fork all over; bake for 15 to 20 minutes. Cool on rack until ready to fill.

FILLING

1 c. sugar

6 Tbs. cornstarch

1 tsp. salt

6 Tbs. flour

4 c. whole milk

2 eggs, slightly beaten

½ pint whipped cream

1 to 2 tsp. vanilla

2 c. coconut

3 to 4 bananas, sliced

Extra whipping cream for topping

To prepare filling: Combine sugar, cornstarch, salt, and flour in a heavy pan. Stir in milk. Bring to a boil over medium-high heat, stirring constantly until thick. Remove from heat; pour a spoonful or two of the hot mixture into the beaten eggs and stir well. Add egg mixture to hot mixture. Bring to a boil, then remove from heat to cool. Stir in the whipped cream, 1 to 2 teaspoons vanilla, and coconut. Line pie shell with sliced bananas. Cover bananas with filling. Top with whipped cream.

Serves 8.

Jenny Oaks Baker began playing the violin at the age of four and made her solo recital debut in 1983, when she was just eight years old. Since then, Jenny has played throughout Europe, Asia, and the United States. She has performed in Carnegie Hall and at Lincoln Center, and has soloed with the Jerusalem Symphony, the San Diego Symphony, the Utah Symphony, and the Mormon Tabernacle Choir. Jenny has received multiple Pearl Awards from the Faith Centered Music Association for her albums. Jenny received her master's degree from the Juilliard School in New York City and hold's a bachelor's degree in violin performance from the Curtis Institute of Music in Philadelphia. She is a first violinist in the National Symphony Orchestra, and lives in Northern Virginia with her husband, Matthew Baker, and their daughter, Laura June.

Chocolate Angel Pie

ELAINE CANNON

As young mothers, we looked forward to book club gatherings once a month; they were an escape from the blessings of baby talk and peanut butter sandwiches with our numerous little children. Twelve of us took turns hosting, with each hostess pulling out all stops to delight the rest. It was on such an occasion that I first tasted Chocolate Angel Pie. I hadn't guessed there could be a way to improve on a Hershey's almond bar, but one of the girls proved it could be done when she served this dessert. It was such a hit that we wanted to have it every month!

MERINGUE CRUST

2 egg whites

Pinch of salt

⅛ tsp. cream of tartar

½ c. sugar

½ tsp. vanilla

CHOCOLATE FILLING

1½ c. whipped cream

3 small Hershey's® chocolate almond bars

3 Tbs. water

1 Tbs. vanilla

1 drop almond extract

Dark chocolate shavings

Maraschino cherry (optional) to top

Preheat oven to 300° F. Beat egg whites until fluffy, with a pinch of salt and cream of tartar. Stir in sugar and vanilla. Handling lightly, spread into a 9-inch glass pie plate. Bake on middle rack of oven for 1 hour. Let cool on countertop while preparing filling.

Whip cream, setting aside 1 cup for filling. Sweeten the remainder of the whipped cream with a sprinkle of powdered sugar; cover and set in refrigerator to use later for topping.

In small saucepan, carefully melt Hershey almond bars (do not scorch); let cool slightly. (Chocolate bars may be melted in a mixing bowl in the microwave for about a minute—time varies according to individual microwave ovens—then stirred to completely soften.) Stir water, vanilla, and almond extract into melted chocolate-almond mixture. Fold in reserved 1 cup whipped cream until blended. Spoon into meringue pie shell and chill in refrigerator for at least 3 hours (but not overnight). To serve, garnish slices with dollop of sweetened whipped cream and chocolate shavings; top with a cherry, if desired.

Serves 12.

Tried-and-True Apple Pie

ELAINE CANNON

Jim and I reared our family on a half-acre property, restoring the farmhouse in the middle of a small orchard. We had plums, pears, apricots, peaches, cherries, and apples and we taught our children about pruning, spraying, picking—and minding the dropped fruit while cutting the lawn. Superb fresh fruit pies and tart plum jam continue to be family traditions. I am something of a connoisseur of apple pies in every land; but this traditional American apple pie is the tried-and-true, best recipe of all—and my favorite!

2 Tbs. flour

2 Tbs. cornstarch

¾ c. sugar

½ tsp. salt

¼ tsp. nutmeg

¼ tsp. allspice

2 tsp. cinnamon

10 to 12 medium-sized, tart apples (preferably Jonathan), peeled, cored, and sliced

Grated zest and juice of ½ lemon (large)

¼ c. butter, cut in pieces

Golden raisins & chopped walnuts (opt.)

Recipe for double pie crust

Blend dry ingredients in very large mixing bowl; add apple slices and gently toss, coating well. Drizzle with juice and sprinkle with lemon zest. Heap apple mixture into a prepared 9-inch shell, peaking apples in the center. Use enough apples so that the pie shell is full and mounded. Before adding top crust, dot apple mixture with butter pieces. At this point, add golden raisins and chopped walnuts—if you really want to! Preheat oven to 425° F. Fold over top crust and slit crust with appropriate design for steam vents. Place crust over mounded fruit in shell and pinch pie crust edges together to seal. Brush crust with cream or lightly beaten egg white; sprinkle with granulated sugar. Bake at 425° F. for 12 minutes. Reduce heat to 350° F.; bake 45 more minutes, until apples are tender and crust golden brown. Serve warm.

Serves 8.

Elaine Cannon has published seventy books in her long career as a writer and editor. A former general president of the Young Women organization, Sister Cannon also lectured for BYU's continuing education program for thirty years and served as associate editor for several Church magazines. Elaine is the wife of the late D. James Cannon and lives in Salt Lake City, Utah. She currently serves as the Relief Society president of the Salt Lake Emigration Stake.

Rhubarb Cream Pie

WILLIAM SMART

Both Donna and I have fond memories of rhubarb pie at home. It is best in my mother's hot, water-lard homemade crust; but since lard is a no-no nowadays, make it with your own favorite crust.

1½ c. sugar

3 Tbs. flour

½ tsp. nutmeg

1 Tbs. butter

2 eggs, well-beaten

3 c. rhubarb, cut up

Pie crust for 2-crust pie

Preheat oven to 450° F. Blend sugar, flour, nutmeg, and butter. Add eggs. Beat until smooth. Pour over rhubarb in 9-inch pastry-lined pie pan. Top with pastry and pinch edges to seal. Cut several slits in pastry top to allow steam to escape. Bake at 450° F. for 10 minutes; then at 350° F. for about 30 minutes, or until browned.

Serves 8.

William B. Smart spent forty years with the *Deseret News*, including fourteen years as editor and general manager. He has subsequently served as senior editor at the *Deseret News*, editor of *This People* magazine, and president of the Utah Innovation Foundation. He served twenty-five years on the general boards of the Sunday School and the Young Men's Mutual Improvement Association. He and his wife, the former Donna Toland, live in Salt Lake City.

Edie's Southern Pecan Pie

JOHN AND LISA ADAMS

Though Lisa's southern roots are on the paternal side of her family, our pecan pie recipe is from her maternal grandmother, Edith Hansen Worley, who came from pioneer stock and was a native of Rexburg, Idaho. Edith cooked and cleaned and ironed like no one else. She loved the ballet, the theater, and the symphony. Edie's pecan pie continues to be a favorite at our table.

¾ c. granulated sugar

1 c. dark corn syrup

3 eggs, slightly beaten

4 Tbs. butter or margarine

1 tsp. vanilla

1 c. pecan pieces

1 9-inch pie shell, unbaked

Preheat oven to 350° F. In a saucepan over medium-high heat, boil sugar and corn syrup together for about 2 minutes. Pour over slightly beaten eggs in large mixing bowl, stirring vigorously. Add butter, vanilla, and pecans. Pour into pastry shell. Decorate with leaves cut from pastry dough. Bake for 50 to 60 minutes.

Serves 8.

John A. Adams, a shareholder in the law firm of Ray, Quinney, and Nebeker in Salt Lake City, is the president of the Utah State Bar for the 2002–2003 year. Both his undergraduate and law degrees are from Brigham Young University. He is a member of the Racial and Ethnic Fairness Commission and on the board of "Friends for Sight." John served a mission in Germany and has served in a variety of callings, ranging from bishop to Blazer leader. His wife, Lisa Ramsey Adams, holds a law degree from the University of Utah. Lisa has served on the board of the Children's Dance Theatre and as a volunteer for Utah's Foster Care Citizen Review Board. She was also an Olympic Winter Games volunteer. They are the parents of four children.

Fluffy Tapioca Pudding

EMMA LOU THAYNE

Born two months apart, Helen Jean and I had been close cousins and friends for seventy-seven years. As young girls we practiced our laughs till we cried and danced about the pot-belly stove to tunes on the old wind-up phonograph. Through high school and college we had classes together, saw boyfriends off to war, and married after graduation. In our third pregnancies we dieted before seeing the same doctor for weighing in, and splurged after with scones in the ZCMI Tea Room.

In any ailing or rejoicing we were never out of touch. Through it all, Helen Jean played the piano—sometimes for me alone. She delighted me with her off-hand and, to me, miraculous renditions by ear of anything I requested—from the theme song of Katharine Hepburn's 1937 *Little Women* to Beethoven, Mozart, or "Home on the Range."

One night in February 2002, I begged her to play. She had broken both legs in a fall on some stairs and was barely walking again. She was feeling lonely and reluctant to be among even the people she loved most. But there I was with my tapioca pudding and tape recorder, expecting. I wanted her music and laughs to play any time I pleased.

Tapioca. What our mothers had built into our belonging. That and the baked custard Helen Jean brought to me daily whenever I was in bed with a disorder or surgery. Comfort food. Love in a dish. Shaking her finger and saying, "No, Emma Lou, you can't record me," Helen Jean sat at her baby grand and began to play. I turned on the tape. Her fingers, knotted with arthritis, played like a girl's—light, persuasive, not a phrase without feeling. Leaning over the keyboard, I cried and we laughed. She was the young Helen Jean, yoo-hooing to me from Castle Crags in the canyon. At one point, she improvised and I scribbled words to her notes, the song: "We Belong." We did. We do. To those trembling years of more than three quarters of a century; to that sturdy joining of hearts which music and tapioca can resurrect on cue. All of it is now splendidly preserved on tape for me to listen to on any nostalgic whim. Oh, and I made a duplicate for her. Of course, she hates her voice, but I suspect listens just as I do, while perhaps wishing for another spoonful of mother's tapioca.

2 c. milk

3 Tbs. Minute® tapioca

¼ tsp. salt

3 Tbs. sugar

3 egg yolks

¾ tsp. vanilla

2 Tbs. sugar

3 egg whites,

Sprinkle of nutmeg

Other garnishes: fresh fruit slices or berries, sugared-slivered almonds, cranraisins, caramel sauce, whipped cream

Heat the milk to simmering. Mix tapioca, salt, and 3 tablespoons sugar in small bowl. In another bowl, beat yolks slightly. Pour into tapioca mixture, stirring. Add a few spoonfuls of the warm milk to the bowl— to adjust temperature and prevent eggs from curdling. Slowly pour tapioca-egg mixture into the pan with warm milk, stirring constantly as it thickens. Do not allow to boil. (Nothing worse than lumpy pudding!) Remove from heat and let stand 5 minutes. Add vanilla, stirring gently. Beat egg whites into peaks, gradually adding 2 tablespoons of sugar. Gently fold beaten egg whites into tapioca pudding. Cool 20 minutes. Stir. Pour into bowl and allow to cool another 20 minutes. Spoon into custard dishes. Garnish with a sprinkle of nutmeg, or top with jelly, as desired.

Serves 5 to 6.

Emma Lou Thayne is perhaps best known for the beloved hymn, "Where Can I Turn for Peace?" (*Hymns*, no. 129). She is a successful writer, having published thirteen books of poetry, essays, and fiction. She has taught English part time and coached tennis at the University of Utah, where she received an Honorary Doctor of Humane Letters in 2000. She also received the David O. McKay Humanities Award from Brigham Young University. She has served on the advisory board of the *Deseret News* and on the Young Women general board. She and her husband, Melvin E. Thayne, live in Salt Lake City and have a family of five daughters and sons-in-law, eighteen grandchildren, and two great-grandchildren.

Custard

JANE F. HINCKLEY

Custard is a comfort food. My mom often made it while we were growing up. I love it, my husband, Richard, loves it, and our children love it. In fact, it has become a tradition for us to have it for breakfast every Christmas morning. It's nice because I can make it the day before. I also love giving it to friends because I feel it is different from what most people give them. Richard's father, President Gordon B. Hinckley, served a mission in England, so he has always liked it.

3 c. whole or 2% milk

3 eggs

1 tsp. vanilla

⅓ c. sugar

½ c. brown sugar

Nutmeg

Preheat oven to 350° F. In blender, mix milk, eggs, vanilla, and white sugar. Sprinkle brown sugar over bottom of small loaf pan. Pour milk mixture on top and sprinkle with nutmeg. Place loaf pan in larger, oblong cake pan filled with an inch of water. Bake for 70 minutes (or until knife inserted in center comes out clean). Remove and allow to cool slightly; then refrigerate for at least 4 hours. Refrigerated, it will keep for at least 1 week.

Serves 4 to 5.

Jane F. Hinckley, and her husband, Richard, were both born and reared in Salt Lake City. Richard received a bachelor's degree from the University of Utah and a master's degree from Stanford University. He owns and operates a small business in Salt Lake City. His Church service includes a mission to Germany, callings as a bishop, a stake president, and as mission president of the Utah Salt Lake City Mission. Jane received a bachelor's degree in math from the University of Utah and was Phi Beta Kappa. She has taught math and guitar lessons for thirty-five years. She was Intermountain Women's Tennis Champion in 1964 and ranked number one in Utah. The couple are the parents of four children and the grandparents of three.

Mary Lund's Chocolate Éclair Pudding

EDWARD R. AND LOTTIE LUND MCKAY

Back when Ed was attending medical school in Philadelphia and living off the sweat of his "Frau," we once invited missionaries and Salt Lake visitors to our flat for an evening of fun. We decided that my mother's Chocolate Éclair Pudding is what we would serve. It took time and money, but we decided to splurge! We shared our favorite treat, and Ed joined the eaters. His face paled and he whispered frantically to me, "Did you taste yours?" I did, it tasted like chocolate motor oil topped with whipped cream and a cherry. I fled the scene and locked myself in the bathroom to cry. When our company left, we discovered that the culprit was a leaky can of 3-in-1 oil that the powdered sugar box had absorbed. Years later, this is a favorite again—sans the oil!

1½ c. miniature marshmallows

1 (8-oz.) can Hershey's® chocolate syrup

1 c. pecans, chopped

¼ c. butter

1 c. powdered sugar

3 egg yolks, beaten

1 tsp. vanilla

3 egg whites

14 whole graham crackers, crushed

In a medium bowl, combine marshmallows, chocolate syrup, and nuts; let stand. Cream butter and powdered sugar in large mixing bowl; add beaten egg yolks and mix together with chocolate-marshmallow mixture. Stir in vanilla. Beat egg whites and fold into the pudding mixture. Sprinkle the bottom of a cake pan with half of the crushed graham crackers. Spread the pudding mixture over the crackers; then sprinkle the remaining crackers over the top. Refrigerate for 12 hours. Serve with whipped cream and top with a cherry.

Serves 12.

Dr. Edward R. McKay practiced as a colon-rectal surgeon for forty-five years. He is a diplomat of the American Board of Surgery and of the American Board of Colon-Rectal Surgery. He was president of the staff of Primary Children's Hospital for two years. He served as a missionary in the East German Mission; he also served with two bishoprics and three high councils. His wife, Lottie Lund McKay, sang with the Mormon Tabernacle Choir until she was called to the general board of the Mutual. A marriage counselor for twenty years, she also worked with students at Highland and West high schools promoting self-esteem. They are the parents of five children.

Persimmon Pudding
with Whipped Cream Sauce

HOWARD SHARP

While serving missions we received several delicious recipes. We came across this one in the California San Bernardino Mission in 1980. Marjorie's visiting teacher gave it to her and said it was from Nancy Reagan. We serve it for special occasions. Persimmons are only in season in the winter. The pulp can be frozen and used at other times of the year. The sauce is very good and can be used on apple crisp, warmed dark fruit cake, etc.

PUDDING
½ c. butter, melted

1 c. sugar

1 c. flour, sifted

¼ tsp. salt

1 tsp. cinnamon

1 tsp. nutmeg

2 tsp. baking soda

2 tsp. warm water

1 tsp. vanilla

1 c. persimmon pulp

2 eggs slightly beaten

1 c. seedless raisins

Whipped Cream Sauce (recipe follows)

WHIPPED CREAM SAUCE
1 egg

⅓ c. butter, melted

1 c. powdered sugar, sifted

Dash of salt

1 Tbs. vanilla extract

1 c. whipped cream

Butter a steam-type covered mold (or, use aluminum cans with foil and a rubber band to cover and seal the tops). In mixing bowl, stir together melted butter and sugar. Resift flour, salt, cinnamon, and nutmeg together; add to butter and sugar mixture. Dissolve the baking soda in the warm water and add vanilla; stir into the batter, along with persimmon pulp. Add eggs, mixing thoroughly but lightly. Add raisins, stirring until blended. Pour batter into mold, filling only half full. Cover mold or cans and place in kettle with water level at two-thirds the height of the mold or cans. With smaller molds or cans, several can be made at once—this way they do not fall over while steaming. Steam for 2½ hours. Cover the kettle with a lid and check the water level occasionally.

To prepare sauce, beat egg until light and fluffy. Beat in butter, powdered sugar, salt, and vanilla. Gently fold in the whipped cream. Cover and chill until ready to serve. Stir before spooning onto pudding.

Serves 8 to 10.

Howard Sharp serves in the temple presidency of the Salt Lake Temple with his wife, Marjorie, at his side as an assistant matron. Howard's medical career includes twenty-five years at the Bryner Clinic in obstetrics and gynecology. In 1983 he joined the faculty of the OB-GYN Department at the University of Utah, specializing in pelvic surgery. He is a member of the Church's Missionary Medical Advisory Committee and took his wife on an eighteen-month humanitarian mission to Russia for their fiftieth wedding anniversary. The Sharps are the parents of seven children and the grandparents of twenty-five.

"Here's Looking at You, Kid . . ." (Blueberry-Key Lime Pie Yogurt Dessert)

JACK WEYLAND

I created this dessert after reading an article about the tremendous antioxidant properties of blueberries. Blueberries are even thought to help maintain eyesight; hence the name "Here's Looking at You, Kid." I enjoy this dessert six days a week. Nobody else in my family will eat it. Preparation time is a mere thirty-five seconds.

1 (6-oz.) carton yogurt, key lime pie
    flavor

½ c. blueberries, frozen

1 banana, sliced

Put the frozen blueberries in a soup bowl and microwave for 30 seconds. Add key-lime-pie yogurt and sliced banana; stir until well mixed. Show your enjoyment by making slurping sounds in front of family members while eating it. Don't mind if someone asks, "What's that slop you're eating?"

Serves 1.

Jack Weyland has delighted hundreds of thousands of readers since writing his first novel, *Charly*. That book has become a phenomenal bestseller and is now the basis for a major motion picture. Jack has since written more than twenty-five books. When he's not writing, Brother Weyland teaches physics at BYU-Idaho, where he is also known for his saxophone playing and his wry sense of humor. He and his wife, Sheryl, have five children and live in Rexburg, Idaho.

Ice Cream Supreme

ARDETH KAPP

Food for Thought: A friend of mine was taken by surprise one day following my invitation for her and her husband to come for dinner with a group of friends. In response to her question, "What can I bring?" I suggested she bring *food for thought*. "What?" she asked. I repeated it. "Like what?" she questioned. "Anything from the basic food for thought groups," I responded, "such as information, inspiration, revelation, and maybe some speculation—and for dessert, socialization. We will feast upon the word."

Oh, such a party was held on that occasion! Each was invited to bring his or her own "recipe book" with favorite passages to share and discuss. It turned out to be a real feast, a smorgasbord, a banquet. The ingredients used did not include flour, sugar, eggs, or favorite spices. This feast was made from different ingredients. Copies of some of the favorites that we feasted upon that evening are highly recommended and can be found in the following references: 2 Nephi 9:51; 2 Nephi 31:20; 2 Nephi 32:3; Jacob 3:2; Alma 32:42. A warning: Following parties of this kind no one is anxious to leave and no one remembers what was served to satisfy the physical appetite, however good it was. But no one ever forgets what they brought to the party and what was placed on the banquet table for all to enjoy. You'll find yourself looking for opportunities to share these favorite recipes with other friends and extending an invitation for them to come to a party and "feast upon that which perisheth not, neither can be corrupted, and let your soul delight in fatness" (2 Nephi 9:51).

Included with the menu for such an evening, I usually serve a good-sized bowl of what has become a traditional favorite, Ice Cream Supreme.

½ to 1 gallon of vanilla ice cream

½ gallon sherbet, raspberry or pineapple

1 (16-oz.) can pineapple, crushed or tidbits

2 bananas, cut into small chunks

1 c. raspberries

Blueberries and strawberries (optional)

½ c. nuts

Soften ice cream and sherbet just enough to stir; combine and blend well. Add fruit and nuts; refreeze in large container.

Serves 20.

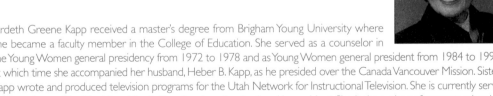

Ardeth Greene Kapp received a master's degree from Brigham Young University where she became a faculty member in the College of Education. She served as a counselor in the Young Women general presidency from 1972 to 1978 and as Young Women general president from 1984 to 1992 at which time she accompanied her husband, Heber B. Kapp, as he presided over the Canada Vancouver Mission. Sister Kapp wrote and produced television programs for the Utah Network for Instructional Television. She is currently serving as matron of the Cardston Alberta Temple where her husband is president. She is the author of numerous books.

Alma Cannon Winder's
Grape Ice Cream

NED WINDER

My parents were married in June 1919 and Mom, like most modest brides, confessed she "couldn't cook." She must have learned somewhere along the way, because among family and friends she had the reputation of being a wonderful cook. One of the things everyone remembers her making is grape ice cream. This wasn't a sherbet, but a full-bodied, delicious ice cream. It may sound unimpressive, but it was so tasty and refreshing it received raves from everyone who tasted it. Early on, this ice cream became a leverage for Mother to get her first electric refrigerator—a Frigidaire. She promised Dad she would make ice cream whenever he wanted, if she could just have a refrigerator instead of an ice box. Of course, Grape Ice Cream became a favorite!

1 c. sugar

1 c. water

½ c. Karo® syrup

2 c. grape juice

¼ c. lemon juice

1 c. whipped cream (may substitute 2 beaten egg whites)

In a large saucepan, mix sugar and water and bring to a boil, stirring to dissolve sugar. Add Karo syrup; stir to blend. Chill; then mix in the grape and lemon juices. Partially freeze in the refrigerator freezer; then fold in the whipped cream (or beaten egg whites). Alternately freeze and stir the mixture until frozen.

Serves 4.

Edwin Cannon "Ned" Winder, aged eighty-one, has been a partner in his family's Winder Dairy business all of his life. After serving in the Navy during World War II, he was active in many civic affairs and was appointed the youngest president of the Salt Lake City Chamber of Commerce. Also active in the LDS Church he has held many positions, including bishop, member of the YMMIA general board, and has presided over three missions: Florida Caribbean, Micronesia Guam, and Australia Adelaide. He currently is a sealer in the Salt Lake Temple and is a stake patriarch. He married Gwen Layton fifty-three years ago. They have seven children, thirty-seven grandchildren, and fifteen great-grandchildren.

Grape Ambrosia Ice Cream

BRENT GOATES

This recipe was originally used by Fern T. Lee, wife of President Harold B. Lee, but it has been added upon by descendants. Still our favorite.

1 (6-oz.) pkg. grape Jell-O®

1 (3-oz.) pkg. grape Jell-O®

1½ c. boiling water

1 qt. grape juice

4 c. sugar

Juice of 3 lemons

Juice of 3 limes

1 qt. whipping cream

1 pt. half and half

2 cans evaporated milk

Whole milk, enough to fill freezer canister ¾ full

Dissolve Jell-O in boiling water. To a 6-quart ice cream freezer, add grape juice, sugar, dissolved Jell-O, lemon and lime juices, whipping cream, half and half, evaporated milk, and remaining milk to fill canthree-quarters full. Stir after each addition. Cover with lid and freeze in electric ice cream freezer, using 3 large bags ice cubes and 3 quarts rock salt. When freezer motor stalls, unplug quickly, remove lid and dasher, cover with waxed paper, recover with lid, and cover with remaining ice cubes. Keep covered with an old towel or blanket until ready to serve. (Homemade ice cream always tastes best if it can ripen four or five hours.)

Serves a crowd!

L. Brent Goates is best known as the biographer of Church President Harold B. Lee. Brother Goates' definitive writings about President Lee include *Harold B. Lee: Prophet and Seer*; *Modern-day Miracles: From the Files of Harold B. Lee*; and *He Changed My Life: Personal Experiences with Harold B. Lee*. Brent has also served as president of the California Arcadia Mission and as a regional representative. He married Helen Lee, daughter of President Lee. They are the parents of five sons and one daughter. Sister Goates passed away in 2000.

Sweet Treats

CAKES, COOKIES, BROWNIES, AND BARS

Butter Crumscious Cake

SHIRLEY RIRIE

I have no idea where I got this recipe. I recently lost it and found it again in my mother's recipe file; thank goodness I had given it to her. It is an easy cake, always moist because of the cream cheese. Also, it needs no icing—so it is fast.

CRUMB TOPPING

¼ c. butter or margarine

½ c. flour

½ c. brown sugar, firmly packed

CAKE

2 c. flour

½ tsp. salt

½ tsp. baking soda

2 tsp. baking powder

1 (8-oz.) pkg. cream cheese

1¼ c. sugar

2 eggs, unbeaten

1 tsp. vanilla

½ c. milk

½ c. nuts, chopped (optional)

Preheat oven to 350° F. Grease and flour a 9x13-inch baking pan. In a small mixing bowl, prepare topping first by cutting butter into flour and sugar until a crumb texture forms. Set aside.

For cake: In another bowl, sift together the flour, salt, baking soda, and baking powder. In a large mixing bowl, blend the cream cheese until smooth, gradually adding sugar. Blend in the unbeaten eggs and vanilla. Alternately add milk and dry ingredients to the batter.

Turn batter into baking pan; sprinkle with crumb topping, along with chopped nuts (optional). Bake for 30 to 40 minutes.

Shirley Russon Ririe is co-founder and artistic director of Ririe-Woodbury Dance Company in Salt Lake City. Her performing career has spanned forty years, with performances throughout the United States, Europe, and Asia. She taught modern dance at the University of Utah for thirty-nine years and has received the university's Distinguished Woman of the Year Award. Shirley is a national leader in the field of dance for children and has produced two dance programs for PBS Arts Alive. She and her husband, O. Rhees Ririe, are the parents of four daughters and reside in Salt Lake City, Utah.

Bavarian Torte

Tyler's wife, Emily, writes: "Tyler's mom, Marsha Castleton, gave us the recipe for this mouth-watering cake, which was a birthday tradition in Tyler's home growing up. He had seven brothers (no sisters), so it seemed like his mother made the cake quite often! When the boys were younger Tyler's mom often hid quarters in the cake. One year she managed to hide an entire gift in the center of the cake! The frosting alone is to die for, and this dessert is a must for any serious chocolate-cake lover. One year for a Halloween party we replaced the chocolate cake with a pumpkin spice cake; the result was wonderful."

CAKE

2 eggs, separated

1½ c. white sugar

1¾ c. cake flour

1 tsp. salt

¾ tsp. baking soda

⅓ c. vegetable oil

1 c. buttermilk

2 oz. unsweetened baking chocolate, melted

1 (1.5-oz.) small chocolate bar

To prepare cake, preheat oven to 350° F. Grease and flour two 9-inch round baking pans. Beat egg whites until foamy. Beat in ½ cup of the sugar, 1 tablespoon at a time. Continue beating until very stiff and glossy. Set aside. In a large mixing bowl, blend the remaining sugar, flour, salt, and baking soda. Add oil and half of the buttermilk. Beat one minute on high speed. Add the remaining buttermilk, the egg yolks, and melted chocolate; fold them into the batter. Pour into the prepared cake pans and bake for 40 to 45 minutes. Let cool on racks and remove from pans.

CREAM CHEESE FILLING

2 c. heavy whipping cream

1 (8-oz.) pkg. cream cheese

⅔ c. brown sugar, softened, packed

1 tsp. vanilla

⅛ tsp. salt

To prepare filling, beat whipping cream until stiff in a medium bowl. Then blend in cream cheese, brown sugar, vanilla, and salt.

Split cakes into 4 even layers. On a large plate, frost the top of the first cake layer. Continue to add cake layers and frosting. After adding the final top layer of frosting, grate the chocolate bar over the cake. Refrigerate immediately until ready to serve.

Serves 8 to 10.

Songwriter and music producer Tyler Castleton is director of artists and recording and music for Deseret Book/Shadow Mountain in Salt Lake City. As a producer, Tyler's credits include award-winning albums for Jericho Road, Hilary Weeks, Kenneth Cope, Cherie Call, and many others. As a songwriter, his songs can be heard on dozens of LDS and Christian recordings by artists including Gladys Knight, Julie de Azevedo, Katherine Nelson, and The Jets. As a songwriter for Reba McIntire's Starstruck Writer's Group in Nashville, Tennessee, Tyler's song "For the Love of a Woman" was recorded by country superstar and RCA recording artist Martina McBride. Tyler was the music producer and a composer for the LDS Church's 2002 Olympic Spectacular, "Light of the World." Tyler and his wife, the former Emily Gibbons, reside in Salt Lake City, with their two children, Bryn and Sam.

© Busath Photography

Chocolate Eclair Cake

BRUCE AND CHRISTINE OLSEN

My husband, Bruce, does not like frosting. He always puts his cake in a bowl, scrapes off the frosting, and pours milk over the cake. So I decided to experiment and put custard—using the same recipe I do for eclairs—over the cake. It quickly became a family favorite. The chocolate sauce was a later addition. This is the dessert that is most requested by all the members of my family.

1 pkg. chocolate cake mix

1 c. sugar

3 Tbs. flour

3 Tbs. cornstarch

¾ tsp. salt

4½ c. milk (warmed in microwave)

3 egg yolks, slightly beaten

1 Tbs. vanilla

1½ c. heavy cream

CHOCOLATE SAUCE

½ c. heavy cream

1 (7-oz.) Hershey's® Symphony
chocolate bar

Prepare and bake the cake following package directions. You may want to substitute the oil with applesauce. Set aside and prepare custard.

Combine dry ingredients in saucepan. Add milk, stirring constantly. Cook and stir over medium heat until mixture thickens and boils. Cook and stir 2 to 3 minutes longer. Stir a scoop of hot mixture into egg yolks; then add yolk mixture to hot mixture, stirring until blended. Cook and stir until mixture barely begins to boil. Add vanilla; cool. Before serving, beat custard smooth; whip cream until stiff, then fold into custard.

To prepare chocolate sauce, heat cream in 2-cup container in microwave. Add chocolate bar, broken in pieces. Continue heating in microwave 30 seconds at a time, stirring between cooking, until chocolate is completely melted.

To serve cake, cut cooled cake into serving-size pieces and place in a bowl. Spoon custard over the top and drizzle with the chocolate sauce.

Serves 12.

Bruce L. Olsen is the managing director of the Public Affairs Department for The Church of Jesus Christ of Latter-day Saints. His assignment includes direction of worldwide government affairs, community relations, and media relations programs of the Church. He has previously held positions as director of corporate communications for Geneva Steel and assistant to the president for university relations at Brigham Young University. His wife, Christine Payne Olsen, is a nurse at the University of Utah Women's Center and has served on the general board of the Young Women organization. From 1982 to 1985, Brother and Sister Olsen presided over the Massachusetts Boston Mission. They are the parents of five children and the grandparents of nine.

Fruit Cocktail Cake

ANNE MARIE OBORN

A favorite from Idaho—the fastest cake you'll ever make.

CAKE

2 c. flour

2 tsp. baking soda

1 tsp. salt

1½ c. sugar

1 (16-oz.) can fruit cocktail

1 tsp. vanilla

To make cake, grease and flour an oblong (9x13-inch) baking pan; preheat oven to 350° F. Mix all ingredients together in mixing bowl and pour batter into baking pan. Bake for about 40 minutes. Pour butter sauce over hot cake.

SAUCE

¼ c. butter

½ c. sugar

¼ c. canned milk

To make sauce, mix ingredients in small saucepan and bring to a boil; then pour over hot cake.

Serve with French vanilla ice cream.

Serves 12.

Anne Marie Oborn is an award-winning artist with training in Russian traditional realism. She is well known for her portraits of children and her ability to recreate the beauty and personality of a particular day and time. She has created numerous commission and gallery pieces throughout her career and is the illustrator of *His Gift,* by Richard Paul Evans and Tracy Michele Evans. A collection of her paintings was recently released in the book *A Mother's Love.* Anne Marie and her husband, Garth, also an artist, reside in Bountiful, Utah, and are the parents of four children.

Grandmother's Favorite Pioneer Family Chocolate Cake

ROBERT GARFF

Kathi's grandmother, Elaine Neff Bagley, was born and raised in East Millcreek, where her pioneer grandfather, John Neff II, established the first flour mill in the Salt Lake Valley. Her mother, Ann Eliza Benedict Neff, baked this cake for birthdays. Kathi's mother, Frances Swan Bagley, and her aunt Marjorie Bagley Turner bake this cake for all family birthdays. It has thus become the center of our birthday celebrations, and is sometimes even sent to foreign countries to satisfy cravings of the family chocolaholics! To do this, it must be carefully boxed and hand carried with much TLC. No other cake holds a candle to this chocolate cake.

The secret is to have all ingredients at room temperature and use only REAL butter!

CAKE

2 sq. bitter chocolate, melted with 5 Tbs. boiling water

1 c. butter, room temperature

1¾ c. sugar

4 eggs, separated (room temperature)

2 tsp. vanilla

2 c. flour

½ tsp. salt

2 tsp. baking powder

½ c. buttermilk

1 c. walnuts or pecans, chopped

To make the cake, grease and flour a 9x13-inch pan or 2 9-inch round pans for a layer cake. Preheat oven to 350° F. Melt chocolate with 5 tablespoons of water over a double boiler. Cream butter and sugar together in a large bowl. Separate eggs and beat the yolks; add beaten yolks to sugar and butter, beating until fluffy. Add melted chocolate and vanilla. Sift together dry ingredients and add to batter, alternately with the buttermilk, beating after each addition. (If you don't have buttermilk, add 1 tablespoon vinegar to ½ cup whole milk or cream; use in place of buttermilk.) Mix 1 tablespoon flour into chopped nuts and stir into batter. Beat egg whites in clean, dry bowl until stiff; fold carefully into batter.

Pour batter into prepared pans and bake for 30 to 35 minutes. Do not overbake. Allow cake to cool before assembling layers and frosting. Push sterilized coins into cake just before icing. The prize is a quarter—the others are nickels and dimes.

CHOCOLATE ICING

1 sq. bitter chocolate

½ c. butter

Canned milk, for consistency

1 tsp. vanilla

Salt, to taste

3½ c. powdered sugar

To prepare icing, melt bitter chocolate with butter and a little canned milk. Add vanilla and a little salt. Beat in powdered sugar until smooth. Add small amounts of powdered sugar or canned milk until frosting reaches the right consistency. If your family favors nuts, decorate the top of the frosted cake with chopped or whole nuts.

Serves 12 to 18.

Prominent community leader Robert H. Garff has served as Speaker of the House in the Utah State Legislature, as chairman of the board for the Salt Lake Olympic Committee, and as chairman of the board of Deseret Book Company. He is CEO of Garff Enterprises, which owns and operates twenty-nine auto manufacturers, thirty-seven locations, five collision repair centers, and three used car centers. He and his wife, Kathi Bagley Garff, presided over the England Coventry mission and are the parents of five children.

Apple and Carrot Wheat Cake

JEFFREY L. ANDERSON

This is a favorite snack when I'm hankering for sweet carbs and a quick energy boost but also want something hearty and healthy. This cake got me through stressful medical school and internship days! (Warning: easily addicting.)

⅓ c. granuated sugar

⅓ c. brown sugar

⅓ c. canola oil

2 eggs (or ½ c. egg substitute)

½ tsp. salt

1 tsp. cinnamon

⅓ c. buttermilk

1 c. whole wheat pastry flour (like Bob's Red Mill)

¾ tsp. baking soda

1 tsp. baking powder

1 c. finely grated carrots

1 c. grated apples

⅓ c. nuts (slivered almonds, walnuts, or pecans)

⅔ c. unsweetened muesli cereal or granola

¼ c. raisins

Grease an 8x8-inch pan and preheat the oven to 375° F. Mix the sugars, oil, eggs, salt, cinnamon, and buttermilk together until thoroughly blended. Stir in the remaining ingredients. Pour into greased pan and bake for about 20 to 25 minutes, until toothpick inserted in center comes out clean.

Serves 9.

Dr. Jeffrey L. Anderson is associate chief of cardiology at LDS Hospital in Salt Lake City. He is also a professor of internal medicine at the University of Utah. He received his medical degree from Harvard Medical School and has worked with the Public Health Service at the National Institutes of Health in Washington, D.C. He has been named one of the best heart doctors in America by *Good Housekeeping* and was awarded a prestigious mastership in the American College of Physicians in 2002. He and his wife, Kathleen Tadje Anderson, are the parents of four children, the grandparents of six, and live in Salt Lake City.

Dark Fruitcake

FLORENCE S. JACOBSEN

This fruitcake recipe belonged to Rachel Ridgeway Ivins Grant, President Heber J. Grant's mother and my great-grandmother. Having made the cake for so many years I now consider the recipe my own. I make six times the quantity of this recipe and share it with friends every year. The candied fruit can now be purchased in one-pound packages.

1 lb. mixed, candied fruit (citron, lemon, orange rind, etc.)

2 c. seedless raisins

1 c. dates, cut into small pieces

1 c. nuts (chopped pecans and walnuts)

2 c. flour

½ c. butter, softened

1 c. sugar

2 tsp. baking soda

1½ c. applesauce

½ tsp. ground cloves

1 tsp. ground cinnamon

½ tsp. salt

2 eggs, beaten

Place a strip of aluminum foil in bottom of two 8½x4½x2¾-inch loaf pans and grease well; preheat oven to 300° F. In a large mixing bowl, add flour to fruit and nuts; mix until fruit is coated. Set aside. In a large bowl, cream together butter and sugar. Stir soda into applesauce, then add to creamed sugar mixture. Stir in spices, salt, and beaten eggs; then add all to bowl with fruit and flour. Mix well. Divide batter between two pans; bake at 300° F. for 1 hour, with small pan of water in oven.

Florence Smith Jacobsen is the granddaughter of two Presidents of the Church, Heber J. Grant and Joseph F. Smith. Sister Jacobsen served as general president of the Young Women from 1961 to 1972. She was also called to preside over the reconstruction and renovation of several major Church historical sites, including the Lion House, the Joseph Smith Sr. home in Palmyra, New York, and the Peter Whitmer home in Fayette. Sister Jacobsen's husband, Ted Jacobsen, served as president of the Eastern States Mission and director of Temple Square. He also had much to do with Jacobsen Construction, which was started by his father, Soren, and has been responsible for construction of several temples and other important Church sites. The Jacobsens are the parents of three children.

Mom's Chocolate Chip Cookies

STEVE YOUNG

When asked to contribute a recipe to this cookbook, Steve turned the whole thing over to his mom, Sherry. "She's got all the good ones," Steve said. Sherry was more than happy to comply and sent in this recipe, one of Steve's favorites—although he likes to turn it into a sandwich. "Steve's cookie sandwich is only for the really brave, and, I must add, is not mother approved," Sherry says. "To make it, take two cookies from the oven, and place a tablespoon of raw cookie dough in between them. He claims it is delicious. He really does this every time."

4 c. all-purpose flour

¾ c. quick oatmeal

2 tsp. baking soda

2 tsp. salt

2 c. solid shortening

1½ c. granulated sugar

1½ c. brown sugar, packed

2 tsp. vanilla

4 lg. eggs

4 c. chocolate morsels

1½ c. walnut or pecan pieces (opt.)

Preheat oven to 375° F. In a large mixing bowl, combine the flour, oatmeal, baking soda, and salt. In another large mixing bowl, beat the shortening, sugars, and vanilla. Add the eggs, one at a time, beating well after each addition. Gradually beat in the flour mixture. Stir in the chocolate morsels and optional nuts. Drop cookie dough by rounded tablespoon onto ungreased baking sheets. Bake for 9 to 11 minutes, or until golden brown. Remove the cookies from the oven and let stand for two minutes. Move the cookies to wire racks to cool completely.

Makes 10 dozen cookies.

Steve Young is best known as the former quarterback for the San Francisco 49ers. His achievements include recognition as the highest-rated quarterback in NFL history, Super Bowl XXIX's Most Valuable Player (MVP), and the NFL's MVP in 1992 and 1994. Off the field, Young is founder and chair of the Forever Young Foundation, a charity devoted to the development, security, strength, and education of children. Steve and his wife, Barbara, are the parents of one son.

Grandpa Glen's Famous Oatmeal Chocolate Chip Cookies

GLEN S. HOPKINSON

When Chloe, Lily, Lavender, Zinnia, Samantha, and Spencer come to visit me, I always enlist them as models. They have a great time getting all decked out in period costumes and I have fun capturing them on canvas. Having some cookies on hand helps when I need to bribe them to stay in costume just a few more minutes. They all vote these cookies as their favorites, and kids know cookies! If you are making these with your grandkids around, you really need to double the recipe.

1 c. butter, softened

1 c. brown sugar, packed

½ c. granulated sugar

2 eggs

1 tsp. vanilla

1½ c. all-purpose flour

1 tsp. baking soda

1 tsp. cinnamon

½ tsp. salt

3 c. old-fashioned oatmeal (don't use quick cooking)

1 c. semisweet chocolate chips

Preheat oven to 350° F. Cream together butter and sugars; add eggs and vanilla; beat well. Combine flour, baking soda, cinnamon, and salt. Mix well and add to above mixture. Stir in oatmeal and chocolate chips. Drop by rounded tablespoonfuls onto ungreased cookie sheet. Bake 8 to 10 minutes, or until light golden brown. Cool on cookie sheet for one or two minutes. Remove to wire rack. Serve with tall glass of cold milk. Expect lots of smiles and hugs.

For bar cookies: spread batter in an ungreased 9x13-inch baking pan. Bake at 350° F. for 30 to 35 minutes. Cut into squares and serve.

Makes 3 dozen cookies.

Glen S. Hopkinson began painting full time in 1971, focusing primarily on historical paintings. His ability to visually tell a good story is one of the most striking features of his art. That skill proved useful in creating the storyboards for the pioneer movie *Legacy*. Glen just completed a book titled *Old Nauvoo through the Eyes of Artist Glen S. Hopkinson*. It is a collection of paintings reflecting the early Nauvoo period. He and his wife, Pamela, live in Mesa, Arizona, and are the parents of five children and the grandparents of nine.

Chocolate Chip Cookies with a Twist

LAURA GARFF LEWIS

Everyone has a favorite chocolate chip cookie recipe, but our family's favorite is definitely a gold medal winner. My mother got it from her friend, Maurine Myrick, many years ago. We have since shared it with countless friends and relatives who love it, too. The Garff girls never had a boyfriend who could resist them. The secret ingredient is freshly grated orange rind.

½ c. butter

½ c. shortening

2 c. brown sugar

2 eggs

1 tsp. vanilla

1 tsp. baking soda

1 tsp. salt

Grated rind of 1 or 2 oranges

1⅓ c. flour

3 c. oats

1 (12-oz.) pkg. chocolate chips

1 c. pecans, toasted, chopped

Preheat oven to 350° F. Cream together butter, shortening, and sugar. Add eggs, vanilla, baking soda, salt, and grated orange rind; mix well. Stir in flour and oats and mix thoroughly. Add the chocolate chips and chopped nuts, stirring gently until blended. Drop by rounded spoonfuls onto ungreased baking sheet. Bake for 10 minutes.

Makes 2 dozen cookies.

Mezzo-soprano Laura Garff Lewis performs with the Utah Opera Company in their "Opera in the Schools" program. She has performed classical and Broadway concerts with the Utah Symphony and has been a soloist with the Oratorio Society of Utah, the Utah Chamber Artists, Temple Square Chorale, Suisse Romande Radio Choir, and the Mormon Tabernacle Choir. Laura received a special honor performing for the queen of Thailand at the Rattanakosin Bicentennial Celebration for Bangkok and sang the "Olympic Hymn" at the closing ceremonies of the 2002 Winter Olympics. She and her husband, Bob, have two children and share time between their home in Salt Lake City and their log home on Boulder Mountain in Southern Utah.

Chocolate Chip Meringue Cookies

KATHLEEN LUBECK PETERSON

This cookie is great for wedding receptions or other fancy events. I made dozens of these cookies for my sister Nancy's wedding reception.

2 egg whites

⅛ tsp. cream of tartar

⅛ tsp. salt

1 tsp. vanilla

¾ c. superfine sugar

½ c. chocolate chips

Preheat oven to 300° F. In medium mixing bowl, mix egg whites, cream of tartar, and salt. Beat together until soft peaks form. Add vanilla and sugar gradually, beating until stiff. Fold in chocolate chips.

Cut brown wrapping paper, ungreased (or baking parchment), to fit cookie sheet. Drop mixture by teaspoonfuls onto paper, 2 inches apart. Bake about 25 minutes. Cool before removing from paper.

Makes 3 dozen cookies.

Kathleen Lubeck Peterson has written magazine and newspaper articles for various publications. She has been a contributor to the religion column in the *Los Angeles Times*, Orange County edition, and worked as director of national media placement in the Church's Public Affairs Department in Salt Lake City. Sister Peterson served on the Young Women general board under Elaine Cannon and later with Ardeth Kapp, and presently serves as media relations liaison for the Church's Orange County Public Affairs Council. She and her husband, John L. Peterson, M.D., live in Irvine, California.

Annie's Almond-Mint Macaroons

ANNE MARIE OBORN

Anything with mint and chocolate is my love, so I combined an Almond Joy candy bar with the added thrill of mint to come up with this original recipe.

6 egg whites

½ tsp. mint extract

½ tsp. cream of tartar

½ c. granulated sugar

1 (14-oz.) pkg. coconut

Chocolate chips

Sliced almonds

Preheat oven to 325° F. Beat egg whites to soft peaks, then add mint extract and cream of tartar. Continue to beat while slowly adding sugar until glossy, stiff peaks form. Gently fold in coconut. Drop by spoonfuls onto prepared baking sheet. Push 4 chocolate chips into each mound and fold over. Top with sliced almonds. Bake for 15 minutes.

Makes 2 dozen cookies.

Anne Marie Oborn is an award-winning artist with training in Russian traditional realism. She is well known for her portraits of children and her ability to recreate the beauty and personality of a particular day and time. She has created numerous commission and gallery pieces throughout her career and is the illustrator of *His Gift*, by Richard Paul Evans and Tracy Michele Evans. A collection of her paintings was recently released in the book *A Mother's Love*. Anne Marie and her husband, Garth, also an artist, reside in Bountiful, Utah, and are the parents of four children.

Chocolate Marshmallow Surprises

DAVID AND JOANNE DOXEY

We were introduced to these cookies in the 1960s while living in Phoenix. The children and I have since surprised many a family with this simple cookie that carries a façade of fanciness. They are so easy and fast to make and use ingredients that are generally on hand. I've had many people comment on having used this recipe after it was printed in the *Deseret News*. A year or so ago at a meeting, I met the wife of the dean of BYU's law school. She said to her husband, "Oh, Honey, this is the Joanne Doxey whose cookies we've been making for so many years."

2 c. flour

½ tsp. soda

½ tsp. salt

½ c. cocoa

½ c. shortening

1 tsp. vanilla

1 c. sugar

1 egg

½ c. milk

20 marshmallows, cut in half

Chocolate Icing (see recipe)

Nut topping, if desired

CHOCOLATE ICING

1½ c. powdered sugar

2 Tbs. cocoa

Dash salt

3 Tbs. milk

1 Tbs. butter

1 Tbs. shortening

Preheat oven to 350° F. Stir together flour, soda, salt, and cocoa; set aside. In a separate bowl, cream together shortening, vanilla, sugar, and egg. Alternately blend in dry ingredients and milk. Drop batter from a teaspoon 2 inches apart on ungreased baking sheet. Bake 8 minutes. Remove cookies from oven, set one marshmallow half on each cookie and return to oven for 1 minute more. Remove from oven and set aside for 1 minute; then drop a spoonful of icing on each marshmallow-topped cookie, letting it drizzle over all. Sprinkle with crushed nuts, if desired.

Makes 3 to 4 dozen cookies.

For icing, combine powdered sugar, cocoa, and salt. Heat together milk and butter and beat enough of it into the powdered mixture, along with shortening, to make a soft icing.

David Doxey presided over the Spain Barcelona Mission from 1978 to 1981. He now serves as president of the Madrid Spain Temple with his wife, Joanne, as matron. Joanne served on the Primary general board and as a counselor in the Relief Society general presidency. They have served together in Church Hosting and in the presidency of the Salt Lake Temple. David was president and property manager of a real estate development company. They have eight children and thirty-seven grandchildren.

The Chocolate Cookie That Tastes like Fudge

SUSAN EASTON BLACK

If you need a break from healthy eating and want calories that are sure to stick, this recipe is for you. To my knowledge the recipe began with my grandmother, who passed it to my mother, and is now read in all ward Relief Society cookbooks. But there is a missing process in the other cookbooks: the secret to a better cookie is in the last twenty-four hours!

1 c. chocolate chips

½ c. butter

1 c. walnuts, chopped

1 c. graham crackers, crushed

1 can sweetened condensed milk

1 c. coconut

These ingredients are the same as a typical chocolate cookie bar; so are the directions. Stir the ingredients together in a heavy pan over medium heat. Bring the mixture to a boil. Pour the batter into an oblong baking pan and bake at 350° F. for about 20 minutes.

Now comes the secret to elevating these traditional cookie bars—almost as common as funeral potatoes and Jell-O—to new heights. After baking, cool the cookie bars slightly; then roll them into bite-sized balls and freeze them for 24 hours. Remove the balls, dust them with powdered sugar, and you've made amazing fudge! Don't be surprised if longtime presidents of Relief Society request your recipe.

Makes 4 dozen cookies.

Susan Easton Black is a professor of church history and doctrine and a past associate dean of general education and honors at Brigham Young University. Dr. Black has received many university awards and fellowships for her research and writing over the past twenty-five years, including the Karl G. Maeser Distinguished Faculty Lecturer Award in 2000, the highest award given a professor at Brigham Young University. She has authored, edited, and compiled more than ninety books and as many articles. Her most recent book is *The Nauvoo Temple, Jewel of the Mississippi.* She is married to Harvey B. Black, and they are the parents of eight children.

Surprise Cookies

DAVIS BITTON

On holidays Mother would bake Surprise Cookies, using a recipe she obtained from Elizabeth Duckworth, English-born wife of our stake president.

COOKIE

1 c. sugar

½ c. shortening

1 egg

½ c. milk

3½ c. flour

3 tsp. baking powder

FILLING

1 Tbs. (heaping) flour

1 c. sugar

1 c. boiling water

1½ c. raisins, chopped

½ c. walnuts, chopped

For cookies: In a large mixing bowl, cream sugar and shortening. Add egg and milk. To that mixture add flour and baking powder, stirring until well blended. Put dough in refrigerator while making the filling.

For filling: Mix flour, sugar, and raisins in a saucepan. Pour 1 cup boiling water over flour and sugar, and bring mixture to a boil for 2 minutes. Add chopped walnuts just before removing from stove.

Remove dough from refrigerator and roll out thin on floured pastry board; cut out with round cutter. Put a dab of filling on one circle and top with another circle, pressing down around the edges. Bake on a greased cookie sheet at 350° F. for about 12 minutes, until lightly browned.

Makes approximately 2 dozen large cookies.

Davis Bitton is an award-winning author and Church historian. His book *George Q. Cannon: A Biography* was the winner of the 1999 Evans Biography Award. He served as assistant Church historian for ten years, during which time he had many remarkable and faith-affirming experiences. His writings include a number of significant historical works, such as *The Mormon Experience: A History of the Latter-day Saints*, which he co-authored with Leonard Arrington, and *Images of the Prophet Joseph Smith*. Brother Bitton is married to JoAn Borg Bitton, and they reside in Salt Lake City.

Lemon Drop Cookies

RUSSELL AND ANN WHITING ORTON

Raising a batch of five children often required an ample supply of cookies—cookies in the oven, cookies on the counter, and rarely cookies sequestered in the freezer. Most of these quickly disappearing cookies bore a Chocolate Chip label, but, always, the search continued for alternative recipes.

At a casual lunch at The Pointe at the Huntsman Cancer Center, Russell and I happened on a surprising new lemon cookie. With my previous food world connections, I thought I could easily retrieve the recipe from the friendly chef. No such luck! The cookies were supplied by a vendor, who was understandably unwilling to part with the carefully guarded secret.

The cookie recipe crusade began: my cookbook review and Russell's Internet search yielded several possibilities. Not one of the newly discovered recipes came close to the original. We then contacted a newspaper recipe search column, which, after three weeks of printed requests produced nary a response. It seemed the only alternative became a kitchen experiment. After six or eight attempts, we created Lemon Drop Cookies. These tasty cookies quickly disappear from cookie trays at missionary farewells, luncheons, showers, and any other family, neighborhood, or ward gathering.

2 c. sugar

1½ c. butter-flavored shortening

3 eggs

2 tsp. vanilla

1 tsp. lemon extract

4 c. flour

1½ tsp. soda

1½ tsp. baking powder

1 tsp. salt

Finely chopped zest of one lemon

1 (6-oz.) pkg. lemon drops, crushed

1 c. powdered sugar

Juice of one lemon

Preheat oven to 350° F. In mixing bowl, cream sugar, shortening, and eggs; add flavorings. Stir in dry ingredients, lemon zest, and crushed lemon drops. Roll into balls, flatten slightly, and bake on parchment-lined baking sheet for 10 to 12 minutes. Be sure to use the parchment paper on the baking sheet or the cookies will stick. Let cool slightly on pan 1 to 2 minutes. Make a glaze by mixing powdered sugar with lemon juice; then brush lightly over the cookie tops. Let cookies cool completely.

Makes 4 to 5 dozen cookies.

Ann Whiting Orton worked as food editor of the *Deseret News* then as the restaurant critic for the paper, in addition to being the Mountain West field representative for the Zagat Survey. She was a contributing author in An *Emotional First-Aid Kit for Mothers*, and the author of two additional books. She is the mother of five living children and the grandmother of three. Her husband, Russell Orton, was the former owner of Bookcraft Publishing. The Ortons recently returned from a mission in Nauvoo, Illinois, and now reside in Salt Lake City, Utah.

Marble Brownies

SHIRLEY RIRIE

When I was working on my master's degree in New York City (having a great time studying with Martha Graham, Merce Cunningham, Hanya Holm, and Alwin Nikolais), my mother sent me a letter with this—my favorite cookie recipe.

1 c. shortening

2 c. sugar

4 eggs

2 c. flour

1 tsp. baking powder

½ tsp. salt

2 c. chopped nuts

1½ tsp. vanilla

2 sq. baking chocolate, melted (for marble layer)

Grease and flour a 9x13-inch baking pan and preheat oven to 300° F. Cream the shortening in a large mixing bowl, gradually adding sugar. Beat in the eggs one at a time beating after each addition. Sift the flour, baking powder, and salt, then add to batter, mixing constantly. Stir in nuts and vanilla.

Divide dough into two equal parts. Pour one portion into baking pan. To remaining portion, blend in the melted chocolate; then pour over light layer in pan and, for marbled effect, swirl several times with spatula. Bake for 45 to 55 minutes.

Shirley Russon Ririe is co-founder and artistic director of Ririe-Woodbury Dance Company in Salt Lake City. Her performing career has spanned forty years, with performances throughout the United States, Europe, and Asia. She taught modern dance at the University of Utah for thirty-nine years and has received the university's Distinguished Woman of the Year Award. Shirley is a national leader in the field of dance for children and has produced two dance programs for PBS Arts Alive. She and her husband, O. Rhees Ririe, are the parents of four daughters and reside in Salt Lake City, Utah.

Rich Fudge Brownies

WINNIFRED C. JARDINE

This recipe is a variation from Annemarie Huste's *Cooking with Annemarie* (New York: Putnam Publishing Group, 1979). It is one of the best and fits all the requirements of my brownie test: it must be of high quality and flavor (calories are too precious to squander on ordinary sweets) it must have nuts to balance the sweetness, and it should never have frosting (frosting interferes with a brownie's elegant flavor; connoisseurs take their brownies plain). Enjoy!

1⅓ c. butter

8 (1-oz.) squares unsweetened chocolate

8 large eggs

4 c. sugar

½ tsp. salt

1 Tbs. vanilla

3 c. flour, stirred, measured, leveled

1½ c. broken walnuts or pecan halves

Prepare a heavy 11x17x1-inch baking pan (larger than a standard 10x15-inch jelly-roll pan) by lining with parchment paper and brushing lightly with oil or shortening. Preheat oven to 350° F.

In double boiler or heavy pan over very low heat, melt together the butter and chocolate. Remove from heat and set aside to cool. In large mixing bowl beat together eggs, sugar, salt, and vanilla until light and fluffy, then add slightly cooled chocolate mixture. Blend well. Turn mixer to low speed and add flour. Stir in nuts. Spread mixture evenly in prepared pan. Bake in preheated oven for 20 to 25 minutes or until top is dry and a small, sharp knife inserted into center pulls out to show consistency of chocolate pudding. Do not overbake. Cool completely in pan, cut with sharp knife into 2½ x1½-inch bars; then refrigerate. To separate chilled brownies, invert pan, peel off parchment paper and take brownies apart carefully. Keep refrigerated or frozen.

Makes 4 dozen brownies.

Winnifred Jardine graduated from Iowa State University in technical journalism and foods and nutrition. For thirty-six years she served as food editor of the *Deseret News*. Prior to that time she served, among other things, as a home economist in the Martha Logan Test Kitchen, Swift and Company, Chicago; as director of home economics at the American Meat Institute in Chicago; and as instructor of foods and nutrition at the University of Utah. She is a past president of the Utah Association of Family and Consumer Sciences and the Utah State Nutrition Council. She is the author of many cookbooks. Winnifred and her husband, Stuart, live in Salt Lake City, Utah.

Snickerdoodles

SHERI DEW

2¾ c. self-rising flour

2 tsp. cream of tartar

1 tsp. baking soda

½ c. butter, softened

½ c. shortening

1½ c. granulated sugar

2 eggs

4 Tbs. sugar

4 tsp. cinnamon

Preheat oven to 400° F. Sift together flour, cream of tartar, baking soda, and salt; set aside. Cream butter, shortening, sugar, and eggs. Stir in dry ingredients. Chill dough for 10 to 15 minutes.

Mix together 4 tablespoons sugar and 4 teaspoons cinnamon. Form dough into balls and roll in sugar and cinnamon. Place about 2 inches apart on an ungreased cookie sheet. Bake at 400° F. approximately 8 to 10 minutes or until lightly browned.

Makes 4 dozen cookies.

Sheri Dew is a native of Ulysses, Kansas, and a graduate of Brigham Young University. She served as second counselor in the general Relief Society presidency from 1997 to 2002, and has also served as a gospel doctrine instructor, a president and counselor on both the ward and stake level, and as a member of the Relief Society general board. The author of biographies of Presidents Ezra Taft Benson and Gordon B. Hinckley, she is also the president and chief executive officer of Deseret Book Company.

Apple Squares

VICTOR L. BROWN, JR.

My job with the daily menu is to eat what my wife, Mareen, cooks. One of my favorites is a recipe using home-canned apples in a flaky crust. It requires some advance planning, unless the canned apples are already on your shelf.

CANNED APPLE PIE FILLING

16 apples, peeled, cored, and sliced

6¾ c. sugar

1½ c. cornstarch

2 Tbs. cinnamon

1½ tsp. salt

½ tsp. nutmeg

⅓ c. lemon juice

To make pie filling: Mix dry ingredients in a kettle and add 15 cups water. Cook over medium heat, stirring constantly until thick and bubbly. Remove from heat and stir in the lemon juice. Pack the sliced apples in a quart jar, leaving 1 inch of head space. Fill jars with syrup, leaving ½ inch head space. Cap and process for 20 minutes.

VINEGAR PIE CRUST

3 c. flour

1 tsp. salt

1 Tbs. sugar

1¼ c. shortening

1 egg

1 Tbs. vinegar

½ c. water

Egg white

3 Tbs. butter (optional)

Cinnamon-sugar sprinkle

To make pie crust: Preheat oven to 350° F. Use a pastry cutter to mix together the flour, salt, sugar, and shortening until pea-sized clumps form. Add egg, vinegar, and water and blend lightly. Roll half of the dough to fit a jelly-roll pan. Brush with egg white and fill with the apple mixture (or with 2 quarts of your favorite apple-pie filling). Dot with butter, if desired. Roll remaining dough and place atop the apple filling; prick with fork. Brush pastry top with egg white and sprinkle with cinnamon-sugar mixture. Bake for 35 to 40 minutes, until crust is cooked. While hot, cover with glaze. May serve hot or cold.

CITRUS GLAZE

2 c. powdered sugar

2 Tbs. butter

3 Tbs. orange or lemon juice

To prepare glaze, mix together powdered sugar, butter, and juice.

If serving this with ice cream, skip the glaze. It is also very good if made the day before serving.

Makes 20 2x2-inch squares.

Victor L. Brown, Jr., has served as director of the Comprehensive Clinic of the Values Research Institute at Brigham Young University and as commissioner of LDS Social Services. He is a respected speaker and author and has served on several state and national committees and boards related to his professional background. He is the author of *Human Intimacy: Illusion and Reality*. Dr. Brown and his wife, Mareen Holdaway Brown, are the parents of six children, the grandparents of twelve, and great-grandparents of two. Brother and Sister Brown live in Riverton, Utah, where he serves as stake patriarch and as an ordinance worker in the Jordan River Temple.

Fudge Bars

MICHAEL YOUNG

This is my all-time favorite recipe. It does not have a particularly exotic story in the making, or at least one of which we are aware.

But, whatever its origins, this is a family favorite and has sustained us across two continents (the U.S. and Asia) and four major cities (Boston, New York, Washington, and Tokyo) where we have lived over the years. It often becomes a favorite of our friends, as well. Indeed, we seem to spread this recipe about as often as we spread the gospel (and sometimes more easily, I must confess). The recipe is clearly somewhat indulgent, but, despite my advancing years and gradual removal of some of the more cholesterol-ridden foods from my diet, these fudge bars remain a staple.

BARS

1 c. margarine

2 c. brown sugar

2 eggs

2 tsp. vanilla

2½ c. flour

1 tsp. soda

3 c. Quaker® oats

FILLING

1 (12-oz. pkg.) chocolate chips

1 can sweetened condensed milk

2 tsp. margarine

½ tsp. salt

2 tsp. vanilla

1 c. chopped nuts

For bars, mix margarine and brown sugar together. Mix in the rest of the ingredients; set aside. Make filling as directed below.

Preheat oven to 350° F. Divide oatmeal mixture in half and press one portion into bottom of a 9x13-inch baking pan. Pour filling over top. Spread other half of the oatmeal mixture on top of the filling. Bake for 25 minutes.

To prepare filling, melt together the chocolate chips, milk, margarine, and salt in a double boiler. Remove from heat when thoroughly melted and stir in vanilla and nuts.

Serves 8 to 10 (unless I am one of the 8 to 10).

Michael K. Young is dean and Lobingier Professor of Comparative Law and Jurisprudence at the George Washington University Law School. During the administration of President George Bush, Dean Young served as ambassador for trade and environmental affairs, deputy undersecretary for economic and agricultural affairs, and deputy legal advisor to the U.S. Department of State. Before launching his teaching career, Dean Young served as law clerk to Supreme Court Justice William H. Rehnquist. Dean Young served a mission to Japan and as president of the New York New York Stake. He is married to the former Suzan Stewart, and they have three children.

Mouthwatering Morsels

MELT-IN-YOUR
MOUTH
CANDIES AND
POPCORN

Fancy Party Mints

SUSAN EVANS MCCLOUD

We have lots of family parties and "teas" with our friends: Valentine's, Summer Solstice, St. Patrick's Day, May Day, etc. These mints are quick and easy to make and will be a nice, refreshing addition to the other treats and refreshments you plan. Use them to dress up otherwise ordinary occasions. I think the result is worth the extra effort! If you want, you can even use a sealing wax stamp to imprint the mints and dress up the occasion even more. I often use a bee, which is a symbol of mine. Or use an acorn, flower, initial, and so on. It is easy to double or triple this recipe for parties or receptions. I have served these for Relief Society affairs when I was in the stake Relief Society presidency, and received numerous requests for the recipe. Don't be afraid to experiment a little with the amounts. I like them rich, so I use a little more butter and milk—resulting in a larger quantity of mints.

1 egg white

2 to 3 Tbs. evaporated milk

2 tsp. peppermint flavoring (or more to taste)

4 drops food coloring (less for light pastel)

1 (16-oz.) bag powdered sugar, perhaps more

2 to 5 Tbs. butter

Combine egg white, milk, flavoring, and food coloring. Beat in powdered sugar and butter with mixer until consistency is right: stiff enough to handle, but not too dry. Roll into very small balls. Flatten with fork dipped in powdered sugar; place on waxed paper sprinkled with a bit of powdered sugar to prevent sticking.

Mints can be eaten immediately or stored on shelf (in Saran Wrap or tin foil) for 24 hours. Can be refrigerated for 2 to 4 days.

Makes about 3 or 4 dozen mints.

Susan Evans McCloud has published more than forty books, including several biographies, children's books, and dozens of works of fiction. Her work also includes several screenplays, tape narratives, and the lyrics to two hymns: "Lord, I Would Follow Thee" and "As Zion's Youth in Latter Days." Susan and her husband, James, are the parents of six children and the grandparents of six. They reside in Provo, Utah.

World's Best Fudge

JANE F. HINCKLEY

My mother and her sisters used to make this fudge when I was young. I loved it. When I was in junior high school, my friends and I used to get together almost every Friday night. We started making fudge on those evenings. After we cooked it, we would sit around the table and talk while it was cooling. Each girl would have a small plate of fudge in front of her. As soon as it cooled, she would beat it with a spoon until it became light in color and very creamy. It would then harden. (Of course, it would often get eaten before it ever turned hard!) We had such fun talking and laughing while we were waiting for it to cool! Forty-five years later, we all got together again, made fudge, and reminisced.

1 c. whole or 2% milk

2 c. sugar

½ tsp. salt

3 Tbs. cocoa

¼ c. butter

1 tsp. vanilla

Mix all ingredients, except vanilla, in large bowl; pour into heavy pan and cook over medium heat until a spoonful of the mixture forms a soft ball (234° F.) in cold water. Do not scrape the sides or bottom of the pan. Pour out onto large, buttered dripping pan until it is cool. Add vanilla; then beat by hand or in a mixer until it changes color and begins to stiffen. Roll into two logs and wrap in wax paper and refrigerate. Slice the logs into bite-sized chunks when ready to serve. (Fudge can also be frozen for up to 3 months.)

Makes 2 large logs.

Jane F. Hinckley, and her husband, Richard, were both born and reared in Salt Lake City. Richard received a bachelor's degree from the University of Utah and a master's degree from Stanford University. He owns and operates a small business in Salt Lake City. His Church service includes a mission to Germany, callings as a bishop, a stake president, and as mission president of the Utah Salt Lake City Mission. Jane received a bachelor's degree in math from the University of Utah and was Phi Beta Kappa. She has taught math and guitar lessons for thirty-five years. She was Intermountain Women's Tennis Champion in 1964 and ranked number one in Utah. The couple are the parents of four children and the grandparents of three.

Peanut Butter Fudge

WAYNE OWENS

This is a secret Owens Family recipe from Panguitch, which we only allow ourselves to celebrate with on special family events three or four times a year. Five children and thirteen grandchildren are unanimous in declaring it our top family event treat. Unfortunately, it is not only heavily caloric but is also totally irresistible, so long as any remains—hence the importance of making small batches. We do not recommend it be doubled; but, with a large enough pot, it can be done. If it were sold commercially, it would require a warning from the Surgeon General if, in fact, the FDA would allow it to be sold in the first place.

3 c. sugar

1 c. cocoa

½ tsp. salt

2 c. milk

½ c. butter

1 Tbs. vanilla

1 (8-oz.) jar chunky peanut butter

Mix sugar, cocoa, and salt in large, non-stick pot. Stir in milk and blend well. Bring to a boil over medium-high heat, allowing it to cook at moderate boil until a tablespoon of fudge forms a ball when dropped into a cup of cold water. Cut up butter into pieces and place in mixing bowl, along with vanilla; then pour fudge over butter. Immerse the bowl in cold water for half an hour; then, while mixture is still warm, beat with electric mixer, while dropping chunky peanut butter into the batter. When it begins to lose its luster and becomes harder to beat, pour it onto a buttered plate and it is ready to be enjoyed.

Serves a medium-sized family.

Wayne Owens is president of the Center for Middle East Peace and Economic Cooperation, headquartered in Washington, D.C. He represented Utah's second district in the United States House of Representatives for eight years, after being on the staffs of Utah Senator Frank Moss, New York Senator Robert F. Kennedy, and Massachusetts Senator Edward Kennedy. His wife, Marlene Wessel, served with him as he presided over the Quebec Canada Mission. They are the parents of five children and the grandparents of thirteen.

Margaret's Caramels

TRUMAN AND MARILYN CLAWSON

My mother, Margaret Romney Jackson Judd, made different kinds of candy, but I think we always liked the caramels best. As her daughter, I was usually the one to stand and stir and drip in the cream. My friends and I usually walked home for lunch from Uintah Grade School. Because our home was the farthest from the school, it was hard for me to eat lunch, turn around, and call for my friends in as timely a fashion as they would like. One day I was particularly late. A fresh pan of caramels had been turned out on the counter. Mom and I cut them into long sticks, one for each friend, and off I went. They were a great peace offering—even though one of the girls pulled out a filling. Another time, when Mom was our MIA teacher, all of the class informed her that they would not be present at the accustomed time for her next lesson as they wanted to attend our East High School basketball game. Undaunted, Mom went with us to the basketball game, bringing each of us a clever container of homemade munchies with caramel sticks protruding out of the top.

2 c. granulated sugar

2 c. white Karo® syrup

½ c. butter

1 c. canned milk

1 c. whipping cream

1½ tsp. vanilla

⅛ tsp. salt

Mix sugar and syrup in a heavy pot over medium heat. When it is boiling vigorously, add butter. Add canned milk and cream a few drops at a time so mixture does not stop boiling. Stir constantly. Cook to firm ball stage (232° F. on a candy thermometer, or when a spoonful of caramel forms a firm ball in a cup of cold water and makes a ringing sound on the side of the dish). Add vanilla and salt. Pour candy into a buttered 7x11-inch pan. Let stand until cold. Cut caramel into squares and wrap individually.

Makes 6 dozen caramels.

Truman Clawson graduated from the University of Utah law school. He is the owner of Clawson Travel Service and is chairman of the board of Hickory Travel Systems, an international travel service organization. He has served as chair of the Salt Lake Convention and Visitor's Bureau and the Utah State Travel Council, as well as vice-chair of Salt Lake Valley Hospitals for Intermountain Healthcare. His wife, Marilyn Jackson Clawson, is a home economist and served a mission with him as director of the Mormon Trail Center at Winter Quarters in Omaha, Nebraska, and the Kanesville Tabernacle in Council Bluffs, Iowa. They are the parents of eight children and the grandparents of fifteen.

Emma Ray McKay's Vinegar Taffy

EDWARD R. AND LOTTIE LUND MCKAY

In days gone by, when Huntsville was bursting at the seams with cousins, and when President David O. McKay and his three brothers and four sisters were all alive, all McKays headed for the family home to celebrate summer holidays. There were four kitchens in the old homestead, and David O's four sisters manned two of those kitchens. Wonderful aromas floated through the house. We soon learned to make the rounds as each sister proudly presented her treat for all to enjoy. Auntie Annie, Auntie Lizzie, Auntie Nettie, Auntie Kitz, and Mama Ray (David O's wife) provided homemade root beer, taffy, best-ever coleslaw, a dripper pan full of warm, frosted cinnamon rolls, and white cake with strawberry ice cream. Their thanks were the oohs and ahs of the many family members, as we enjoyed each one's specialty of love.

2 c. sugar

1 c. water

3 Tbs. vinegar

Few grains salt

1 tsp. vanilla

Dissolve the first four ingredients in saucepan and stir until mixture boils. Wipe down sides of pan with moistened pastry brush. Insert candy thermometer and cook over medium heat without stirring. When temperature reaches 270° F., pour taffy onto a large, buttered platter or marble slab. Fold in vanilla. When finger leaves an imprint on top of candy, it is cool enough to begin pulling. Lift from platter with hands at either end of taffy and pull gently with fingers—stretching apart and folding back and pulling again—until the taffy is almost too stiff to pull anymore. Then pull out, twisting into a rope, and mark with knife into desired sizes. When struck with a knife, the taffy will break where marked.

Dr. Edward R. McKay practiced as a colon-rectal surgeon for forty-five years. He is a diplomat of the American Board of Surgery and of the American Board of Colon-Rectal Surgery. He was president of the staff of Primary Children's Hospital for two years. He served as a missionary in the East German Mission; he also served with two bishoprics and three high councils. His wife, Lottie Lund McKay, sang with the Mormon Tabernacle Choir until she was called to the general board of the Mutual. A marriage counselor for twenty years, she also worked with students at Highland and West high schools promoting self-esteem. They are the parents of five children.

Pecan Brittle

HEIDI SWINTON

I love to make desserts—anything sweet seems worth making and eating. My most decadent treat is Pecan Brittle. Every year at Christmas I order thirty pounds of fresh pecans, shipped to my house in a great big box. I measure out the pecans for this candy into Ziploc bags and keep them in the freezer for use all year. But, I must admit, I use more than half of them in about three weeks at the end of November and the first of December. This candy is really good. So good that I can eat a whole batch by myself; although, given the ingredients, I wouldn't advise that anyone do the same.

1¼ c. butter (do not use margarine)

1¼ c. granulated sugar

⅓ c. brown sugar

3 Tbs. water

2 Tbs. white Karo® syrup

¼ tsp. salt

3½ c. whole pecans

1 tsp. vanilla

Melt butter in a heavy, large saucepan over medium heat. Stir in sugars and blend until the mixture looks like caramel. Add water, Karo syrup, and salt. Place a candy thermometer on the side of the pan and let mixture cook over medium heat.

Butter two cookie sheets and place in oven set at 275° F. Put pecans in an oven-proof bowl, and place them in the oven as well. Watch the cooking candy—it will bubble. The next few steps require that you work fast. Stir candy occasionally with a clean spoon until the thermometer reads 270° F. Then stir candy constantly until it reaches 290° F. (this isn't very long). Remove pan from heat and stir in vanilla. Take cookie sheets and pecans from oven and place on counter. Pour pecans into the hot candy. Stir to mix in nuts and *quickly* pour out on warm cookie sheets. Spread the mounds to the edges using the back of a rubber tipped spatula in a stretching motion, working from the center to the edges.

Cool. Break into pieces and store in an air-tight container. Best after 2 or 3 days.

Heidi S. Swinton is an award-winning author and screenwriter. Her work includes *Sacred Stone: The Temple at Nauvoo*, which is the companion book to the PBS documentary *Sacred Stone: Temple on the Mississippi; American Prophet: The Story of Joseph Smith*; and *Trail of Hope: The Story of the Mormon Trail*. Heidi graduated from the University of Utah and attended Northwestern's Graduate School of Journalism. She and her husband, Jeffrey, have five sons.

Caramel Corn

BARLOW BRADFORD

A young missionary gave this recipe to my family while we were living in Michigan in the 1960s. We have enjoyed it ever since—especially during the Christmas season.

2 c. sugar

1 c. white Karo® syrup

2 c. whipping cream (no substitute)

1½ to 2 c. popping corn

In a large saucepan, combine the sugar, corn syrup, and whipping cream. Bring to a boil and cook to the soft ball stage (approximately 225° F.). Stir continually while bringing to a boil. Pop the corn into an extra large bowl. Sift out the unpopped kernels. Pour caramel syrup over the popcorn (without scraping the pan) and stir gently to distribute throughout.

Barlow Bradford is the music director of the Orchestra at Temple Square, associate conductor of the Mormon Tabernacle Choir, and music director of Utah Chamber Artists. His live performances and recordings have been heard in many parts of the world. His compositions and arrangements are performed by orchestras and choirs throughout the United States. Brother Bradford lives in North Salt Lake with his wife, Jean, and children, Katie, Anna, Christopher, and Amy.

Sugared Popcorn

ALBERT AND MARILYN JEPPSON CHOULES

A neighbor used to bring this to us at Christmas when I was a child. As a popcorn lover, this continues to be my favorite popcorn treat.

2 Tbs. butter

2 c. granulated sugar

½ c. hot water

2 qt. popped corn (white, plain)

Melt butter in saucepan. Add the sugar and water. Mix thoroughly and cook to a soft ball stage (without stirring). Then stir quickly and thoroughly, using a large wooden spoon. Pour the hot syrup over the popcorn in a large glass bowl. Stir through the popcorn until kernels are lightly coated throughout.

Makes 2 quarts.

Albert Choules, Jr., has been a member of the Second Quorum of the Seventy, a Regional Representative, and president of the New York, New York City Mission. He is the senior vice president of Coltrin and Associates, a New York City-based public relations firm. He was married to the former Rosemary Phillips, who passed away in 1984. Albert married Marilyn Jeppson in 1987. Marilyn has a Ph.D. from BYU and is a counselor in private practice in Salt Lake City. Together, the Choules have twenty-two grandchildren.

Honey-Buttered Popcorn

JOE J. CHRISTENSEN

This is the one recipe I know—because I created it; but frankly, I had never written it down. The invitation to actually put it into writing intrigued me; but how was I going to explain to anyone the exact amount of each of the ingredients to put into it because I measured things out by how much it "felt" like I should add.

During the past forty years or so, there has rarely been a family gathering at our home where we haven't had some of the one and only recipe I know: Honey-Buttered Popcorn. Often, one of the first things the grandchildren say when they come to the house is "Grandpa, will you make some popcorn?" Call it serendipity, luck, or just the product of laziness that it was invented, because it is so much simpler than any other recipe for popcorn balls or caramel corn. In fact, it is so easy that I am almost embarrassed to reveal the secret of how to do it.

12 qts. popped corn

¾ c. honey

1 tsp. salt

½ c. butter

We use a forced air corn popper that does not require oil. Put the kernels in the popper and wait for them to pop out into a large container. The younger grandchildren are usually interested in "helping" with this part of the process by putting hands full of popcorn kernels in the popper and, consequently, there are often some unpopped kernels that end up scattered on the floor. Pop 12 quarts of popcorn. Our old, round plastic container is just right. Once the corn is popped, if you really want it first-class and eater-friendly, you put the whole batch in a large paper bag and shake it until the few kernels that did not pop go to the bottom and can be eliminated.

Put honey in a saucepan over high heat. Add salt and a stick of butter. Bring the whole batch to a lively boil, stirring constantly, until it becomes a bubbly, frothy, yellowish color. The cooking process takes about 5 minutes. Pour the mixture around on top of the popcorn and, with a long-handled wooden spoon, mix or fold it into the popcorn to assure an even distribution of the topping. That's it—the concoction is ready for immediate consumption. We pass around bowls and napkins and each family member returns to the source for refills until it is gone. If any is left over, it is put in plastic bags and given to the families for a treat to take home. You may want to vary the amount of honey, butter, or salt used, but it is hard to have a failure. Give it a try.

Tip: Occasionally we have mixed a small batch on the side to meet the needs of a family member who does not tolerate dairy products. In that case, in place of butter we substitute an appropriate amount of virgin olive oil, and it seems to work fine.

Joe J. Christensen is an emeritus member of the First Quorum of the Seventy and was recently released as president of the San Diego Temple, with his wife, Barbara, as matron. President Christensen has previously served as associate commissioner of education responsible for the world-wide administration of seminaries and institutes of religion, as president of Ricks College (now BYU–Idaho), president of the Mexico City Mission, and served for four years as president of the Provo Missionary Training Center. He is the author of four books on Church-related topics. He and his wife are the parents of six children.

Index

C